INTERACTIVE STORYTELLING FOR THE SCREEN

An invaluable collection of essays and interviews exploring the business of interactive storytelling, this highly accessible guide offers invaluable insight into an ever-evolving field that is utilizing new spatial and interactive narrative forms to tell stories. This includes new media filmmaking and content creation, a huge variety of analog story world design, eXtended realities, game design, and virtual reality (VR) design.

The book contains essays written by and interviews with working game designers, producers, 360-degree filmmakers, immersive theater creators, and media professors, exploring the business side of interactive storytelling – where art meets business. Contributors to this book will share their perspectives on how to break into the field; how to develop, nurture, and navigate business relationships; expectations in terms of business etiquette; strategies for contending with the emotional highs and lows of interactive storytelling; how to do creative work under pressure; the realities of working with partners in the field of new media narrative design; prepping for prototyping; writing analog and digital.

This is an ideal resource for students of filmmaking, screenwriting, media studies, RTVF, game design, VR and AR design, theater, and journalism who are interested in navigating a career pathway in the exciting field of interactive storytelling.

Sylke Rene Meyer is a writer, director, media artist, performer, educator, and co-founder of the performance group Studio206 in Berlin (2007), extended in LA (2019). In 2018, she also co-founded the performance group "Family Room Collective" in Los Angeles. She is a Professor of Creative Writing and the Director of the Institute for Interactive Arts, Research, and Technology at the California State University in Los Angeles.

Gustavo Aldana is a musician, media artist, and educator. Their projects have involved the combination of electronic music, interactive visuals, and the creative use and manipulation of myriad forms of digital media as forms of resistance. They are a graduate student in Television, Film, and Media Studies at California State University, Los Angeles.

PERFORM: Succeeding as a Creative Professional

Series Editor: Anna Weinstein

The PERFORM series aims to offer engaging, uplifting, and expert support for up-and-coming artists. The series explores success in the arts – how we define success in artistic professions and how we can prepare the next generation of artists to achieve their career goals and pay their bills.

The books in this series include practical advice, narratives, and insider secrets from industry professionals. Each book will include essays by and interviews with successful working artists and other professionals who represent, hire, or collaborate with these artists.

Ultimately, the goal of this series is simple: to illuminate how to make a living – and a life – as an artist.

Directing for the Screen
By Anna Weinstein

Acting for the Stage
By Anna Weinstein and Chris Qualls

Writing for the Screen
By Anna Weinstein

Acting for the Screen
By Mary Lou Belli

Producing for the Screen
By Amedeo D'Adamo

Interactive Storytelling for the Screen
By Sylke Rene Meyer and Gustavo Aldana

For more information about this series, visit: https://www.routledge.com/PERFORM/book-series/PERFORM

INTERACTIVE STORYTELLING FOR THE SCREEN

EDITED BY SYLKE RENE MEYER
CO-EDITOR – GUSTAVO ALDANA

Routledge
Taylor & Francis Group

LONDON AND NEW YORK

First published 2021
by Routledge
52 Vanderbilt Avenue, New York, NY 10017

and by Routledge
2 Park Square, Milton Park, Abingdon, Oxon, OX14 4RN

Routledge is an imprint of the Taylor & Francis Group, an informa business

British Library Cataloguing-in-Publication Data
A catalog record has been requested for this book

Library of Congress Cataloging-in-Publication Data
Names: Rene Meyer, Sylke, editor. | Aldana, Gustavo, other.
Title: Interactive storytelling for the screen / edited by Sylke Rene Meyer ; editorial assistant Gustavo Aldana.
Description: Abington, Oxon ; New York : Routledge, 2021. | Series: Perform | Includes bibliographical references and index.
Identifiers: LCCN 2020043263 (print) | LCCN 2020043264 (ebook) | ISBN 9780367819989 (hardback) | ISBN 9780367819972 (paperback) | ISBN 9781003011293 (ebook)
Subjects: LCSH: Digital storytelling. | Interactive multimedia. | Narration (Rhetoric)
Classification: LCC QA76.76.I59 I583 2021 (print) | LCC QA76.76.I59 (ebook) | DDC 808.2/3--dc23
LC record available at https://lccn.loc.gov/2020043263
LC ebook record available at https://lccn.loc.gov/2020043264

ISBN: 978-0-367-81998-9 (hbk)
ISBN: 978-0-367-81997-2 (pbk)
ISBN: 978-1-003-01129-3 (ebk)

Typeset in Garamond
by MPS Limited, Dehradun

CONTENTS

FOREWORD

Anna Weinstein

The PERFORM book series is built on the premise that there is a growing need for artists to understand not only the possibilities of their *craft*, but also the practicalities of their *business*. Far too many creatives turn away from their dreams before they give themselves a chance to figure out how to make a living from their art or even just how to balance their creative work with other income-generating activities.

There is a perception of the hobbyist versus the expert, the amateur versus the professional. At what point *can* you call yourself a professional?

When it comes to creative fields, those of us who identify as *makers* simply want to participate. At all stages of our practice and careers, we want the doors to be open. Certainly not locked shut, even just a sliver of light will do.

However, what if instead of just a single door cracked open, there were double doors wide open and welcoming?

Whether on screen or on stage, there is but one prevailing force behind any mode or type of performing art:

Story.

We humans have a common need for a story. We process our emotions, experiences, and yearnings through story, both in the telling of and consuming of stories. Moreover, recently, we have entered this age of storytelling where interactivity is commonplace. In so many cases and in so many ways, we no longer blindly consume stories; we actively engage! We are not alone in our consumption of creative content; we are connected to the content and to other audience members. We are, in fact, *participating*.

It is with enormous pride and gratitude that I introduce this volume. From the very first conversation I had with Sylke Meyer, her vision for the book was clear, and her passion for interactive storytelling was contagious. Sylke, with the help of her editorial assistant, Gustavo Aldana, has brought together a remarkable collection of essays that details the history of interactive storytelling, the many different forms this type of engaged sharing of stories can take, the technologies involved thus far, and the exciting possibilities for the future.

Nonetheless, most importantly, what she has created with this collection is an accessible way for established and aspiring writers to learn how to work in industries that seek out interactive storytellers. There are opportunities for internships, entrepreneurship, and landing paid positions at companies advertising job openings. There are opportunities for transitioning from one type of storytelling work to another, from stage to screen to virtual reality (VR) to the gaming industry – the list goes on!

The perspectives and insights in this tremendous collection of voices across the many industries where interactive storytelling is flourishing will no doubt get the wheels turning in your mind. If you are merely curious about the possibilities, considering entering an industry where you can use your existing skills and talents, or toying with the idea of transitioning your more traditional storytelling practice into a technology-driven interactive form, then you will find this book a treasure chest of wisdom.

One of the most motivating aspects of this volume, which I hope you will find useful, is the detailed descriptions of the many ways you can use interactive storytelling to accomplish humanitarian goals. Woven throughout this volume is a tapestry of inspiring stories of creators using interactive storytelling to further a cause – for instance, using immersive VR experiences to walk audience members through the horrors of the Holocaust or taking participants on a journey by walking a day in the life of a transgender person.

You will learn about building theme park rides, using "space" in interactive storytelling, VR, intellectual property, improvisational theater, video games, and large- and small-scale transmedia projects for social impact. You will hear from storytellers in New York and Los Angeles, from Canada, Germany, and France.

Whether you are already trained in building interactive stories or just beginning this journey now, I am certain you will find invaluable insights in this book. Speaking from personal experience, I have learned so much from this volume, and I cannot wait to take this with me to the classroom and to my own storytelling practice. I hope you find this book as inspiring as I do!

Thank you for taking this journey with us. Here is to wishing you the very best in your career.

Anna Weinstein isthe series editor of *PERFORM: Succeeding as a Creative Professional*.

ACKNOWLEDGMENTS

We are deeply grateful to the contributors for being part of this adventure and for taking time out of their busy schedules to share their perspectives and expertise. We also like to thank the photographers and graphic designers who allowed us to include their artworks in this book. We wish to thank the "PERFORM" series editor – Anna Weinstein – for her invaluable guidance and advice; Astrid Kahmke – the director of XR4ALL and the member of the jury for the #VeeRFutureAward at #CannesXR for her generous support; Samantha Mariano for her time, spirit, and last-minute transcriptions; the Institute for Interactive Arts, Research, and Technology (InArt) at the California State University in Los Angeles for its support and leadership in the creation of this book.

INTRODUCTION PERFORM: INTERACTIVE STORYTELLING FOR THE SCREEN

Sylke Rene Meyer and Gustavo Aldana

PERFORM: INTERACTIVE STORYTELLING FOR THE SCREEN includes essays written by and interviews with working game designers, producers, immersive theater creators, 360-degree filmmakers, and media professors who are exploring the business side of interactive storytelling – where art meets business. Contributors to this book share their perspectives on how to break into the field; how to develop, nurture, and navigate business relationships; how to formulate expectations in terms of business etiquette; how to devise strategies for contending with the emotional highs and lows of interactive storytelling; how to do creative work under pressure; how to accept the realities of working with partners in the field of new media narrative design; how to begin prepping for prototyping; how to start writing analog and digital.

The term interactive storytelling came into being only in the late 1970s and early 1980s of the 20th century, and it has been credited mainly to the game design pioneer and interactive storytelling researcher, Chris Crawford. In his 2005 book, *Chris Crawford on Interactive Storytelling,* Crawford uses the term "interactive storytelling" to refer to an experience that is a hybrid between a video game and a story.

"Moviemakers see it (interactive storytelling) as a form of cinema; videogame people claim it as an extension of their own field; computer scientists think of it as part of the broader field of artificial intelligence; experts in the art of improv consider it to be the computerization of their skills. The truth is that interactive storytelling is not an extension of or variation in any of these fields; it must be approached as something new and unique. An appreciation of all these fields (and several more) certainly helps you appreciate the challenges of interactive storytelling, but to use one of these fields as a platform from which to launch your thinking is a grievous mistake."[1]

Today, interactive storytelling is not constrained to digital media. Instead, interactive storytelling includes and draws from a variety of sources that are analog and digital. Interactive storytelling inductively moves towards new ideas of usership, escapology, gleaning, slack space, spectatorship, or working on a 1:1 scale – as discussed by Stephen Wright in *Towards a Lexicon of Usership*.[2] New forms of do-it-together include roleplay games, narrative games, improvisational theater, immersive experiences, activism, and many types of collaboration.

Interactive storytelling is arguably the formative media of the 21st century and will shape our social relations and economic prosperity in the future. The Accrediting Council on Education in Journalism and Mass Communication currently accredits 113 professional programs in the United States and outside of the country.[3] With the recent advances in technology in the past years though, and the ease with which people can now design, showcase, or upload their work, there is a rise in nontraditional education to prepare for the fast-growing industry of interactive storytelling and game design. With free design software available and an enormous passion amongst new media storytellers, there is also a large number of young independent artists and designers at work who create and upload on sharing platforms like "Steam," create miniature worlds for live projection storytelling or build up followers on their Youtube™ channel where they comment on games and VR experiences.

Often, interactive storytelling is embedded in narrative explorations that are described with terms such as "immersive," "cross-media," or "trans-media". These terms are often used together but have varied meanings. "Immersive" describes a narrative experience where the user actively enters a story world and experiences the narrative from their specific perspective – either from a first-person perspective or through an avatar. Cross-media, trans-media, and multimedia content refer to a system of narrative placed on different platforms. The terms are typically used in marketing to describe cross-platform concepts that perform story-building around a specific brand. For example, a design team develops a concept for a documentary about bird migration, along with a game about birds and nesting, and an online fan magazine for bird watchers. The concept is a transmedia concept because it approaches a story world on three media platforms: film, game, and blog/text.

Interactive storytelling is a rather new field and includes game design, VR design, new media filmmaking, content creation, a huge variety of analog story world design, and eXtended realities. With all of this said, designing user-centric forms of narrative not only offers a wide range of professional opportunities, but is also the medium to communicate new ideas and stories for the future. Our world becomes more interconnected, and the global saturation of personal media devices increases; interactive storytelling will become essential to narrative traditions. The broad adoption of smartphones, touch screens, and other new interactive tools continues to expand the possibilities of interactive storytelling. As technology becomes more affordable and accessible, so do the tools used to make media for these devices. This opening up of the playing field allows for new kinds of stories to be told and more diverse voices will be heard.

In this book, you will read tales of the successes, challenges, and journeys of interactive artists. You will learn about many different forms of interactive storytelling, and you will also learn about many different functions. While interactive storytelling has obvious links to the entertainment industry, you will also notice that some of the approaches and projects in this book are also historical, educational, and political. As an interactive storyteller, you have the power and the responsibility to tell stories and create experiences that can have a real impact on your audiences. Your work has the potential to have real-world effects and outcomes and to construct new and exciting worlds and experiences.

While there are many differences amongst the diverse group of creators featured in this book, a common thread is that inspiration is the mother of invention. This book will help you to see how others have used inspiration and worked through their ideas. As you read, think about how and where you find your own inspiration to create. Think about how you can use inspiration and creativity to tell your own stories.

In Chapter 1, we will be investigating some ways of entrepreneurship and creative thinking that can help you to find your niche in interactive storytelling – including improvisational theater, virtual reality, augmented reality, and more. In Chapter 2, you will have an opportunity to learn about how other interactive artists have been able to turn setbacks into success. In Chapter 3, we will investigate some of the creative ways that artists have adapted to the ever-changing landscape of interactive storytelling – including designing large-scale experiences, adapting to changes in academia, and finding funding for your projects. In Chapter 4, you will get the chance to hear from creators who are using transmedia approaches to interactive storytelling to have a social impact through projects related to science, education, history, and social justice. In Chapter 5, we will take a look at how creators are pushing boundaries in interactive storytelling through video games, alternative approaches to narrative construction, and the application of interactive storytelling to address issues regarding social consciousness and social justice.

As you will see, interactive storytelling encompasses old and new ideas and technology. The adoption of new technology and media formats in conjunction with more traditional forms of media makes this subject matter endlessly interesting: the story of interactive storytelling is still being written, and the art form is very much alive. Whether you already have a good idea of your own process, or you are just hearing the words "interactive storytelling" together for the first time, this book is an excellent tool for expanding your knowledge and awareness of the wide and wonderful world of interactive storytelling.

Notes

1 Crawford, Chris, Chris Crawford on Interactive Storytelling, New Riders, 2005, pg xii.

2 https://museumarteutil.net/wp-content/uploads/2013/12/Toward-a-lexicon-of-usership.pdf

3 "Critical Thinking." Editor & Publisher, vol. 150, no. 7, Editor and Publisher Inc, July 2017, p. 15.

CHAPTER 1

GETTING STARTED

Interactive storytelling, as a practice, has been carried out by humans through a myriad of forms for generations. From oral traditions to modern digital methods, people have sought out ways to tell their stories. However, as natural as storytelling may seem, the broad history of storytelling and the overwhelming variety of storytelling methods and forms may seem daunting. As a newcomer to interactive storytelling, the breadth of options, and the constantly evolving nature of the industry can seem like serious impediments to the beginning of your interactive storytelling career.

With so many options available, how and where do you begin?

The oral traditions of the earliest storytellers came naturally through the power of the spoken word. However, with the advent of the increasingly interconnected nature of humans and digital tools, we are no longer limited to the old ways of storytelling. With so many tools at your disposal, you can become an interactive storyteller using whatever talents you might have – whether these are in live theater, computer sciences, visual arts, or elsewhere. As an interactive storyteller, you get to decide what practices and methods work best for you in order to succeed. The ever-evolving nature and longevity of storytelling as a practice means that you have the freedom to choose your own path.

A career as an interactive storyteller offers rather open-ended opportunities in terms of your approach to your practice. Luckily, there are professionals who have provided insight into how they have managed to forge their own ways in the industry and write their own stories. By learning about their journeys and experiences, you can begin to learn about what your own adventure might look like.

In the first chapter, you will learn about:

- Ways that the industry has evolved with the advent of emergent technologies
- Planning out the earliest phases of your interactive storytelling projects
- Techniques for creating your own works using new digital tools
- Differences among some of the many new mediums for interactive storytelling
- Methods for creating successful collaborative works
- Strategies for making professional connections as a newcomer
- Business strategies for making your way in the industry
- What you can do to make your way into your chosen niche of the industry

To begin, let us take a look at some of the ways that the approaches to interactive storytelling have evolved over time.

WE ARE BUILDING A BRIDGE AS WE ARE WALKING ACROSS IT

▶ Ingrid Kopp

Ingrid Kopp is a co-founder of Electric South, a non-profit initiative to develop virtual reality and immersive projects across Africa. She also curates the Tribeca Storyscapes program for interactive and immersive work at the Tribeca Film Festival and produces Immerse – a publication for Medium on emerging storytelling – in partnership with MIT Open DocLab and Dot Connector Studio.

Figure 1.1 Ingrid Kopp

My background is in documentaries and television. I started at Channel Four Television in London in the early 2000s just as everything was moving to digital. A lot of new prosumer cameras were coming onto the market. I was interested in storytelling and became interested in how different kinds of technology were enabling different kinds of stories to be told and new filmmakers to enter the space. During my time in television, even though I was not doing interactive work, I started to think about how technology enables things to happen. I was involved in trying to get cameras like a Sony PD150 accepted for broadcasting. At the time, we realized that certain filmmakers were making films with those cameras, but they were not considered to be broadcast quality. We were starting to see new, emerging talent in the TV world, enabled by access to cheaper cameras. That, for me, was the beginning of technology and storytelling coming together in my career.

Then, I moved to New York and started working more on the web development side of things while also being involved with the film community, and running the US office of the British organization, "Shooting People: Independent Filmmakers Network." Through that experience, I began teaching digital boot camps, supporting traditional filmmakers in social media, or using the internet to promote their films and build a career. Over time, I became more interested in interactive storytelling as an art form in itself, as I started to see projects emerging around 2007 or 2008. I started seeing more interactive work on the web, such as web documentaries like "Gaza Sderot," a web documentary that really inspired me.

I saw web documentaries like this and became interested in the idea of using the internet as a medium and not just a platform for traditional media. Casper Sonnen of the International Documentary Film Festival Amsterdam [IDFA] DocLab is a big inspiration: he talks a lot about using the internet as a creative medium. With accessible internet, mobile phones, and smartphones on the market, as well as cheaper digital equipment, it seemed like an exciting time for new forms of work to emerge. I started writing a column about these ideas for a British movie magazine *movieScope*. In 2010, the Tribeca Film Institute in New York hired me to advise on a proposal for a program to fund interactive filmmaking and interactive storytelling. We received a grant from the Ford Foundation, and I found myself running a new department at the Tribeca Film Institute.

Thus, in 2011, I started full-time funding interactive work and became part of the emerging interactive immersive space. Low-tech and high-tech have always interested me. I love high-tech stuff with all of the bells and whistles, being on the bleeding edge of the coolest things technology can do, with high production values. It is very exciting for me, but I have also always been rather interested in ideas, access, and audiences as well. Who is the audience, and who is getting to see the work? Instead of just who is going to make the work. One example was the "Quipu Project," which was about women who were sterilized against their will in Peru. I loved the project because it involved workshops with women in the communities in which they lived. It was a workshop with the women affected, and they had a phone line that women could call and leave messages on. There was also a beautiful website that they created. Another one was "Priya's Shakti" which is an ongoing project. It includes AR-enabled comic books. They also did murals in India that were AR-enabled, but even if you did not have a smartphone, you could still access the project in other ways. The comic books were distributed for free. We also funded the "Nanny Van" project by Marisa Jahn – a public art project dealing with the economy of women working in homes as nannies and as domestic workers.

The idea of collaborative collective work and having different points of entry into a project for audiences was something that really interested me, but it is challenging too. I know why a lot of this work feels unfinished to people who are accustomed to traditional films – because you do not have the three-act structure.

You do not have the beginning, the middle, and the end. Sometimes, it can feel unfulfilling in a way, but it enables you to challenge the dominant narrative of how a story should be and who gets to tell that story. I kind of love the unfinished side, because some of these stories are so loose that it feels like they can go on forever.

I like what they were enabling people to do, but I also think that was one of the challenges in making this kind of storytelling mainstream. It does not engage audiences the way that a lot of stories do. That means it is a little harder to interact with. We did start to get a lot of proposals and ideas sent to us which were very much about crowdsourcing or having crowdsourced material. One of the things that I noticed is that mostly the crowd would not contribute. Most people will contribute to the network that they are already on. People are making TikTok videos, and they are on Instagram. They stay in the communities that they are already in.

If you set up a website and say, "I want you to send me your stories," it usually just does not work. That is something that a lot of filmmakers and storytellers really misunderstand. That is the flip-side of this rather lovely idea of collective work. It is very possible to do it, but I think there have been a lot of bad experiences with crowdsourced storytelling where the intended "crowd" never uploaded anything because they did not feel part of the project.

Funding became really tight for a lot of non-VR work after 2014. A lot of early transmedia and interactive excitement went away, and not all of it was replaced by new sources. In 2012, the new wave of VR was just starting to emerge. The first VR experience that I saw was in Sundance 2012. In 2011, we were funding web documentaries, mobile experiences, mobile storytelling apps, and more transmedia experiences. As VR started coming onto the scene, we started funding more 360 and immersive, room-scale VR, but that did not begin happening until about 2014. All of the money for web documentaries kind of disappeared with this new focus on VR. I do not think it is coming back. VR sucks up a lot of the oxygen in the room. There is new money in the space — mostly around VR. Although, even for VR projects, we are noticing that there has been a dip. A lot of the funders have gone away. With private or commercial money, it is hard to know where it is unless you are already part of that world. People have to think clearly about how their project is going to fit into their career, and how else they will support themselves. A lot of people will break the bank making their one project, and they will not make another one; they will not build on their craft. This is something that is very close to my heart. It is important that filmmakers and artists get to make more than one project, get better and better, and have a sustainable career.

There are a few production companies that are doing well. There are a few artists who are good at getting money and have a body of work. However, most people have to support themselves with other jobs. The market for story-based work is rocky. That pertains to the market in general. The headset market is smaller than everyone expected or wished for. Also, for a lot of projects, it is very hard to charge for them. You can charge for a big A-list game, but it is hard for the small, interesting storytelling projects because people will not pay. They expect the project to be free. In the current infrastructure, we do not have a lot of distributors, sales agents, or all of the other things that get traditional films put out there. Nonetheless, there are people who are figuring it out. There are some entrepreneurial artists, like Briege Whitehead, who is an Australian filmmaker. She made a beautifully shot 360 project about Antarctica, and it was distributed to Australian museums with great success.

You just have to be really smart about how you will fund your project in the first place, and what you think is going to happen once the film is out in the world. You cannot expect to automatically attract a big audience, and that everyone is going to pay $30 for the film because it does not work that way. With Electric South, which is the nonprofit that I co-founded in South Africa working with African artists, we have been careful about how we work. We can get screening fees from festivals. We license the films. I would not say that it has big bucks, but we are definitely making sure that there is income for the filmmakers and that, because we funded the project, they are never out of pocket. It has enabled them to continue working in their practices; however, their practice is defined, because we work with interdisciplinary artists. You have to be really smart about reality and not just hope that something is going to finally change.

When thinking about a project, there are two things to consider: One, be really smart about how you do a project. For example, Marshmallow Laser Feast is making sure that they are scoping out the work they make. They do not make a project and hope that it is all going to work out. They scope out everything. They work out things like how long a piece should be because you will have to get x number of people through every hour. How long will it be? How much can they charge? How many headsets do they need? Will they need extra headsets in case some break? They figure all of that out before they make the project. They know exactly what they need to break even. Then, they design their release schedule around that. It is very expensive for projects to go to festivals. Installations are rather expensive. Often, the festival will not cover all of the travel and accommodation costs. Be especially smart about the real costs, not just the costs when you are at the beginning of the project – the real cost to get out into the world and reach audiences. That is the key. Second, it is important to map out who is funding and where the support is. There are some public media like the point of view "POV" series, which is a part of the US Public Broadcasting Service (PBS). There are some commercial companies in the advertising world doing experiential marketing, so there are opportunities there. There are certain interesting immersive theater crossovers as well. Some of the philanthropy foundations are a source of funding. There are some governments that fund this type of work quite well, like France and Canada. There are exciting things happening in China around VR. There are cities and regions that are trying to bill themselves as "the city of VR" or "the region of VR," and they are investing huge amounts in VR parks and other initiatives. There are a lot more arcades, but I am not sure this model will work everywhere.

You have to be entrepreneurial and figure out where the money is – not just money, but resources as well. There are certain rather interesting stuff happening in the academia around VR and immersive storytelling: Gabo Arora at Johns Hopkins, Jessica Brillhart at USC, Sarah Wolozin at MIT Open DocLab. There is not always money for production available, but there are resources there. In this space, it is not necessarily about a single discipline but, rather, about converging.

You are now in a space where you are with people from the immersive theater, the game industry, film, and journalism. There are a lot of journalism 360-degree projects. Those areas will overlap, and there are a lot of opportunities there because you can tap into their network.

One of the things I have found rich about this space is I have been able to network with other folks who are in adjacent industries. I love that you can work with people doing artificial intelligence, academia, and theater folk in the course of one day. I was part of a World Economic Forum VR council this year (2019). That, for me, was quite interesting, because it made me realize that I am in my independent storyteller mode all the time, and I have not been paying attention to the ways that this technology is being used in other fields. It was eye-opening because I realized that I am always thinking about story-telling and the mostly small grants here and there. However, there is this whole other world with millions of dollars, and big things can happen. They are interested in the future of education. How are we going to learn in the future? How is the economy changing? When are robots coming? With artificial in-telligence, what does work look like? There was a lot of talk about VR and what VR may become as a tool for education. Everything is changing ex-ponentially, so you have to "reskill" endlessly. There are a lot of discussions about therapy and medicine. What does the future of medicine look like? How will VR, AR, and immersive technology work with surgery, therapy, and also military training? How about training to fly jets? Things like security and surveillance? Nonetheless, I still want to hold space for the role of storytelling and art.

One of the things that we are trying to do with Electric South is to explore all of these issues, but with an African perspective. We hope to address all of the things that we have been talking about – what does access look like? What does it look like when different kinds of people get to play with these new tech-nologies? Are the stories different? What does that lead to? We work with African artists across the continent. We run an annual residential lab where we train the artists in all kinds of VR, AR, and 360 filmmaking: whatever it is that they are interested in exploring. After that, they will go and make projects. We fund some of the projects, and we also help with distributing internationally and continentally. We are looking at what African distribution for VR looks like. We do pop-up experiences. We work with museums and other cultural spaces. There are challenges around exhibition and distribution, but there are also solutions. Where are people already experiencing culture? How can we make stories that are not just about famine, war, and disease? Perhaps, they are about those, but they have the freedom to experiment and innovate like ev-eryone else and not have Africa be defined by outsiders. That is not just a VR concept. People want to have room to experiment and play.

We work with artists across many creative disciplines. We have had architects, journalists, filmmakers, and photographers, and they all are bringing different experiences to the VR space. If they are in Lagos, then they are going to have a very different experience compared to those in Johannesburg, Nairobi, or anywhere else. Their experiences depend on their geographic location in the continent – this is huge, and this varies. That aspect is fun to explore. We do not want it to be just South Africa. This is something that the artists have said: they want to be a part of what this space becomes. It is important that we do not wait and hope that some of it trickle down. They want to be part of designing the headsets for African audiences. They are thinking about what a VR exhibition with a lower bandwidth setting would look like; what experiences look like when the electricity goes out for however many hours a day; when the Internet is not so great. How can we work around those problems? I am not denying that there are challenges. Right now, almost all of the money for this work is coming from overseas, and we would like to change this.

When considering interactive storytelling, I also think of the idea of "playing." A lot of the experimental projects that I have seen are about getting adults to play. They are not necessarily games because you cannot win, but there are gaming elements to them. A lot of people are taking elements from these different disciplines, unpacking these, and figuring out what that might feel like. The market and the infrastructure for games is a different world, but there are definitely crossovers. There was this beautiful game called "That Dragon, Cancer." It was so moving. It was made by a parent of a child who died of cancer. It was quite incredible. Of course, a lot of filmmakers that I work with would never consider making a game. It would not even occur to them. They do not see themselves as moving between those worlds at all. That comes back to how these experiences can feel a little bit unsatisfying, because when you unpack some of these structures and play with them and experiment with them, sometimes you end up with something interesting but difficult for audiences to engage with. If you cannot win, you do not know how long something is, or you do not know exactly what shape it is, then the experience it can be really frustrating for audiences.

I have definitely lost myself in weird experiences that are neither one thing nor another. I have been completely transformed and transfixed by being part of another world. I went to Punch Drunk's "Sleep No More" in the week, that it opened because a friend of mine was working with them. There was hardly anyone there. The audience was minimal. I had never been to a Punch Drunk show. I had not even really been to an immersive theater show. I did not know what to expect. I was on my own, and I just had the most amazing time. I did not know what was going on. I was lost in that space. I went back, subsequently for two more times, and the experiences were so different.

However, I have also had experiences where I say, "just tell me what you need me to do or what you need me for. I need to know what's expected of me," because I get really frustrated. I do not know how big this story is, and I do not know where I am in it. Is it ever going to end? I guess that is sort of the downside. I have this conversation a lot with my colleague at Tribeca. At the Tribeca Film Festival, I curate interactive work, and my colleague there – Loren Hammonds – loves to explore in VR. He is always trying to open doors. When you see him in VR, he is often on the floor. He gets enjoyment out of trying to break the game or the experience all of the time, whereas I often enjoy the experience more during the second time because I want to know where I am at and what is expected of me. We both have very different approaches, and we both hugely enjoy these. I like to know where the boundaries are, and he likes to break the game and set his own boundaries. Audiences are often somewhere in between those two extremes.

There are many interesting museums, libraries, and other cultural communal spaces that are beginning to explore these types of things. There are also new opportunities. The BBC did a bunch of VR experiences in libraries. A lot of museums are looking into showing these experiences. Oftentimes, I feel like the world is shrinking, but as funding disappears, other spaces open up. Whenever I am starting to feel like I am in a terrible moment – such as when funding is being pulled – I try to remember that when one door closes, another one opens. This space is ever-changing, and we realize that we are part of making those changes. That is part of the exciting thing for me. We are building a bridge as we are walking across it.

NARRATIVE DESIGN: A WINDING PATH, A WILD ADVENTURE

▶ Michael Yichao

Figure 1.2 Caption: Michael Yichao

Michael Yichao is a Narrative Lead at Wizards of the Coast.. Past titles include League of Legends, Legends of Runeterra, unnamed R&D games, and Wild Rift (Riot Games), Guild Wars 2 (ArenaNet), Magic: the Gathering and Dungeons and Dragons (Wizards of the Coast), Ava (Social Cipher), and Port of Mars (Interplanetary Initiative: Arizona State University).

There is a Far Side comic that I think of often. In it, a kid with glasses plays a console game while sitting too close to the TV. Behind him, his doting parents imagine (via a thought bubble) a classified section set in the (then) far-future date of 2005. The classifieds page is rife with postings seeking "Nintendo Experts" and "Good Mario Brothers Players," with outlandish salaries such as $100,000 or $80,000 – plus a free house! I wonder if Gary Larson – the comic's creator – had any idea how prescient he was, or what he makes of the existence of Twitch nowadays and of streamers like "Ninja" – the 28-year-old gamer that, at the time of writing, is a ubiquitous and (in)famous player with multi-million-dollar deals and numerous lucrative revenue streams to his name.

The work

Gaming has blossomed into a robust field for those interested in interactive storytelling. There are many design roles in game development that sit at a crossroads between hard sciences and creative work. Math, programming, and game mechanics intersect with storytelling, emotional/experiential design, and intuition – all to craft stories where audiences are not just passive observers, but also active participants.

As a narrative designer and game writer, my writing output has ranged across a variety of media – from story content in the games themselves (e.g voiceover scripts, cut scenes, art descriptions, narrative arcs, and world and character development) to things surrounding the game (e.g. promotional cinematics, short films/anime, comics, prose short fiction, and novellas). Each narrative touchpoint offers varying degrees of interactivity with our audience of players, and even some of our more traditional media outputs have player input possibilities.

In many ways, the stories I craft serve as backdrops for the stories that the players themselves generate – stories about their experience and interaction with the narrative, about their play experience with their friends, about their personal relationship and affinity to the characters, etc. My story about a masked swordsman in League of Legends, as an example, is as tangible and relevant to a player as the story they will tell of their encounter with a memorable opponent playing the said character.

At the same time, while game writing offers many unique opportunities in the kinds of stories that it can best tell, there are also many different challenges that demand the writer to creatively problem solve and craft around the various restrictions that emerge. As a writer who entered interactive storytelling from more traditional media, there was a definite learning curve of how to apply the narrative instincts that I built in prose and film into gaming and how to best craft a story that is *experienced* and *played through* rather than just *watched* or *read*.

Additionally, narrative design for games is an intensely collaborative endeavor. Even more so than film (and certainly more so than novel writing), narrative design is done in deep cooperation with other disciplines. Much of my day-to-day is spent in close conversation with artists, gameplay designers, tech leads, and engineers about what is possible and what we are all working to make – not to mention product leads and production coordinators who help keep the vision and keep us on track and on schedule. A good portion of my work is coordinating narrative vision across teams, sharing the story out among creatives, and attending meetings so that everyone from our model riggers to the marketing folks crafting the campaign around a specific narrative beat all have a clear vision of the story we are trying to tell.

Writing for games also has had unique writing challenges that I have not encountered in any other creative space. Below are a few samples of some, rather, *fun* (okay, harrowing) things that I have been told over the years:

"Hey, we have changed the layout of the dungeon, so that 90ish seconds you had for characters in the party to talk while the player runs down the corridor? That already super tight scene where you had to lay out most of the expositional weight of the mission via incidental banter? It is now 30 seconds."

"Listen, I know we are about 80% of the way through development on this new character, but one of his gameplay abilities just was not working, so we completely changed it. Instead of a defensive ability, it is now hyper-aggressive with clear supernatural overtones. I know our setting so far has not ever included any magic or supernatural elements, but you can explain this power in his backstory, right?"

"The scope of the cut scene is getting cut back dramatically. We are overbudget on the number of voiceover lines overall, so we need a 30% reduction in the script length, and rather than custom animations, due to time crunch, we will have to use in game existing actions which means much of this needs to get reblocked. Also, please remember, this is the emotional climax of the story, so please maintain that as we reconfigure the scene."

Finally, my personal favorite example when illustrating some of the challenges of interactive storytelling in games is this question I was asked when interviewing with a company working on an MMORPG [Massively Multiplayer Online Roleplaying Game]:

"A hypothetical: let us say the narrative you have created for a quest has come to an emotional, personal conclusion. The player is delivering painful news to an NPC [non-player character] about her son – giving her back a medallion recovered from his body. How do you create and preserve the emotional integrity of this moment… when there are 20 other random players running around the area, spamming dancing emotes while standing on mailboxes, and shouting random things via chat?"

The challenge of the job is to constantly craft and deliver content that allows for player expression and participation yet remains flexible and robust enough in its structure so that it can bend but not break under player scrutiny and interaction. All in all? It is a pretty fun job.

> It is quite delightful and surreal to have "Very Serious Business Meetings" about how scary the dragons should be, whether we think the way the giant soul-reaving mace hits *feels* satisfying and right and *is* that how a demon spirit would look when vanquished by a cursed blade?

The past

When I was a kid, I just wanted to be a writer when I grew up. At the time, this meant I dreamed of writing books – books like the ones I would hide away under the covers and read by flashlight far past my bedtime. However, I also loved video games. Even though I was not allowed to play them until late middle school, I played them at friends' houses, at sleepovers, and in stolen moments huddling with a friend as they played their GameBoy after school. A wild amount of my hours as a kid disappeared into games.

I also came across a fantasy card game called "Magic: the Gathering," where players collect unique cards and build decks to battle each other in strategic, turn-based gameplay. As my fandom (and card collection) grew, I learned that the designers of the game wrote regular articles on the topic of design via their website. Learning about the design and thinking behind the cards fascinated me, and I quickly devoured the article backlog and began eagerly awaiting

Mondays – when the newest article from the head designer would be published. Nonetheless, even as I grew more interested in the design behind the games, becoming a game designer was still a fantasy I, at best, briefly entertained in daydreams – like being an astronaut or a famous actor. It did not seem like a *real* job for *actual people* to do.

When I started college, I fell in love with writing and performing. After getting my BA in Theater and English, I attended the California Institute of the Arts, where I would eventually get my MFA in Acting. CalArts also offered unique opportunities with coursework in theme park development, featuring instructors from Disney Imagineering and other theme park design firms. Upon graduation, I stayed in Los Angeles, and in between auditioning for gigs, I did contract work for themed entertainment. An internship in school with Disney Imagineering had led to a gig writing script coverage and ultimately led to a surreal phone call on a random Thursday to come in for a pitch meeting for a new stage show for Disneyland Shanghai. ("Are you available next Tuesday for a brainstorm session with executive producers and directors?" "Let me check my calendar: YES, I AM FREE.")

At the same time as that contract (which spanned two years in totality), I continued to audition and to write plays, was hired on a Chinese TV sitcom, and wrote for other theme park developments. The themed entertainment work broadened my understanding of interactive storytelling spaces.

Then, as my Disney contract was wrapping up, a friend reached out to me about a job opportunity. She worked at Wizards of the Coast in Seattle, and they were hiring a copywriter for their web team. Wizards made "Dungeons and Dragons", and that little card game, "Magic: the Gathering." I applied, interviewed, and before I knew it, everything was set up for me to move a thousand or so miles up the coast. "It is a six-month contract to scratch this nerd itch," I told myself. "I'll be back in LA in no time."

Two and a half years later, I was working as a narrative designer at Wizards and had contributed as a game designer as well by helping to make new Magic cards. One of Wizard's greatest strengths was its flexibility in allowing folks opportunities to flex outside of their roles and contribute creatively to the game, regardless of their main job at the company. Though I started on the web and community team, I regularly expressed my interest (and had the encouragement and support of my manager) in contributing to design and narrative. As fate would have it, they also were overloaded with prose stories that they needed to write, and I had an opportunity to write a piece of fiction that would be part of the canon Magic universe. When that story did incredibly well, I was given more opportunities to write – ultimately leading to an offer to move into a role on the team.

Since working at Wizards, I have had the opportunity to write for ArenaNet (the makers of Guild Wars 2) and Riot Games, where I worked on Legends of Runeterra, League of Legends, and other new games. Outside of my work with large studios, I also served as the narrative and gameplay designer for Port of Mars, an Interplanetary Initiative project sponsored by Arizona State University that is "a social experiment disguised as a board game." I also was the narrative writer for Social Cipher's Ava, an independent 2D-platformer adventuring game that features an autistic protagonist and is targeted for use in classroom and counselor settings. As my experience grew, so did the variety of opportunities that came across my path – ultimately leading to a return to Wizards as a Narrative Lead on Digital Publishing, and my current career in games.

The how

When folks learn that I write for games, I almost always get one of two follow up questions:
"Video games have writers?"
Or,
"How do I get a job doing that?"
Here are the answers:
Yes.

And...

1. *Write. A lot.*
   Do not wait for permission. Start doing the thing you want to do today. Write. Write all kinds of things. Write fanfiction of your favorite properties. Write branching and interactive fiction using tools like Twine (twinery.org) or Ink (Inklestudios.com/ink). Build your creative muscles making work – independent projects, freelance projects, just-for-you projects. If you can, take classes. Form a writing group with friends. Seek feedback from mentors and peers you trust.
   Some of the things you make might make it into your eventual portfolio. Some of it you may wish to never see the light of day. (There are web series on YouTube that I penned that I hope remain buried at the bottom of search algorithms.) By continuing to write, you will only grow

your skills.

Work leads to work. However, for that to start happening, you have to start putting in the work.

2. *Play. A lot.*

This is what many people think is the easy part. "Play more games? Hell yeah!"

It is more than just playing, however. Play with a critical eye. Take notes. Do your homework. Ask *why*, a lot. Seek out answers. Dig deeper online. Read critiques of the games you play. Be critical of the critiques of what you play. As a writer, there is a constant tension between carving out time to write and carving out time to consume media. The former strengthens your creative skillset. The latter strengthens your creative *taste*. What works, what does not, what do you like, what do you not like – and more importantly, how did the design of the thing you played, watched, or read succeed or not in making you like or not like a thing?

When hiring, we often ask about a candidate's thinking on games or to give examples of games that did X or Y element well or poorly. Being able to speak intelligently on games demonstrates your familiarity with the medium and empathy for the player experience – essential skills for the job.

3. *Build a portfolio.*

Pull samples of your best (and most high-profile) work. Different studios will look for very different things from your samples and will often specify examples of what they are looking for. Regardless, you should always strive to showcase your best and, barring rare exceptions, your most *brief* work. Remember, the hiring manager is likely wading through possibly tens, if not *hundreds* of applications. Leave them wanting to see more.

4. *Practice interviewing.*

Ask your friends and peers to help you prepare. Think through examples of your past work that you would love to bring up and practice working them into answers. Do your homework on the company: what is their mission statement? Values? How does your past experience and work demonstrate your competencies around those and in the field, in general? Practice how you would frame your answers and work in shining moments from the past to showcase your abilities.

Companies may even provide you with examples of how they interview or the types of questions they ask – familiarize yourself with them! Look up the STAR interview method and rehearse answering in that format.

You have worked hard to have the resume and the experience and the portfolio to get to the conversation. Give yourself the preparation and practice you deserve to put your best foot forward.

5. *Know someone.*

Every single one of my biggest jobs and opportunities, other than the Chinese sitcom, began with an introduction or recommendation.

While there are plenty of folks who get hired from an open pool of submissions, having someone who can vouch for your work is rather helpful, especially when you are starting out. Of course, a recommendation or introduction can only carry you so far. From there, your writing sample, skillset, experience, and interview have to carry you through. However, the industry is tiny, and the more you build a positive reputation, the more opportunities and doors you may find open a little more easily.

6. *Don't "network."*

I know. This seems to sit in direct opposition to the previous point but hear me out. Perhaps it did not start this way, but the very term "networking" has come to carry with it a connotation of connecting with someone with the expectation of a return; you "network" by talking to people who could potentially benefit or help you out. It is the worst feeling when you are talking with folks and it feels like they're sizing you up and seeing if it is worthwhile to "befriend" you. Those conversations feel icky and slimy, coated with a veneer of false niceties and manipulation.

The thing is, those conversations are unpleasant to be in on either side. People can also see and sense disingenuous motives from a mile away. Even when "networking" is done within a professional setting and construct, it can still feel artificial and weird.

> Instead of networking, make genuine connections. Build genuine relationships. I know – on the surface, this sounds like semantics – but the key difference between networking and building genuine connections is one of intention. It is the difference in asking "What is in it for me?" versus "What can I learn and offer?"

Approaching someone you admire is hard. Approaching someone who potentially has the ability to open doors and big opportunities for you is harder. What is the (not-so) secret way I found?

Ask them to lunch. (Who does not like lunch?) Then, talk about their work, not yours.

All along my path and growth and as an artist and professional, there has been one constant. People go above and beyond to help you out and lift you up. Seriously, it is pretty amazing. I am where I am because of the generosity of talented people further along on their career paths helping me out, serving as mentors, and giving me amazing guidance, advice, and encouragement. Asking for a bit of their time to chat – over coffee, a sandwich, or (less preferable) an email, call, or even Twitter direct message, has allowed me to build some great friendships and relationships. Do not network. As the proverb says, "do good and throw it in the sea." Befriend and reach out without the expectation of return and be surprised as you reencounter the good you put out along your journey when you least expect it.

The future

The games industry has grown and expanded in wild ways. I feel fortunate to get to tell the stories I do with the companies that I do it with. The industry also holds many opportunities for young aspiring creatives. The future is quite wild and unknown. If you are interested in joining, well … let us grab lunch and chat.

AUGMENTED REALITY DESIGN

A Brief How-To of Reality Creation

▶ ## Dr. Holden Holcombe

Dr. Holden Holcombe focuses his artwork and research on the place of transgender individuals in respect to the self, society, and social media. He has exhibited his work internationally using a variety of media – including AR/VR, video, animation, sound, and experimental music.

Figure 1.5 Dr. Holden Holcombe

In the last decade, time-based storytelling has radically advanced in sync with developing technologies and can be seen in the inclusion of extended realities as a staple in contemporary narratives.

> In contrast to virtual reality, augmented reality alters the world and spaces around us rather than creating whole new environments.

These alterations can be accessed through a mobile device or tablet or through specific augmented reality devices. It can be connected to a QR code or image, or it can be programmed to exist without a marker. As AR is becoming more a part of our everyday experiences, it is becoming readily available for artists to begin crafting allegories that allow every audience member, regardless of location or physicality, to become an interactive component of the story.

In my own journey as an artist, I began experimenting with augmented reality in 2015. Prior to finding AR, I had worked mostly with experimental video, animation, sound, and installation as tools for unraveling concepts of identity, especially in underrepresented stories of the queer community. Despite my relatively late interest in extended realities, I had the privilege of learning from one of the pioneers of fine art augmented reality – John Craig Freeman – while I was an undergraduate at Emerson College. In his 2012-work *Border Memorial: Frontera de Los Muertos*, Freeman uses AR to visualize the exact locations where the remains of people trying to cross the Mexican-American border have been found. This work, when activated on a smart device, such as a phone or tablet, shows hundreds of skeletons across Southern Arizona. These skeletons remain hidden to passersby and can only be found by those specifically searching for them.

In my work, I use this concept of hidden stories in AR to discuss the journeys of transgender men and women and aim to use the technology as a means of bringing lightness to heavy subjects. My 2018 series, *This Is How It Feels*, allows viewers to participate and learn about transgender culture while engaging with social media and embracing humor. Without AR, I fear that my stories would be too dark to successfully educate and expand people's understanding of different points of view. AR also allows viewers to become a part of a story and a world that they otherwise do no participate in. In *This Is How It Feels*, heteronormative cisgender people were placed into the viewpoint of transgender men struggling with the social expectations of transition. For most cisgender individuals, this is not a view of the world they would ever have, but, through AR, I was able to bring one person's story into another's world. Augmented reality allows artists and storytellers to make their audience

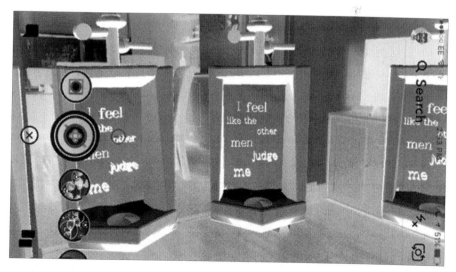

Figure 1.3 | I Feel Like the Other Men Judge Me, Augmented Reality Documentation, 2018

members "trade glasses" with another way of life and become a part of that other world, even if only for a moment.

Creating your own environments

When creating an augmented reality environment, there are dozens of apps to choose from – some being free, others requiring a one-time payment, and some needing a subscription.

One of the best software tools – and interestingly enough, one of the earliest created – is the ARToolKit. This is an open-source database to assist in creating environments. While it is somewhat user-friendly, working knowledge of CS comes in handy when constructing your app. If you are less familiar with programming languages, then I highly recommend using one of the three apps featured below.

Prior to choosing your application, however, it is important to consider what the purpose of your AR environment and narrative will be. Do you want to create AR using video, sound, and other traditional time-based media techniques? Do you want to create three-dimensional (3D) models that appear in the real world? Do you want your environment to be connected to social media and be instantly shareable? Do you want to scan a barcode or an image marker, or do you want your AR to be site-specific? All of these features need to be considered when choosing your application.

Membit

Membit is an AR photo-sharing application created in 2016 that uses a Human Positioning System (HPS) and was originally designed as a "geolocative photo-sharing app that allows pictures to be placed and viewed in the exact location where they were captured" (Membit, 2016).[1] Membit, conceptually, has a great potential in storytelling to connect place, memory, and narrative in a "tangible" way. While it does not currently allow any 3D objects in an AR space, it does allow access to your camera roll rather than simply streaming, so it is possible to import from your device in order to create the illusion of imagery in a location. This is extremely useful for site-specific AR that can be easily accessed by the public.

The application's greatest strength is how incredibly user-friendly it is as an AR platform. Once you open the app, you are brought to a screen with a featured map that shows where you are on the HPS and highlights any other public AR environments created on the app near you. To add an AR photo, press the large plus sign at the bottom of your screen. You will be prompted to create an account and to allow for the app to use your camera, camera roll, and location services – all of which need to be on in order for the app to function properly. If you are taking a photo with your camera rather than importing from your camera roll, then it is important to note that only a small area of your screen will be saved as the AR image.

In 2020, Membit released Aery, which is targeted towards the business end of fine art but has great potential for creation as well. Although the HPS and geolocation aspects of Membit provide opportunities for storytelling, the final AR is flat and does not embrace the strong qualities of augmented reality in fine art. Nevertheless, it is an excellent starting point for storytellers to begin experimenting with the nuances of augmented reality. As a potential project, try creating an AR image for every hour of your day. Experiment with the idea of creating hidden stories that need to be searched for in order to be seen. Embrace the interactive qualities of AR and become familiar with how site-specificity can be used to engage your viewer.

Roar

Once you become more comfortable and confident with the concepts of AR storytelling, an excellent second application to experiment with is Roar. Roar is an image-recognition based AR app that was created in 2015. The application is free for a certain number of AR environments and views, but once you have filled that quota, a subscription is required. Image-recognition-based AR has been used in several industries – including fine art, education, and retail – and, while profit-based industries are Roar's target audience, the app functions well for artists in a sense that it allows for environments to be accessed without scanning a code, but rather a specifically designed image or surface.

While Roar does give users a massive amount of free reign in creation and has an intuitive online platform, it does have some difficulties. The biggest inconvenience with Roar is its cost. While the free version is great for experimenting and becoming familiar with the platform, a purchase is needed in order to create lasting works. This can range from $99 per year for educators and up to $300 a month.[2] The possibilities of the app for image-recognition-based AR are seemingly endless, however, and it is worth the purchase if an entire exhibition or narrative utilizes Roar.

In order to create an AR experience with Roar, create an account either through the Android or IOS application or on the Roar website.[3] You use this online interface to create your AR environments, but this is not a space to create your content, unlike with Membit. Your videos, photos, sounds, animations, or whatever augmentation will be appearing in your environment needs to be created externally. I highly suggest having these prepared prior to experimenting with Roar if you are using the free version, since you only have a certain number of scans and tests available. It is important to note that videos with too large a file size will not load properly with Roar.[4] Consider which features are most important to you and your work.

After registering and logging in on Roar's online platform, simply hit the "Create AR" button to start building. This will bring you to another window where you must choose what type of AR you want to create. This can be image-recognition-based AR (as described above), or one of the two beta versions that Roar is constructing. This includes an ARKit that allows 3D objects to sit in the physical world without a marker and the WebAR that works through a link. I suggest selecting image-recognition based AR for fine art purposes, but, as Roar evolves, other features will certainly become useful to artists.

Once you select "Target Image AR," you will be directed to another page where you will be asked to assign your marker. This can be uploaded directly from your desktop and should be either a JPG or PNG file. After the upload, you can edit your marker within the platform to a particular size or color, but remember that the more you edit the image, the higher the chances are that it will not scan in the physical world. After your marker is assigned, Roar will process your request, and if the marker is acceptable, then this will bring you to a fourth window. In some cases, your marker may be denied – including if the image is being used by another artist or if the quality of the image is too poor.

If accepted, the fourth window will show your image marker in the center of the page with two toolbars surrounding it. The left toolbar features your content, or what you can add to your AR environment, while the right functions almost as the layer window in Photoshop, where you can see what you have placed onto the image. Once you have added content onto your marker, you will notice that it appears to cover at least some segment of your image – this is what appears after you scan the marker on the mobile application. You will also notice that the content is proportional to the image. In other words, it is highly likely that your video (or other content) will seem small in comparison to a high-resolution image. You can easily scale this by dragging the corners of the content. Once you are happy with the placement and size of content, you can connect to a URL or file in the right toolbar, test, and then save your AR environment publicly or privately.

As an experiment, try adding a Roar video environment to the cover of a book. This content can be a live video of flipping through the pages, an animation of the story being told, or any other element of the narrative. Prepare your files – including the content and the image marker – prior to entering Roar.

> Play with how the content sits on the cover and how it will shift as you physically move the book through real-world space.

Like all AR storytelling platforms, Roar is dependent on the concept of content and the physical, tangible interaction with space – ensure to give equal importance to both.

Snapchat

The last application to consider as you start creating AR environments is Snapchat, a multimedia messaging app created in 2011. It works on both Android and IOS devices and was originally created just to share photos and simple text messages back and forth between contacts. As the app developed, AR filters became an essential and attractive feature. Lens Studio, created by Snap Inc. in 2017, allows users to create their own AR lenses and import them directly into Snapchat to share with millions of users worldwide. Unlike Roar, Lens Studio and Snapchat are completely free and have no limit to the number of lenses you can create, share, or test.

In addition to allowing users to create and upload their creations, the app also provides extremely detailed guides and tutorials ranging from importing to texturing, lighting, and even basic scripting. Lens Studio, much like Roar, is not a platform for complete content creation, but rather for transforming models into AR environments. It is directly compatible with 3D programs like Maya, Blender, 3Ds, Cinema4D, and Qlone, as well as any other program that exports in FBX or OBJ files. If you have never used a 3D program but are interested in AR, then it is worth dedicating some time to familiarizing yourself with one of these programs in order to fully embrace the features of Lens Studio.

In order to use Lens Studio, you must have a Snapchat account which can be created online or via the social media app. Once you have your account, download Lens Studio onto your desktop and Snapchat onto your mobile device. If you are new to creating AR environments, then I highly recommend creating from a template – as this allows you to simply delete and replace objects, rather than coding or manipulating the space significantly. As you become more comfortable with the program and AR storytelling, creating off-template may serve your work better.[5]

Lens Studio provides over twenty templates to choose from in both "face" and "world" settings. The "face" settings are built for the camera looking at the users, almost like a mask, while the "world" settings are made to look away from the viewer, more similar to Roar. As an artist, I prefer to use the "world" camera that allows me to add to the physical space around us, rather than alter the filters of the viewer's face – but this choice depends on the AR story you want to tell. I suggest viewing each of the templates within Lens Studio and testing them on your mobile device in order to make an informed decision on which style of environment you want to create.

For your first AR lens in Lens Studio and Snapchat, I suggest using the "World > Static Object" template. This will provide you with everything you need to import a 3D model as an AR environment. This template comes prepared with folders labeled "to be replaced" and others labeled "to be edited." These can be seen on the left toolbars in the "Objects" and "Resources" tabs. These function similarly to layer menus in Adobe programs. In the center of the program, there is a 3D grid often featured in modeling programs. Along with the grid, this screen holds your objects, shadows, and a small blue camera that represents the camera lens on the mobile device in Snapchat. Where you place objects around this blue camera will impact how viewers will see them in the augmented reality. On the right side of your screen, there is a preview of your AR environment in a simulated real-world scenario. You can change this scenario via a drop-down menu in the "Preview" tab.

At this point, if your content is already built and appropriately exported, then you can import by right-clicking on one of the "Replace Me" folders in the "Objects" tab and selecting "Import Object." You can experiment, alter, and play with your imported object as it relates to the space, the grid, and the camera. At any point, you can test the lens on your own device by selecting the "Push to my Device" button above the "Preview" tab. This will automatically send the lens to your Snapchat app and can be accessed by holding the outlined circle in the bottom center of your screen until the featured lens appears. Your lens will not update on your device as you make changes in Lens Studio, so it is necessary to continuously push your lens to your mobile.

It is important to note that there are a few requirements within Snapchat that you must abide by, including the size of your lens. Lens Studio and Snapchat will not support lenses above 4MB, and although this seems small, your original OBJ or FBX must be quite large in order to reach this capacity within Lens Studio. You can always check to see your file size in the "Project Info" tab on the top left of your screen. Here, you can also alter the title of your lens and the featured icon – this is what will sit in the middle of your QR code. Unlike Roar, you cannot scan Snapchat AR from an image marker; it must be scanned via a QR code generated from Snap Inc. or shared directly through the app.

Once you are content with your lens, your work must be vetted by Snapchat. To do this, you select the "Submit Lens" button above the "Objects" tab. This will prompt you with a pop-up window asking you to confirm your submission and agree to Snapchat policies. Inappropriate material will not be allowed on the app, so if you are aiming to tell stories on the border of political correctness, as I often am, be prepared to have a few lenses rejected.

This rejection does not impact your ability to create or work in the app, but it

Figure 1.4 This is How It Feels, Exhibition Installation View, 2019, Cica Museum, Gimpo-si, Gyeonggi-do, Korea

does provide an interesting sense of censorship to one of the most progressive art forms of our time. As your Snapchat experimentation, consider creating an AR environment that tells an underrepresented story. Play with translating a serious subject onto such a jovial social platform. Find a way to skirt the boundaries of correctness in the project. This, for me, is one of the most compelling components of working within Snapchat. Not all of my stories have been allowed in the app, and, by now, I must be on their "watch list," if they have one. However, perhaps this reveals more about the medium of augmented reality than Membit or Roar – will it just be for the stories of the masses, or will AR serve as a way to promote change?

> Augmented reality provides a new type of story-telling, dependent not only on what we are saying and how we say it but also on how we interact with it. Unlike more traditional art forms, AR forces the viewer to become fully engrossed in a narrative in order to participate at all. AR stories do not exist without the viewer contributing or without the viewer searching for them, and that is what interests me so immensely as an artist.

I aim to use augmented reality to discuss hidden, forgotten, and untold stories in a light and playful manner. However, as seen with the censorship in Lens Studio and Snapchat, AR may not evolve to reach its true potential in story-telling. How artists use augmented reality in the next decade will determine if the medium becomes a technological gimmick, or if it can be used to serve a greater purpose.

The apps discussed in this chapter can be used as a jumping-off point for storytellers and creators interested in extended realities. While at a first glance, the technology behind AR seems daunting, you will be able to create new worlds and experiences for your viewers in using Membit, Roar, and Snapchat. Nonetheless, remember, technology is just a tool, and all too often, stories are lost in the flash and façade of machinery. Create wisely.

Notes

1 "Membit." Membit Inc., 2016, www.membit.co/about/.
2 Prices vary depending on subscription. Data as of May 2020.
3 www.theroar.io.
4 All step-by-step instructions are based on May 2020 version of application.
5 All step-by-step instructions are based on May 2020 version of application.

YOUR AUDIENCE IS WAITING

▶ Margaret Moser and Esjay Wonderly

Margaret Moser is a professor at the USC School of Cinematic Arts, where she teaches interactive design, game development, and production practices for creative projects. She has spoken at the Game Developers Conference and curated for the IndieCade game festival. She holds an MFA in Design and Technology from Parsons.

Figure 1.6 Margaret Moser

Esjay Wonderly is a transmedia creator with previous experience in documentary production and film marketing. She earned her MFA in Interactive Media from the University of Southern California's School of Cinematic Arts and is obsessed with creating participatory experiences that promote narrative agency and humanist ideals.

Figure 1.7 Esjay Wonderly

The internet is history's biggest story machine. Every day, millions of people post photos, tweets, videos, polls, and a thousand other forms of content – telling the story of their own lives: a new haircut, a hot take on pop culture, a silly thing that their cat did. As a creator, you can use it too – not just to share your latest screenplay, but also as a new way of making stories.

There is an enormous audience for interactive storytelling: those who would not consider themselves gamers but would love to engage with a story the same way that they already engage with content online – following links from one piece of content to the next, whether it is to get more detail or to see a different perspective.

You can meet these audiences where they already are through a transmedia approach to storytelling. It is a medium that is practically made for the internet, with limitless and largely unexplored possibilities for storytelling.

What is it? Transmedia storytelling (also known as multiplatform storytelling) is simply the name that has been given to telling stories across multiple channels within the same story world. Examples of potential channels include social media sites, webcomics, books, film, television, graphic novels, video games, and apps. If you can use it to communicate with an audience, then there is room for it in a transmedia project.

Scale

Right now, the main place where we see transmedia is in massive IPs like Star Wars or the Marvel Cinematic Universe – with mountains of high-production-value content: movies AND games AND comics AND action figures all tied together by branding and monetization strategies. Powering these highly polished, worldwide properties requires directors, animators, programmers, and even package designers, along with a staff to approve storylines and maintain consistency. No wonder why it can sound daunting!

However, it would be incorrect to assume transmedia work has to be produced on a scale only industrial systems can manage. While it certainly *is* used for large IPs, children's programming, brand marketing, and so on, it is also a creative approach that scales down quite well. What might be most exciting for creators is that you no longer have to compete for the attention of gatekeepers to get your pieces produced and published.

With a transmedia approach to storytelling, small teams and individual creators have ultimate agency: you can engage your audience directly, and you can build your own platform based on what you already know how to make.

For example, when Esjay began her most recent project, Moss Haven, she did not have a team at all.

"When I started out, I did not even know what transmedia was. I was just trying to find a way to do everything I wanted creatively, because I did not want to be dependent on anyone else for production or publishing. I came from a film and television production background; I am a narrative person, first and foremost. However, I saw how much more meaning and playfulness interactivity could bring to these narrative worlds and moved over to interactive work – as a student first and then as an artist.

Previously, I worked in edutainment, marketing, documentary, and comedy, so creating transmedia work is just sort of a natural progression in utilizing all of these perspectives and my love of worldbuilding. It is just a really accessible and natural way to work for someone like myself who likes having a lot of options for creative outlets."

What is Moss Haven? It is an adorable town of miniatures inhabited by live costumed snails. The town's story unfolds across short videos, a website, and social media. The audience has many options for engaging with the story world through its different channels. On the town newspaper's website, for example, they can write to the advice columnist or browse the classified ads. There are periodic online polls where they can vote as a member of the town council on issues like fixing the town fountain. In the short videos, they can make choices to follow one narrative path for a character or another.

The main story arc is sent out in installments, so the audience can respond to each part via polls, and their input influences the next installment. Between installments, Esjay makes smaller pieces that help build out the world and character arcs. In her words, "It is really like building a creative relationship with the audience."

Affordances

Media critics are fond of pointing out what different forms are good at in terms of their "affordances." A novel is great for a story with a lot of interior layers that can be read off and on, while a film is better suited for showing action and interaction between characters in generally one sitting. Since transmedia storytelling can include any other form, it is supremely adaptable. However, it also has some affordances of its own, which we will outline here.

World canon
As you saw above, all the channels of a transmedia story exist within the same story world. Information specific to this world is its "canon." Any previous works referring to these storylines, to their places, characters, plots, and so on

become part of the world canon. The narratives may overlap but never conflict with each other.

This means if we have two channels of the story taking place in the same era and location, then they had better be pulling from the same canon. If flying cars exist in one channel, then they must exist in the other. Working within a canon is not just a restriction. It means that you can draw from numerous perspectives and outlets to build your story. If Star Wars were released today, then we might learn about Darth Vader being Luke's father through a private journal entry that he accidentally uploaded to Soundcloud!

Short cycles

If you work with easy-to-use tools and publish as often as you like, then you can take an experimental approach. You can try out different writing styles, different perspectives, and different kinds of interaction like simple online polls. With no gatekeepers, you can try publishing on longer or shorter cycles to see what sustains interest. Moreover, best of all, you have direct access to your online audience, so you can get immediate feedback from the people you are making it for.

Interactivity

Any story can have multiple levels of interaction. There is interpretive inter-action, where just by reading a book you are bringing your own perceived meaning to it. With choice-based interaction, like *Choose Your Own Adventure* books and most games, you choose a path through premade content. The deepest kind, adaptive interaction, is where the audience participates in adding to or changing the text in some way.

That last kind is rare but rather interesting. The best example is probably tabletop role-playing games. In something like *Dungeons and Dragons* or *Lasers and Feelings*, players can try pretty much whatever they want by deciding what they want their character to do – whether that is fighting an orc or growing a pumpkin – and the "game master" then decides what the result will be. (There are set rules for certain things like combat, but the game master has total discretion about when and whether to apply them.) Even if the result is not what the player wanted, whatever they tried becomes part of the story. It becomes a collaborative creation.

Transmedia storytelling can be any combination of the above. The audience can join in story creation, or it can be a simple, self-contained experience.

Ephemerality

For a long time in film and television, you had to show up while it was playing or miss it forever; you could not replay an episode if you missed it nor download the movie later. Anticipation was part of the experience; speculating what was to come was a pleasure of its own.

Now, once something is published, it is (generally) available forever. The audience can choose when and how they want to consume it – whether by binge-watching a whole series or by playing a single console game over the course of several months.

However, what if that audience had to show up within a certain time frame in order to *influence* a story? It raises the stakes, draws the audience together, and creates anticipation for each new opportunity to weigh in. Each member who weighs in has a sense of ownership of the story, however, attenuated, because they were present in that specific moment.

It is a little like going to an exciting baseball game. Everyone who was there for that walk-off homer now has something in common with the rest of the crowd. They could meet years later, and they would have something to talk about. People who go to every home game can become a strong community because of the long-shared experience of being a fan. They look forward to each game and talk about what might happen and share their opinions afterward, all based on being there in the moment.

That shared anticipation and response is a powerful tool for a storyteller. While it is not necessary for every project, it can add excitement for your audience and build buzz around your work, whatever its form may be.

Getting started

Trying something new can be all kinds of weird. Do not know where to start? Do not worry, we have got you covered. We have outlined some helpful approaches (which are, by no means, rules) that can help get you going on your transmedia narrative.

Inspiration

It is easy to get started: just focus on what you love. Think about the types of stories and types of play you enjoyed most as a kid. Maybe you had semi-interactive bedtime stories with your parents, or you put on puppet shows for your friends, or you loved telling scary stories around a campfire. Whatever it is for you, it can help you imagine the kind of relationship you can build with your audience and the emotions you want to cultivate with your work.

Esjay's favorite pastime has always been brainstorming and producing creative projects with friends, so Moss Haven was designed with collaborative improv as the main point of engagement for the audience. Maybe you loved collecting things as a kid – you could tell your story with baseball cards or build your own wiki for that detail-oriented little collector who still exists inside you. Maybe you could build out a whole mystery or caper story where items go missing, and their images are replaced with clues that lead you through the story world.

Get it? Pick what you love and build around it. You will have more knowledge than the average Joe on your subject matter, and you will be working on something that you really like rather than wasting your time trying to build something you *think* other people will like.

You can start from scratch or adapt something you have already been working on; it just depends on how flexible you want to be with your idea. (Attention, all you screenwriters with passed-on scripts: dust off your favorite and figure out what formats work best to get its story out to your audience!)

Decide on your experience goals

Not all transmedia projects need to be interactive. However, there are some specific techniques that interactive designers and storytellers use to develop ideas that not all writers would know about. One example is what is called an experience goal.

When you make something interactive, you are not "telling" a story anymore so much as you are creating a story system for your player to explore. The way that the player finds or interacts with your story is important and is often as important as your actual content. Accordingly, as you create, you will want to have a very clear statement about how it all feels to the player – the content, the interactions, the sequence of discovery, all of it together. This is an experience goal.

Your project might aim to make the player feel epic and powerful like a Star Wars game, or frustrated and depressed like Anna Anthropy's *dys4ia*, or confused and frightened like *Inside*. Maybe they will feel triumphant as they dig a clue out of an evil character's journal entry or intrigued by hearing the end of a story before the beginning.

Of course, you can have different goals for different parts of your work. Nonetheless, an overall experience goal will help make your project feel cohesive and intentional to the player.

Here is Esjay's description of the experience goal for Moss Haven:

> "I wanted Moss Haven to be a place where busy ladies could immerse themselves in a weird little world for a short time and feel excited about determining narrative direction. It is part storytelling and part having your friend over to play dollhouse."

Find your audience

Who is going to get the most enjoyment from your work? Having a specific audience in mind as you plan out your transmedia projects will help you immensely. Every subculture has its own community esthetics – their customary tones, visuals, and in-speak. People who like Jim Henson's work will be drawn to fun and thoughtful ensembles with crafted esthetics, very different from James Bond fans who would prefer heroic exploits with an ultra-slick look.

Inventory your tools and resources

Once you have got your idea and experience goal, how do you actually make your project? The first step is to take stock of available resources: your skills, potential collaborators, and any useful equipment, as well as how you like to work, and how much time and energy you have for the project. If you know that everything that is readily available, then you can custom design an approach that can meet your project's experience goals but remain accessible to you as the creator.

> Do not overlook existing social media sites, mobile apps, and software – these are powerful tools for easy content creation. Maybe you can think of an unconventional way to use these that will delight your audience with their novelty.

For example, an anonymous Amazon user a few years ago wrote a whole series of reviews in character as a down-in-the-dumps divorcee, gradually including details that revealed a (clearly fictional) story. Imagine having access to this character's Instagram and freshly minted dating profiles and seeing how these are updated over time. Maybe the different sites reveal different sides of his character; maybe he orders outlandish shoes and then his dates are more (or less) successful. Finding this information across multiple channels lets the reader construct the story, leaving space for them to imagine their own "meet cute" moment.

Every opportunity for communication out there is a transmedia device just waiting for you to make use of it. With a little creativity, you can give yourself a variety of ways to make content and give your audience a variety of ways to encounter and interact with it.

While we are talking about tools, there are some great ones for writing interactive work that you might not know about. Someone new to making interactive work – such as a screenwriter – might find Inkle Writer is a good first step; it is free, visual, and very intuitive, with a great step-by-step tutorial. Furthermore, there is Twine which is just text and is not much different from writing in Word or Final Draft, except that you can easily make links from one chunk of story to another. Neither requires any deep technical knowledge or skill to get started. Consider trying them out for a morning – you might find that you love imagining all of the ways one story could turn out!

Make it quick and easy

You have lined up your inspiration, your experience goals, your target audience, and your resources. It is time to make some content! You will want the first few things you send out into the world to have an immediately intriguing or delightful appeal, something that makes the viewer want to go down your rabbit hole willingly. For Moss Haven, a costume designer made hand-drawn portraits of the main snail characters in their costumes (top hat, pince-nez, and so on). They were beautiful all on their own but also highly shareable – everyone who saw them wanted to know more.

Maybe you are worried because you do not have any visual skills. You can still find a way to meet or subvert your audience's expectations in your content! When you get away from studio platforms, expectations for polish really loosen up. By intentionally creating for people who love the same things you love, you will be able to speak more clearly to them through any format you choose, because they will understand where you are coming from on an authentic level.

Maybe your photos or videos are mediocre. You can turn them into comedy gold with clever captions or by superimposing thought bubbles... or both. Do not stress it. People are very accepting of low-fi work when they know it is being produced on a small scale.

Whatever the form, that first handful of things should not ask for more than a minute or so of your viewer's time. Once you build interest and trust from your audience, then you can start to make longer works and start adding other channels into the mix.

Where to go from here

Transmedia storytelling really is for anyone who has a story to tell. There is an audience waiting for you and no gatekeepers to stop you. Be creative, be adaptive, have fun, and really make a point to work in areas authentic to you!

- For a more nuanced (but still accessible) explanation of what transmedia is and how it came to be, we recommend Henry Jenkin's "Transmedia Storytelling 101".
- To learn more about how interactive designers work, *Games, Design, and Play* by Colleen Macklin and John Sharp is a good introductory text with a practical approach to the nuts and bolts of making a game.
- If the idea of levels of interactivity made you curious, then you will enjoy the work of Espen Aarseth. His book *HyperText* is a short, clear presentation of this framework.

PLAYING IMPROVISATIONAL THEATER IN LOS ANGELES

▶ Josh Simpson

Josh Simpson is a comedian, actor, writer, and social media mischief-maker living in Los Angeles, California. He has worked for CONAN, Funny or Die, Comedy Central, FX, and Participant Media, and he started the @BPGlobalPR Twitter account in 2010 to satirize BP's public relations tactics during the Deepwater Horizon oil spill and to raise money for the Gulf Restoration Network.

Figure 1.8 Josh Simpson

When I first started doing improv, I did not think of it as getting into the business of it. I liked comedy of all kinds in college. I tried out for the improv troupe at Syracuse University. From there, we started doing short form. I discovered Upright Citizen Brigade (UCB) through one of my friends in the group. Upright Citizens Brigade is the name for comedians from Chicago who moved to New York to try to get a television show. Amy Poehler is one of the founding members. Adam McKay was a founding member. He directed and wrote *Anchorman*, *Talladega Nights*, *Step Brothers*, and more recently he has done more directing, such as *The Big Short* and *Vice*. Then, there is Matt Besser, Matt Walsh, and Ian Roberts. They had a television show on Comedy Central. They used a bit of their notoriety there to start a theater and make a place for long-form improvisation in New York. Long-form improvisation during that time was mostly done in Chicago and maybe a little in Toronto. They kind of brought it to New York and started their own theater. The ethos behind the theater was "cheap shows." All of the shows were perhaps five bucks when they started or free.

We took a trip to New York, saw a short-form improv, and saw what UCB was doing. It was instant, for me especially, but I think it was unanimous that everybody wanted to do what we were seeing at UCB. We saw "The

Soundtrack" on Friday nights, which I assume they still do. That started the journey.

What attracted me was that it seemed like they were doing it for the love of the game. They were doing risky comedy. They were allowed to take chances since the model of the theater was that there was not really a financial incentive. I think they made their money through their classes. You could tell, especially back then, that they were a small devoted group of people that were doing really weird, good, creative work in comedy. It started out of this ethos that they wanted comedians to have a place to do stuff without being screwed over by the venues or theaters they would rent. They made it easy to do shows that you could take risks in.

Improv in Hollywood

In 2005, UCB moved to Los Angeles. As soon as I moved to Los Angeles, I started taking improv classes at UCB in Los Angeles. I knew that I wanted to do stuff in comedy, and it seemed that learning improv, learning sketch, and being around that community was the place to do it. I took my first class in 2004. I started going there, got on teams, started teaching, and it all happened organically. Like most things with improv, the more you put yourself out there, the more it keeps happening. It started organically with a broader goal of doing comedy in mind. Improv was something I had a knack and love for, so I just kept on with it.

UCB has since grown quite a bit. I do not think it would still be considered to have the punk rock ethos that it embodied in the early days. I do not think it has gone full Hollywood, but I will say that Hollywood has come to it. "Broad City," for instance, is a UCB show that goes to Atlanta and Abbey. Basically, the whole cast is UCB people. People are getting on Saturday Night Live, with Amy Poehler being the face of it now. Everyone thinks, "Amy Poehler did improv. Steve Carell did improv," but they do not really know what that looks like. Now, you see Middleditch and Schwartz on Netflix. I have definitely watched UCB turn from a hole-in-the-wall theater to a place where agents and managers say, "You should take a UCB class to get good in comedy." When you improvise, you learn. The way I explain to my students about how you get better at improvising is that you do a thing ten times and figure out which move works best. I cannot even tell you how many improv scenes I have done at this point. When I am in a scene, I have a general sense of what is missing, how I can further the fun, or how I can push the scene forward in a way that either entertains me or clarifies what is going on for the audience.

By improvising a lot, you learn to do that quickly. You can find fun or find humor in scenes that are maybe struggling just by improvising a lot. To apply that to a writers' room or interactive storytelling, improvising trains your brain in a way. It is almost like a guiding light. You have an instinct for what could be funny, exploratory, or useful in the pursuit of both an improv stage or a writers' room. The pursuit is to be funny. If you could do it at the moment, then you could probably apply that to the page. The other thing that helps in terms of comedy writing is, if you are willing in an improv scene to share the responsibility of writing with your scene partner, then you are more likely able to work with other writers in a writers' room. Writing can be a lonely profession, but in a writers' room, it is a team effort. Sometimes, there may be people who are not the best writers. They are not going to sit down and pan out a brilliant script from their mind. However, there is value in being a person in a writers' room who hears an idea and adds to it.

I have a friend who got into Pixar because he related his experiences in improv to how they set up their writers' room. They basically had a thing called "plussing." They do not judge their ideas. They add to them all together and take the ones they like. There are writers' rooms where people can become competitive and attempt to stake their claim, get their joke in, or get their script idea through. The Pixar process is more collaborative and tries to "plus" ideas rather than everyone pitching and fighting for their own.

UCB teaches how to find a premise and play it in improv, to write a premise, to sketch, to write, and to perform a character in their character classes. It has become a hub.

Improv, acting, and storytelling

Improv is interactive acting. You have to listen and respond to your scene partner, and that is 80% of the battle with acting. What I am learning in an acting class is how to prepare for a role and how to use what I learned in improvisation and apply it in a useful way to a scripted scene. Much of what I learned in the acting classes is how to put myself in the right headspace and how to understand my character so that I can enter a scene and basically improvise with some idea of the lines I am going to say. I view improv as my core acting work. If we were doing a scripted scene and your line was, "Let's go on a vacation," and you said it in that tone of voice [chipper] for ten times in a row, but then for the eleventh time, you said it in a glum tone of voice, as an improviser, I would know how to respond to each one of those. The moment you change it to being glum I would respond, "What's wrong? Do you not want to go on a vacation?" Whereas someone only focused on the acting side of their work or the preparation of acting in a scene might stick with the thought, "Well, they said it glum but the work I have done tells me I should respond 'Heck yeah! Let us go to Florida!'", rather than responding honestly to what is in front of them. Improv is the training ground.

If you want to become a comedic actor in Los Angeles, then you are probably going to go to UCB. Once in a while, I will get stopped after a show. Someone will ask me to audition for a show. With everything, when there is a new batch of performers on Harold Night, which is like their house teams that they cycle new performers into, oftentimes the industry will attend. However, that is not really on my mind when I am performing there. I would recommend having an agent, at least if you want to get auditions. The relationship is pretty simple. They send me on auditions, and I go. I would tell young people to definitely get to work and find people who could help you get work. You do not always want to jump on the first thing that comes your way. Like with any business, you have to make sure that whatever you choose is right for you. Especially in the world of commercials, a lot of times, you just need an agent. You need somebody to put your headshot on a casting director's desk. I met my theatrical and commercial agent through the same company. You can put a packet together, submit it to people, and go to meetings. You can be referred to by a friend. I got my first agent through UCB because she was basically taking all the people who had a stamp of approval from the UCB. There is not really a blueprint for finding an agent. I wanted to be a comedian. Now, I want an actual career, so I better learn how to be good at the business part.

The general way an audition will go, for instance, is they will say, "We will be doing a Toyota commercial. We need this type: male, 20s–30s". They will indicate whether you should be good at comedy or have a comedy background. Most of them default to that. If they say, "male in their 30s for a Taco Bell ad," my agent would take my profile and submit me for the role. I have profiles set up on different casting sites. LA Casting is one of them. The agent's job is to look through all of the job listings and submit their clients who fit the roles or who they think might be a good fit for what the casting is asking for. You go in for an audition. If you are lucky, then you get a call-back. If you are very lucky, then you get booked.

Sometimes, the auditions are nice. Sometimes, they are not nice. Sometimes, they are in a nice facility with a parking lot. Sometimes, you have to park half a mile away and walk to it.

Actors do not tend to get a lot of respect throughout the process. We do not get paid to audition or to do call-backs. You show up at the office, and there are a lot of people who look like you. You receive a run-down of what you are doing that day. You walk into the office. You read for it. A lot of times the comedians or improvisers tend to be good at the auditions, because we are funny, or we can add a funny line that is not in the script. So much of it, honestly, comes down to how you look. I have booked stuff in which I did not think I did well at all during the audition. I think I was booked because they wanted someone who looked like me. I have booked a lot of alcohol commercials, but sweet alcohols – think, sweet ciders or cinnamon whiskey. That is my look – a sweet drinker, and I do not even drink. It is humbling. They certainly do not pull the punches on you when they are casting you. Sometimes, they will be like, "We want the best friend type. Not too attractive. Maybe chubby." My agent will send it to me like, "Perfect!" Women have it worse than men in that department though, especially with commercial acting.

Funny business

The business model of being a comedian is dependent on the person. For instance, on UCB Harold Night, shows ["The Harold" is an improv long form] are a $7 ticket or free for students. There are sixteen performers on the stage because there are two teams of eight people. They have full-time employees that manage the theater. They have the rent. It would be great to set up a system where performers are paid. I have a couple of ideas on how you could actually do that. Some of my friends are great performers. They have improvised for ten years. After a certain amount of time, they decided that they would try to write for television. Some of my friends are more on the acting side, and they do not write much at all. One of my favorite performers is a landscape architect. He works 9–5 at his landscape architect job. Then, he performs at night and has a well-rounded life with a family. Did I picture myself in my 30s making most of my money from teaching improv? That was probably not my aim when I came out here at the age of 18. However, I feel very fortunate to be doing it.

The way it looks for me is I have a baseline of income where I teach through UCB, and I teach independently myself. I teach my own workshops. I pay my bills. Then, I leave my days open to try to have television pilots that I could pitch to or sketches that I do to show that I can still do work. The last two years have been good for acting, so that has been a good supplementary income. For students coming out of college, you will have to decide that for yourself when you are ready to decide that. One of the best realizations I had out in Los Angeles is that no one is going to ask you to do anything unless you do it yourself. If I want to be booked on shows where people come out and do comedy characters, then I cannot expect to be asked to do the shows. I have to start putting out my own comedy characters wherever I can and making my own space to do that. When people want to book a comedian who does characters they will think, "Josh does characters!" Start doing stuff so that doors will open and, hopefully, you will find things that you love to do.

I would put "getting paid" to the back of your list if you are doing improv. If you want to perform at UCB, then it could be kind of difficult to get a slot. There are a lot of different stages, but if you want to get on the main stage, then you definitely have to pass a few tests. It is hard to say how to find your group. You have to find people who are doing the kind of work that you like and those who have a similar sense of humor. Another thing to remember, especially in the beginning: people try to get it perfect or get it exactly right how they dreamt it right out of the gate. Getting into a group could take a second, and it gets harder as you get older. People get busier or have their own established groups. In the beginning, you just need people who are going to show up and be humble enough to take notes from a coach, be willing to work on the team or themselves, or prioritize the work they are doing in their life so that it is not a waste of time for everybody. A lot of it is dependent on the chemistry and the willingness to show up. Keep working at it.

Funny games

My biggest outlet for my improv is my podcast, "The MEAT Improv with Josh Simpson and Jake Jabbour." My podcast comes out every Tuesday, and I record it every Monday. You have to put up consistent good work. When you tell the average person that you do improv comedy, they do not know what long-form improv is. They probably think of "Whose Line Is It Anyway?" or "Comedy Sports." They probably do not imagine that you could do an improvised set that is a 30-minute play. My intention behind starting a podcast was to create a space that I was in charge of, and no one could take it away from me. No one could say, "your show is canceled." I am the producer. I also thought there was a lack of improv podcasts at the time we started it in 2016. I like to have fun onstage. I like to be goofy, take chances, and wing it a little bit. I also wanted to incorporate the idea of people telling meaningful stories or talking about interesting, meaningful things to inspire the improv. The idea with the podcast being called "The Meat Improv" is that the guests come on, and they each share a meaty story or we talk about a meaningful topic of conversation, we get honest about it, and then we release the pressure of what are sometimes heavy conversations or what are sometimes just silly stories. Then, we do improv inspired by it to sort of laugh. That is the kind of show I wanted to do. Improv is such a fleeting performance to do. Most of the shows I have done have been for small crowds in a theater in Los Angeles. We wanted to find a way to put it on the record, so my friends back home could listen to my work. We have had a couple of hundred-thousand listeners over the years.

A lot of people are trying to figure out how to do improv online, myself included. D'n'D [Dungeons and Dragons], larping [LARP=Live Action Role Playing], and online games are just people playing. Improv is like structured play. The goal of improv is to be funny. The goal of D'n'D is to have fun. I will tell you that there is definitely a lot of overlap. There are a lot of improvisers who like D'n'D. The one thing we all have in common is you have got to be a nerd about something in order to play with other people to do it. To do VR, we would have to step out of the traditional form of improv and into the digital territory. I do think that is beginning to happen. I have some friends who do shows on Twitch. A lot of people from my improv team are putting on shows on Twitch. Twitch is a good way to broadcast your set. One of my teachers is Seth Morris, and he is doing a show called "Brighter! Comedy" where he plays a character who is a hippie in a basement. He dresses his set so that it looks like it fits his character, and he interviews people from his building, which is just a character grab bag. He is working on a way to give the show a feel or excuse as to why they are all in these boxes. I look forward to it. I think these kinds of new things help to level the playing field.

CHAPTER 2

STICKING IT OUT

Sylke Rene Meyer and Gustavo Aldana

Your career as an interactive storyteller will be a quest through the hills and valleys of success and challenges. It is often said that we learn and adapt through experiencing failure. As you climb the mountain on the way to achieving your dreams as a successful interactive storyteller, you will need to have the strength and fortitude to persevere through the valleys of setbacks.

Interactive storytelling is a career path that may seem quite natural, considering the human propensity to tell and listen to stories, but like any other career in the entertainment industry, the path to success is not straightforward. The open-ended nature of interactive storytelling provides many opportunities for you to find your own way. While the industry is full of opportunities to make money and win accolades, there are many ways to get lost as well. You could have mastered technology through a proprietary application, only to find that new technology and application has taken over as the industry standard. The industry is constantly changing, and you will need to work to keep up.

While the ever-changing nature of interactive storytelling presents a unique set of challenges for finding success, there are common threads that tie the stories of those who were successful together. The professionals who have found success have had perseverance, and they have kept an open mind to new technologies and methods in interactive storytelling. As you read about some of these tales of fortitude in the face of adversity, you may find yourself inspired, challenged, and questioning your own abilities. Do you have what it takes to grow as an artist and a professional along with the industry? Will you have the strength of spirit to stick it out when new challenges and technologies arise?

In this chapter, you will read about:

- A detailed description of the ways that academia has evolved in approaching interactive storytelling
- Experiencing the evolution of technology from the perspective of industry veterans
- Challenges in funding and producing interactive storytelling projects
- Ways to implement your personal challenges and experiences into your work
- What to do to persevere when you face those inevitable setbacks
- Working within an appropriate scope to increase the odds of success
- Methods for working with and maintaining a working collective
- How to keep going after experiencing failure

Learning about ways that others have conquered their own failures will help you to fight your own battles when they arise. What if you were an interactive designer and want to start up your own company?

NAVIGATING THE INDUSTRY AS AN INDEPENDENT CREATIVE

▶ By Lena Thiele

Figure 2.1 Lena Thiele

Lena Thiele is the artistic director of the Berlin-based media company, Miiqo Studios, and has been conceptualizing and producing digital media formats for over 20 years. Her projects received numerous awards, such as the SXSW Innovation Award in the category Best Visual Media Experience. In 2016, Lena Thiele was appointed professor for "Digital Narratives – Art and Design" at the ifs international filmschool cologne.

I always wanted to be independent. The big challenge for an entrepreneur and creative is how to make a living while still doing the work you love. There is a constant tension you have to keep in balance among your artistic work, your personal, ethical, and social compass, and the need to care for your everyday life. My personal experience, methods, and tools are what I can share with people who are willing to look for their own path.

I graduated from high school in the mid-1990s, but I had no clear plan regarding where and how to start my professional career. I started to work in a very small advertising agency, which, back then, did creative work with clients like MTV. It was my first experience working at an agency, and I remember it being a very tough job with long nights, working overtime and on weekends, organizing pitches, and learning how to level the stress between creative work and pressure.

After my internship ended, I got the opportunity to work at a big, German private TV broadcaster. I started as a runner, carrying everything that needed to be delivered in-house, sometimes literally running around with the videotapes to get them to the studio in time, only moments before the live broadcast was on the air.

The positive aspects: you get to know everyone in the building, which allowed me to have my first sessions in learning 3D modeling, as I was offered to just sit and learn through their night shifts. I applied for a job in the art department at the film studio in Babelsberg. This job was my first insight into how to create the illusion of worlds for big Hollywood productions, as well as for exhibitions and theme parks. Most of the work was manual work done without computers, and I was able to acquire a solid knowledge of a very old craft, which I still appreciate, before moving into the digital area of the media industry.

The end of the 1990s was the rise of the new economy Together with family and friends we set up a small start-up business in Berlin. We realized that the internet was at a point where pictures, visuals, and moving images were becoming a natural part of the new digital identity. We strongly believed in the power of creating communities online around shared visual experiences. Our platform "lieblinx.net" offered live-streaming of mainly sport events connected with a simple community tool. At that time, consumer internet connections were still very slow with mainly a 56k bitrate. However, we developed an idea for technology to actually allow users to stream live events in decent video quality with a chat tool attached to it to allow for events, communities, or meetings to be interactive. We started in our small 60-square-meter flat – living and working together: my brother, my boyfriend, the cat, and me. Later, we moved to a very small one-room office in former East Berlin, looking at the still no-man's land of the former Berlin Wall from our window. I was still a student, but at the same time, I prepared pitches and learned how to write business plans. We continually ran out of money of course, but we really believed in our product. The time felt right. We began looking for funding. There was a business plan competition by the investment bank of the city of Berlin. We won a package for free consultancy, and that opened many doors.

> I found myself participating in meetings where I got a certain color wrist band symbolizing "looking for money," and I talked with so-called angel investors with different colored wrist bands symbolizing "I have money."

I was often the only woman in the room, especially when the meetings were technology-based. I never thought about questioning my competencies,

I wasn't broad up like this, and it really took me a while to understand why I am good for a drink, but not good enough to talk business – just because I am a woman in my early 20s in a tech-related environment. Back then it seemed like it did not matter that I co-developed the whole product. Such experiences have to make you even more confident in your work and motivate you to stay with your idea. Back then, there was a range of funding programs that were specifically for tech-related start-up ideas. We almost achieved funding right before the Dot-com bubble popped. However, based on this situation, the US cut us off. These were very interesting and weird situations back then, because you sometimes had no idea how to pay your rent, yet you were pitching for millions in funding. After the cut-off from the US market, we had to stop working for the company, because we ran out of money. My brother stayed with it and created websites for smaller businesses. My husband went on to work for a digital agency. A paid job was essential for my upkeep. I applied to work for an event agency and started as an event manager and creative for commercial brands, for the next two years.

Doing what you love

This experience initiated a major and still lasting shift in my work: first, to learn about experience design for real events. Creating huge, interactive, and visually striking live events is still an experience that I add to my current work constantly as you create immersive experiences for a diverse audience. Nonetheless, that also comes with responsibility. All my creativity and all my energy supported something that I did not want to support. The client I was working for did not represent a company that I wanted to have a better standing with in the world. I understood the power in the work that you do, the power of immersive experiences, but also the responsibility that comes with it. The day after one promotion party, I quit my job and decided to focus on our own independent artistic projects, although that is clearly not the sector where the big money is. My brother, my husband, and I teamed up again. Why not start over with your own company again?

> As an entrepreneurial spirit, I guess you just think of yourself being in business, and I never thought about being employed long-term.

I grew up in this atmosphere, as my parents owned a company for events, event technology, and equipment. I assume I am quite used to dealing with the ups and downs of self-employment. When we started again, we were always at the intersection of using new technologies to create special experiences by integrating all kinds of media formats – including the connection between real and virtual space. It was, and still is, a huge playground.

We began developing VJ software for live events that integrated the visuals of the audience. People could feed in their own images on location and their choices were put into a queued timeline, and then they were played when the DJ was finally on set. The audience was literally creating the visuals for the event. Those were interconnections that I was and still am very interested in: how to make your work engaging, inviting for participation, and not simply creating interaction – using creativity from the fields of software development, narrative design, artistic expression, and entrepreneurial spirit. All of our approaches were integrating different platforms and technologies. Back then at around 2006, we developed our first cross-media approach: how to think from the topic to your audience, how to create a media framework that allows you to roll out on different platforms, and how to engage your audiences on different levels. In addition, we initiated and implemented different production structures combining production processes from software and game development, like Scrum, to creative processes that you apply in the design-thinking method. These agile developing processes allowed us to stay flexible with our products and, by rapid prototyping, apply and test new technologies.

In-house, we started to restructure the company based on the different main competencies, software/web-development, communities, and games. At a certain point, we split the companies apart: with the gaming company, we aimed to create our own products and IPs, while the web-agency was mainly doing work for clients. Both branches did support each other with the endeavor to create engaging fictional and playful worlds and products by trying to let people connect. We started quite small with eight people, and during its peak, we had about 40 employees working in several offices. We went from a very small space where everything was handmade to a three-floor enterprise.

In 2007, we created our first game, a multiplayer strategy game for mobile phones, and we continued with external licenses. When the App Store was launched, we jumped on this market. Due to the possibilities of self-publishing, smaller gaming studios felt liberated from the pressure of big publishers. You could self-publish your games not only in the AppStore, but also even in the stores of the consoles for the Nintendo DS, for PlayStation, or for Nintendo Wii without a publisher being the middleman. However, if you are self-publishing, then you are also self-marketing. The big publishers still had to sell shelf spaces in the big market, and they have the contacts for the right people in the App Stores for things that are featured. Even if you hire a marketing specialist, that does not imply the person has the necessary contacts; you are still a very small player. Nevertheless, there was always the story of THE ONE small studio who made millions with their own small game. We published several smaller games, even on Nintendo DS, including a multi-player trading card game with beautiful graphics and rather good reviews, with a full cross-platform concept including real card decks to be sold and connected to the gaming console. Even so, we never made more profit than what was needed to recoup our costs, and all of the remaining profit went directly into new projects.

Starting over again

Both company branches became insolvent, which was extremely hard to deal with. Especially as a family business, this pushes you into a deep crisis – financially and emotionally. In other countries, this kind of crushing experience is part of entrepreneurial life. In Germany, it feels like a failure, and you feel like a failure instead of acknowledging that you tried and it just did not work out. However, you learn from your failures, and we learned a lot, even if this was the hard way.

As our heart is in the creation, our energy always went into the development of the best product we can think of. On the other hand, marketing and business were not our strongest suit, at least from my perspective.

When inventing a tech product, the only way you can put that into a business model as a company is to develop a framework or technology that you can reuse. You develop the next product based on the same technology, the next game based on the same engine, and you start licensing your work.

However, that is often not how we worked. We always kept inventing, not selling. When you are a small team, you devote all of your energy to pushing your product to the highest quality. After that, you do not have the energy left to push it into the market and to keep it alive.

From the entrepreneurial side, we took too big of a risk. We lost plenty of money with a few really huge projects. Additionally, you have to keep your team and be able to keep the cost of a company that is working on several projects in parallel. That was the moment where we were not able to make any artistic decisions anymore because you are under immense pressure to acquire the next project in order to pay your monthly costs. Back to square one: my husband went back into an advertising agency. I was hired by a documentary film production company because they wanted to extend their content to interactive and digital formats. Even if this step was very painful, this new work was a beautiful new challenge: to connect the film industry with digital narratives and technologies.

Keep it small and flexible

Entering the film industry reminded me of the long history of hierarchical structures and linear development processes. What I call world-building and systemic thinking – as well as agile development and production processes – could not be further from the approach I was confronted with. Integrating the different co-creation processes of the development and production structures was a huge effort, but it was also highly interesting on many levels. It was not only about making the project succeed; it was about bringing people together that work differently and being open to interconnecting completely different mindsets and experiences to create new forms and formats with high-quality content. After two years of work at the production company, I became sick and had to leave work for over a year. This was not only a physical crisis but also a mental one. It was hard to recognize what value all of those experiences could possibly have, and I was not sure that I wanted to stay in this business – always following the pressure of constant change, rapid development, and the need for visibility and success. Feeling weak and vulnerable was a very important learning process. It was about reorientation and allowing myself to be fragile, but also about being resilient.

After a long healing process and a reevaluation of what we wanted, my husband and I decided to start a new company in 2012 with just the two of us. We were aware that the most precious and most important value for both of us was to keep as much creative freedom as possible and to work on the topics we believe in. Staying flexible and agile was the highest priority while being aware that there will be limits to growth, limits of project sizes, limits of budgets, and the necessity to focus. We are in the fortunate position to build on a network of amazing people who we knew and could trust from our work in different segments and projects over 25 years. This network is the basis of where we stand today. We are still curious about inventing, and we are not bound to any form, topic, or technology. That is the strength in what we are doing because we can allow ourselves to think free, as we have the experience to be aware of the consequences in production costs, time, technologies, and requirements, and we are able to consult highly creative people from our network.

> Integrating the financing and revenue-model in the concept phase is also key to be able to get bigger projects off the ground. All of our bigger projects work from a systemic and world-building principle with the audience in mind. This gives us a range of different products we can define and scale to different markets, audiences, and partner needs. To allow financial fundament for huge projects, we make them scalable.

We offer a core product that requires a minimum amount of money, as well as a concept for the bigger picture. This story-world approach combined with a cross-media framework for us is not only a "buzzword," it is still something that is very valuable. This is why the concept work including financing, revenue, and audience engagement is quite important in the beginning. Think of it as a system of breathing organisms of the project.

These breathing organisms also allow you to think creatively around business models and consider how to recoup. This is still one of the biggest challenges. On one hand, we can be very flexible with our formats, audiences, and markets, but on the other hand, we are not a known player in a solid infrastructure. For example, if you are a game studio, then you are developing for a market with established revenue models, distribution channels, and sales options. If you are developing highly artistic media frameworks, then you have the opportunity to be creative with your revenue models and implement existing strategies from different industries. You need to give potential partners their link to your project and an opportunity to say, "Listen. It is interesting for you because …" That is where you need an open door to your project. It can be tough for someone who is just entering this field of work, as you need the experience to have this kind of helicopter view of your own work. Additionally, you need the experience to handle the production process. That is why I consider a solid knowledge of methods, processes, and skills to be essential to allow you to handle a project from multiple angles.

We are now in a position where we have been working in interactive narrative design, immersive digital technologies, and art for over 25 years; we have received numerous awards and international recognition for our work, and yet, despite having a good network, it is still tough. For the entire developmental process, you need to have financial resources or another project you work on profitably to pay your bills. However, that also takes energy. We are continuously trying to create a balance. Furthermore, the only constant thing that I experienced over all of those years is change. My job description ranges from artistic lead, author, creative director, narrative designer, transmedia producer, creative technologist, story architect – you name it. When I have to explain what I am doing I keep it simple: I am an artistic director at Miiqo Studios, and I hold a professorship for Digital Narratives Art and Design at the ifs international film school cologne.

Very personally and despite all of the challenges, I see the beauty in being able to create, invent, and take risks to co-develop a constantly changing area of immersive narrative frameworks at the intersection of art, design and technology, and socially relevant topics.

> I was exhausted, frightened, and disappointed, but also and most of all always inspired; I am surrounded by amazing people, and I am never bored.

If you have the gift to create an environment that allows people to change perspectives for a second, to create empathy, and build a systemic view of the world, then it is always worth taking the risk. My students often ask me to teach them what they need to do to be successful in this industry, to explain the clear steps of a career path, to tell them how I got to where I am. The ideal picture is that it was and will be a straight path: that I started with a clear vision and goal in mind and a fixed job description. The reality is very different.

SPACES ARE ALSO AUTHORS

▶ By Sean Patten, Sarah Thom, Simon Will, and Berit Stumpf

Gob Squad is a British-German collective based in Nottingham and Berlin. They have worked collaboratively since 1994 in the fields of performance, video installation, and theatre.

Gob Squad is one of the most influential contemporary performance collectives that came together in 1994 at Nottingham Trent University. Permanent members include Johanna Freiburg, Sean Patten, Berit Stumpf, Sharon Smith, Sarah Thom, Bastian Trost, and Simon Will (Freiburg and Stumpf also belong to the tribe of She She Pop). The group is currently based in Berlin, Germany.

The group became famous in 1997 when they performed at the documenta X art exhibition in Kassel, where they presented the performance *15 minutes to comply*. In the performance, a dog is chased in a video loop at a subway train stop, while the performers perform a strange waiting dance live on the platform until the tram arrives, and they disappear into it. Since then, the group has become one of the most influential performance groups worldwide. Gob Squad has put out 48 productions, most notable are *Super Night Shot* (2003), *Gob Squad`sKitchen* (2007), *Saving The World* (2008), *Revolution Now!* (2010), *Before Your Very Eyes* (2011), *Western Society* (2013), *My Square Lady* (2015), *Creation* (2018) and *I Love You, Goodbye!* (2019). The group works as a collective and develops work interactively, often including the audience, as well as real-time live footage.

This interview was conducted with the group in December 2019 in Berlin, Germany at their office.

> When you all share authorship, what is your common story? Once it is not from one person's vision, how can you share that in a piece of work? Somehow, just the fact that a five, six, or seven-headed monster creates the work somehow forms the process because it is not just from one person's vision.

Sarah: We met one another in Nottingham in what was, back then called a contemporary art program. All of the British people in the company have been in that program and visited a festival in Giessen [in Germany]. We developed a relationship with some of the people there. We recognized that there was a bridge to Nottingham. Our practice was very interdisciplinary. In Giessen, it was very theoretical, but somehow it felt like we were informing each other in a way that felt productive.

Berit: I knew much more about *how* I wanted to work than *what* I was going to do. I wanted to work in a team and in a group, knowing this is how I can thrive. Finding one another – that is when it clicked: We knew how we wanted to enter a process together.

Sarah: I think that, early on, we realised that this was a group of people that wanted to work collaboratively. It cannot be overstepped – the fact that we were encouraged in the Nottingham program to work across disciplines in groups that collaborated. We were developing a muscle of how to work in a group without a director and that we could all share authorship.

Sean: I would say that right from the very beginning, we placed an emphasis on a truthful, honest way of telling a personal story. It is about telling a truth in the hopes that a spectator can empathize with it and, therefore, form a social connection with the artist.

> If we are telling stories, then at no point did we set out to tell a fiction, but to tell a truth as a way of making a connection.

Simon: There is no singular interpretation of a work. In its creation, it is already in a prism of interpretations. "To me, this means this; to me, this means this." What is that overlap? Or can it mean both things? Furthermore, that is also kind of an offering to an audience and a viewer. Part of the interactivity is that they also become an interpreter in the project.

Sarah: Sometimes, the audience members also become authors.

Sean: The starting point is: what is the social situation that we are constructing here? What can we do with it? Maybe we are going to pretend to lock the doors of the theater and use all of the energy in the room to communicate to one TV outside – is that the social situation? On the other hand, we are in a hotel room. The audience is there to help us make it through the night. It is the site, which sometimes can be a theater and a social situation between us and the other people in the piece.

Sarah: For example, when we worked in a shopping center in *An Effortless Transaction*– it was a furniture store. We spent a lot of time going in there, seeing what was there first, and we had to negotiate with the shop. Basically, we wanted the shop to stay exactly the way it was, and we would play within it during the opening hours and the rules that came with it. The people there said: "You can come here every weekend for four weeks and present your work, but if we notice that we are selling less stuff, then you will have to stop."

Sean: First, we sent anti-consumerist messages through their shop loudspeaker system, while they were selling sofas.

Sarah: We were also allowed to use their shop windows. What's really interesting about the whole thing in terms of creating whole narratives is the question: what do you find first, and how much do you go in and change a place. The piece became about transactions because that is what the space led us towards. Moreover, when we went into the theater, later on, we also approached it in a similar way and thought, "what is contained in this space?" We always think of that, every time we walk into a space. This space has its own language before anyone enters it.

Simon: In a way, those spaces are also authors.

Berit: This is where Gob Squad comes from: site specific work. People often ask us: "What kind of text do you start with?" and we say that rather the site is our script, our starting point. We can create a situation within that. Find routes; find the parameters; find a rhythm - and often also content. The space or site provides us with a reality and we ask each time: What is the given reality of this situation we find ourselves in?

Sylke: How do you make a living? Do you get a production commission?! You do not have anything to sell. Especially in the beginning, or even now, I would assume that it is kind of a struggle. If you do not have other resources, then how do you do it?

Sarah: I remember in our program in Nottingham, we had lectures in professional practice. I remember one of the lessons where someone handed me a phonebook and said, "I'm giving you a phone. You can use the phone for free. Here is a phonebook to get anything for what you are working on now. Get it for free." I remember thinking, "of course!" I just started going through the phonebook, and I managed to get someone to lend me suits, someone to lend us a place to do a performance in – just by phoning up. In a way, it was that sort of thing in that professional practice place where they would say, "Let us start applying for some money. Let us start writing proposals." That was in my first year of college. I think that most of us realized that you have got to hit the ground running.

Simon: Growing up in Britain in the 1980s and the 1990s, it was drilled into you, and it was even part of our program, to sell yourself. That is still a very big cultural difference between the United Kingdom and continental Europe. Many people in the UK are on Twitter, Instagram, and other platforms. All of that is part of the fabric in the US too. You have to "feed the feed." It is absolutely necessary.

Sarah: You have to feed the baby. Gob Squad is the baby. It needs some food. It needs some money. It has to keep going.

Simon: It is precarious. I have lived in Berlin for 20 years and now, and I try to think back to the first decade when I was in Berlin. To be honest, I cannot quite actually remember how I did it, because we were not getting anything.

Sean: For the first few years, we were on unemployment benefits. We were making artwork secretly. One of our projects was called *Work*, and we had to build into the structure of a 40-hour performance the time for everyone to go to the unemployment office. Of course, we thought that it would be great to accompany that with video. It would have been so fitting to the piece, but we could not do that. We try to make one or, occasionally, two projects a year. Sometimes, there is one off-site project, but mostly they are projects that can tour and happen again. We make them; we hope that they are good; we hope that people would want to book them and see them again. We keep them in our repertoire as long as people are interested in booking them. Sometimes, we retire them because we are fed up with them. There are some projects that are 16 years old that are still in our repertoire.

Sarah: In the early days every time when we applied for money and got it, we generously handed it out absolutely evenly between all of us. But we always had what was called the "Gob Squad Tax", and we never left it just for us. We never emptied it all. Thinking: "well this will pay towards a camera, a computer, keeping the office running, or paying the person going into the office everyday."

Sean: When we went to documenta X [an exhibition of contemporary art which takes place every five years in Kassel, Germany] in 1997, it was a great honor to be asked to go there. It became very clear that, "We do not have a fee for you." The documenta X had money to make an underground train and an entire train station available, but the artists do not get paid, and we said, "we do not think we can come, because we have to sign off the dole. We need some money to live on or we cannot come." They had to work out a way to give us a small amount of money or we would have had to say "no thanks."

Sylke: Many collectives do not survive. You were not forming a group to do specific work but to work collaboratively. I wonder how you managed to do this for 20 years, 30 years?

Simon: 25 years.

Sean: 48 projects.

Sylke: 48 projects together and nobody got killed.

Sean: Sometimes, it feels like we are close to it. [Laughter]

Sarah: We have since been learning about each other. We are dealing with those differences and putting them out there.

Simon: In terms of the production area, we have what is called an organigram [an organizational chart]. It is everything from press, housekeeping, acquisition, to finance, and everyone within the collective is usually in two or three of these different areas of company development. Every now and then, we try to shift it around. To a certain extent that also transfers into production as well. When we make a production, we will usually have — we use the German term – *Ansprechpartner* like a go-to person for a department.

Sarah: A contact person.

Simon: Yes, as the group's link to a particular area, so, "I will be the contact person to the sound artist." The group feeds into that person, and then they take the consensus to the sound artist. The sound artist, at the end of the day, have a partner that can help form the ideas and the practicalities.

Sarah: Every now and then, we have a meeting to report back from all of our different places of work and everyone can discuss them. It does not mean that if I am in team press that I am making all the press decisions. A lot of that is the same, as Simon was saying, with the production. You carry through what the whole group wants to happen.

Simon: Before the organigram, there was a point of conflict because, sometimes, a lot of work would be burdened because there was no way of seeing it.

Sarah: We try to make sure that all of the departments have at least two people in them which also helps to prevent feeling lonely.

Berit: There also have quite a few basic rules in place. For example, every 6–8 weeks, we have a group meeting where all of the members should be present, and that is when we make all the - strategic and artistically: big decisions what is on the agenda, what needs an answer, what do we want to do, what do we not want to do?

Sarah: We also check in with how we are.

Berit: At least once a year, we have group coaching where we go through some kind of counseling together to look at our issues and conflicts within the group and bigger things that we feel like we get stuck with. We seriously take a look at all these things knowing that it is important to look after the body of the group as much as the artistic work. If we do not do this on a regular basis, then it fires back. Also, once a year we go on a retreat – not necessarily going away, but we withdraw. We take a step back from the everyday calendar and think about future visions, sometimes looking at what has gone by and how that sits with us. It is about taking a step back, looking at the bigger picture, drawing into ourselves, and coming to the center of why we want to do this. These things have become part of the regular planning of our calendar where we feel like we need to make time for an overview. Then, there are regular admin meetings every week or every other week for the daily business.

Sarah: When we do a project, often, we have what is called the drivers. To see through a project – sometimes, that can be a small project or a very big project – we recognize that certain requests come in. I might be like, "Okay, I can drive that." Usually, it is two people. If it is a small thing, then one person can be the driver of that project. Then, they have the overview, and they will sometimes meet and set up production meetings.

Berit: For the artistic process, we always try to come up with a final result that we all own, and we all feel happy with. It is sometimes hard to get there, but everybody needs to be on stage in the final piece with a feeling of "This is mine. I can own this I am responsible for this. I am standing here as one of the faces of this production and I am completely okay with this."

Sarah: We all learn more than one role in each piece. Generally, let us say that the piece has four roles in them, and there are seven people in Gob Squad. Most of us will learn at least two of the roles or two of the journeys. That means that when we come to do gigs, often you do not know exactly what the constellation will be. The piece that you saw might not be with the same people and the same constellation as somebody else. Because you bring your own journey through it, it might even have completely different text in it. For example, in *Kitchen*, when I am playing the person in the scene who does the kiss, and Simon is K1 (the first person in the kitchen), and we meet in a scene we may say, "Wow, we have not done this in ages!" This improvisation is very fresh. It keeps it interesting. It keeps it alive for us.

Berit: This is something that we actually created for our own needs at the time, and now it is a very big principle for our work: replaceability. It came out of necessity, but now we see it as a crucial and important part of our work.

Sarah: It is about watching and doing. We do that all the time. If four people are performing, then the rest of us are watching. We watch the improvisation for about 20 minutes, or we have some sort of structure rehearsal situation. Some of us will watch it, and after a while we swap. You might do something very similar to what someone else has just done, but you try how it feels on you.

That is how we make the piece.

> This frame did not just enable us, but also enabled the public to come into that frame and into the game that we were setting up with this frame. It allowed for interactions that would have been not possible outside of that frame.

Berit: At the same time, it broadens the pool of possibilities. We always talk about a suitcase that we take on the pathway with us for a certain part. This suitcase has been filled by a lot of people during the process and everything in it belongs to everyone. You might pick pieces out of it that are useful for you on that night, with this audience, under these circumstances.

Sean: Other projects have a more algorithmic or decision-based structure. If "this" happens, then "this" happens. If "this" does not happen, then in circumstance A do "this", and in circumstance, B do "this." There is a project, "Revolution Now," where we say that the show ends when we find someone. The audience is invited to join us. If after 40 minutes, we have not found someone, then we go to do "this" part.

Simon: Also, a key concept is there is a "task", and that operates differently from piece to piece. For example, in *I Love You, Goodbye*, the task is quite clear: you are a chef, and you have to cook. That is the beginning, middle, and end. I am going to cook beans on toast, and that is going to take me through the 15 minutes. In another performance, like *Western Society*, the task may become something a little more poetic like, "We found this video, and we are going to reconstruct this video." That is our task, but actually, the journey that you will go on is a journey of us trying to fulfill the task in "this" way and then deciding rather theatrically that we need you from the audience to fulfill this task and then doing it in another way. That is a more poetic understanding.

Sylke: Earlier you have spoken about the omnipresence of images today and how cameras have lost their authority to some extent. Any sense of how your practice is changing or moving into a different realm?

Berit: When we started using cameras and technical filters we realised that they enabled us to do things that we would never do in a direct way, or that we did not want to do, without that filter in between. We also needed the screen between us and the audience to start with. We had that for ages. There was always some kind of separation or technical filter that enabled or allowed, in the end, an intimacy that would not have been possible without it. And let the audience in pieces like *What Are You Looking At?* or *Close Enough to Kiss.* come really really close without us even noticing.

Sarah: The aesthetic was something we started to negotiate. We would go, "What is happening? Why is this so seductive? Why am I looking here and not here? The live person is here, but why am I choosing to look here? What is it enabling me to do as a performer and as a witness?"

Berit: Later on, we would also take the camera out to the street, so the light would look supernatural and everything felt like a movie. That frame enabled us to do things out there that we would never do in public.

Sarah: We have never wanted to use digital technology as a gimmick. It has to be integral to the work. It has to mean something. It has to be, "This piece cannot work without it." We do not have video as a rule. We have it because it is part of our vocabulary.

Sean: It is the same way as interactivity – it is there if it makes sense to the concept.

Figure 2.2 Gob Squad

TEACHING INTERACTIVE STORYTELLING AND GAME DESIGN

▶ By Gundolf S. Freyermuth

Figure 2.3 Gundolf S. Freyermuth

Dr. Gundolf S. Freyermuth, is a Professor of Media and Game Studies and the Founding Director of the Cologne Game Lab at TH Koeln–University of Technology, Arts and Sciences, as well as a Professor of Comparative Media Studies at the ifs international filmschool cologne.

I returned to Germany from the United States in 2004, when I was offered a professorship of media studies at the ifs international filmschool cologne. My Ph.D. had been about the cultural consequences of digitalization, with focus on digital film and games. Thus, I experienced it as a kind of culture shock to see how little everyday life in Germany and, in particular, universities dealt with the possibilities and means of digital technology. All things digital were seen to a high degree as something unpleasant, if not threatening, that had to be avoided as long and as far as possible. As much as I enjoyed the lively artistic atmosphere and the engaging intellectual debates at the ifs, the practical part of filmmaking was still taught in very traditional ways – both technically and aesthetically. Among my fellow film professors, there was not much awareness of the fact that linear media – such as film and television – not only had to enter the digital realm but also had to confront the new digital competition, especially the internet as a medium of distribution and digital games as a new and powerful medium of audiovisual narration.

Over the past decade, of course, things have changed. Back then, in the zero years of our century, I sometimes felt as if I had traveled back in time ten, twenty years to one of the many movie sets that I had visited as a scriptwriter and film reporter during the 1980s and early 1990s. At some point, I met a like-minded colleague, Bjoern Bartholdy, who taught audiovisual media at the Design School. We agreed that in Cologne – actually, all over Germany – there was a lack of artistic and academic education for digital games. After some futile efforts, we managed, in 2009, to get a government grant for a further education master course in "Game Development and Research." One not insignificant reason for our success was that earlier that year, Cologne had managed to attract Gamescom – the biggest gaming trade fair on the planet. On the side of the regional government, there was suddenly an economic interest to create a "games-friendly" environment for this prestigious and lucrative yearly event.

With the government grant and a few research funds that we also secured, we were able to start the Cologne Game Lab (CGL). To anchor our new institute in the research community as well as in the games industry, we established an advisory board of academics and industry practitioners. One of the first who agreed to support us was Odile Limbach, the then-CEO of Ubisoft Bluebyte. Today, she is a professor of Economics and Entrepreneurship at CGL. After a few successful years, we received new and permanent funding from the university. Now we could hire additional colleagues, start a bachelor's program called "Digital Games" in 2014, and become full-time professors and directors at the CGL ourselves. Today, the institute has ten tenured professors, a dozen research and teaching assistants, and over 300 students from more than 40 nations. In 2019, we added two MA courses that we organize together with partner institutions. We offer the consecutive master course "Digital Games" partially as a joint program with the French game school Enjmin of the National Conservatory of Arts and Crafts in Paris. The Master in 3D Animation for Film and Games we run together with the ifs.

I think, with now one Bachelor's degree and three Master's degree programs – all of these taught in English – we have not only by far the most comprehensive range of games education in Germany, but the CGL has also become one of the leading teaching and research institutes in the field of digital games in the European Community, alongside the Game Research Lab founded by Frans Mäyrä in Tampere, Finland, and Espen Aarseth's Center for Computer Game Research at the IT University in Copenhagen, Denmark. In the US, there are, of course, some games educations that seem to be even better positioned – for example, at USC with Tracy Fullerton, at NYU with Frank Lantz and Eric Zimmerman, and at Georgia Tech with Janet Murray and Ian Bogost.

Our most popular course is the seven-semester BA "Digital Games." We have around 400 applicants every year, of which we accept 40. The course has

> three specializations: Game Arts, Game Design, Game Informatics. Media and Game Studies form the scholarly foundation. Each semester – with the possible exception of the fifth semester – our BA students make a game or at least a playable prototype.

In the first semester, they start with a ludic game; in the second, they develop a narrative game, and so on. The fifth semester is structured as a "mobility window," in which students can move to study abroad, do an internship, or concentrate on a self-initiated project – which is usually based on one of the games that they did in the earlier semesters. When they return to CGL for the sixth semester, the students develop a serious or impact game. In the seventh semester, they primarily work on their bachelor project. It can be done individually or in teams, and this consists of two parts – an academic thesis and an artistic work (i.e. a game, or at least elements of a game such as a design document or concept art).

Generally speaking, the bachelor's course can lead to three different results. One outcome is that our graduates create a start-up. Already during their studies, the best project teams have the opportunity to join the CGL incubator financed by the city, the university, and other benefactors. In the incubator, they receive mentoring by industry experts and learn many of the practical skills that they need, starting with how to incorporate. So far, the CGL has produced several dozen start-ups that have been both successful in the market and won numerous awards. A second outcome is that our graduates find themselves employed by one of the big game companies. Each semester, we invite several representatives of the industry from the region and Germany for guest lectures or workshops so that students may build their networks. Again and again, we face the "problem" that the industry wants to hire our students even before they have graduated. Today, dozens of CGL alumni work for regional and national game studios – for example, Ubisoft in Duesseldorf and Berlin, Cloud Imperium in Frankfurt, and many, many others. The third outcome is, of course, that the graduates continue studying in one of our MA programs. The students in the consecutive MA "Digital Games" are half of our own graduates and half are graduates who hold a degree in games from other national and international universities.

In the two further education masters, the situation is different. Applicants do not need to have a degree in games. They must only have game-related practical experience of at least one year. Most are programmers or designers who want to specialize in games. Many, however, come from other fields and professions – we have had a film director, a film producer, fine artists, journalists, an archeologist, an opera singer. These applicants usually intend to use games or elements of games to enhance their original field of expertise – to make museums more interactive, to experiment with nonlinear audiovisuality, to gamify the opera, and so on. Of course, master students have the same three options upon graduation as bachelor students do. They can be admitted to our incubator during their studies and create a company, they can find employment that is usually at a higher level, or they can complete their education with a PhD.

At the CGL, we currently have just under 20 doctoral candidates. Some of them, we employ in program management, teaching, and above all, in our research projects. Basic research, as well as applied research, has been the second focus of our work from the very beginning. In the ten years that the CGL has existed, we have completed almost 30 research projects with a cumulative budget of several million euros. Currently, we are carrying out four projects. The two I am co-leading deal with game literacy, including the development of open-source workshops, and with the design and realization of an interactive VR experience for a German museum – a virtual time travel 30 years into the future.

Storytelling has always been at the center of my artistic and academic interests. On one hand, telling stories is a human activity and desire that transcends art forms, media, genres. There are a lot of common elements that you have to learn and know if you want to tell a good story. Storytelling is a transmedial craft. On the other hand, as a storyteller, you have to acquire specific skills depending on the medium and the ontological mode you have chosen (i.e. whether you want to tell fictional stories or factual stories in literature, theater, film, or games). Two aspects have always been of particular concern to me. First, the relationship between literary and audiovisual storytelling. In literature, the narrator can dispose of space and time as desired. You can cross centuries and continents in a single sentence. In the theater, for example, you cannot manipulate time and space that easily. From the limitations of the stage, the aesthetics of the unity of time and space emerged. Second, I am fascinated by the intersections and divergences of storytelling in audiovisual media, the differences between theater, film, and games. Furthermore, now, of course, there is VR. That is why it was and is exciting for me to teach both games and film students.

Film, as a linear medium of audiovisual narration, can manipulate space and time to a far greater extent than theater. This was the source of the fascination that the movies immediately exerted on the industrial masses. Movies could capture the new industrial life – the big city, its crowded boulevards, its chaotic traffic, speeding railroads, cars, airplanes; everything modern that could not be put on the pre-modern medium of the stage. However, the movies could also manipulate this representation of contemporary existence in a heightened way. For example, an actress is sitting on a couch, and at the other end of the room, there is a door. The actress has to leave through the door. On the stage, the actress will get up, walk to the door, open the door, close the door. Then, she will be gone. In a movie, the actress begins to stand up. Then, there is a cut. The actress never reaches the door. She is gone; the room is gone. We are somewhere else in a different place and a different time. We might see the actress now in another room or on another continent, or we might see someone else or something completely different. In this way, the film as a medium expresses the shocks of industrial modernity that Walter Benjamin spoke of.

Digital games, in contrast, represent digital living conditions and culture, gradually emerging new forms of work and communication – whatever that may mean in detail. To remain consistent with the above example:

> In most games, I or my avatar have to go to the door. Games do have cameras – unlike the theater or, at least, unlike pre-digital theater. However, they cannot manipulate space and time for their narrative purposes in the same way as film does.

Much depends on the genre, but in comparison to the movies, games evoke other rhythms of the perception of time and space. Even more profoundly, films and games differ in the authorship of the stories that they tell. In a movie, a story is encoded into the final cut. Each time you watch a movie, you might discover new elements – details you had overlooked before. However, the story that a film tells always remains the same. The various authors – from the scriptwriter to the editor – make a definitive decision on which story is presented to the audience, again and again, each time the film is screened or broadcast, or streamed. Games, on the other hand, primarily provide action spaces for possible stories.

> The players have to "realize" the different options embedded in a narrative game. Two players who play the same game independently of each other can then tell different stories afterward.

The basic requirements for making games may not be very different from those for writing novels and producing movies. If you want to write a novel, then you have to read many novels, analyze, and reflect. If you want to make a film, then you have to watch many films, analyze, and reflect. Furthermore, if you want to create a game, then you have to play many games, analyze, and reflect. Nonetheless, the essential difference is, of course, that novels are written, and movies are written – to a certain extent – whether by a single author or a whole room of writers. Games, however, are not written at all. They are designed.

> You can write for games, but you cannot *write games*. You have to create prototypes and then let people try them out. Playtesting is a constitutive element of the creative process in game development because nobody is able to foresee entirely and in detail how people will act.

You create choices, you offer participation and interactivity, but there is no way to know beforehand what the players will be doing in the environment and with the options you provide. For games, because of their mechanics and interactivity, the involvement of actual players is constitutive to the story-telling.

These specific circumstances of game development, as well as the fact that each player realizes the possible stories afforded by the game in different ways, turn the players – the play-testers as well as all the people who later buy and play games – into co-authors of the stories they experience. Such co-authorship has been reinforced by the democratization of the tools for producing digital games over the past decade, particularly game engines. As these development environments became more affordable and easier to use, modding games and even developing games and other interactive experiences from scratch turned into a realistic option for more and more fans. This democratization benefits games education at universities not at the very least.

Today, our students can produce games with hardware and software resources that would have been beyond our financial means a decade ago. What makes studying at the CGL different from all amateur efforts, however, is the combination of organized, artistic practice with scholarly knowledge transfer and critical reflection. Such a combination of theory and practice, of academia, art, and the industry is also at the heart of our annual research conference "Clash of Realities – International Conference on the Art, Technology, and Theory of Digital Games" that we have been hosting at the CGL since 2015. Every year, it attracts about 60 presenters, scholars, and artists, and 300 guests from academia and culture, politics, and industry. The basic idea is to avoid the separation among artists, academics, and industry professionals in the field of digital games, which exists in the older arts, such as literature and film. On the first day, there are summits on Game Studies, Game Development, Media Pedagogy, and other changing topics such as history in games, sound design for games, or on the relation of film and games. On the main day, however, the various specialists come together in one room, our large auditorium. Here, artists, academics, and industry practitioners, who otherwise rarely meet, discuss with each other. Last but not least, our students benefit from the fact that with the "Clash of Realities," we bring the world's foremost game studies scholars and game practitioners to the CGL – unique artistic and academic talents like Janet Murray and Tracy Fullerton, Jesper Juul and Frans Märyä, Espen Aarseth and Eric Zimmerman, Alison Harvey and Celia Hodent, Nick Montfort, Mark J.P Wolf, and Ian Bogost. Because of our diverse faculty and students, the CGL is an international venue all year round. Nonetheless, during the days of the "Clash," we experience special magic: how the passion for digital storytelling brings together artists and scholars from all over the world.

THROUGH THE EYES OF
The life and practice of an interactive storyteller
▶ By Paisley Smith

Figure 2.6 Paisley Smith

Paisley Smith is a Canadian filmmaker and virtual reality creator from Vancouver, British Columbia. She is the creator of Unceded Territories, an interactive VR film with artist and activist Lawrence Paul Yuxweluptun, which premiered at the Tribeca Film Festival 2019. She also created "Homestay," an interactive VR documentary produced by the National Film Board of Canada. Homestay is the recipient of "Best XR" for Change at the Games for Change Festival 2019. She is a 2021 Civic Media Fellow with the Annenberg Innovation Lab at USC. During these times of extraordinary change, she is using her worldbuilding skills to design solutions for deep, meaningful connections and to imagine our Feminist Future. She lives and works in Los Angeles.

My life changed when I shot my first film on a digital video camera in grade 9. At 15 years old, my teenage mind was blown, and I started identifying as a storyteller. Prior to that, stories in all forms had been an intrinsic, deeply important part of my life, but it had not even occurred to me that it might be something I could DO, you know, for life. Our teacher, Chantal Drolet, had given us the assignment of shooting a film "Through the Eyes Of" someone, or something, else. This simple assignment provided a profound opportunity. She taught us how to turn on and operate our digital cameras: how to properly insert our mini DV tapes, listening for the soft buzzing sound as it lowered into the body of the camera. She taught us the importance of a script and a shot list. We got into teams. Suddenly, we were free to go out and shoot. I will never forget that Canadian winter with my friends, holding the camera, running around Vancouver shooting that first film assignment and taking turns acting in each other's scenes. It was absolute magic. This was my first taste of creative freedom, and I have been hooked ever since.

The magic that emanated from "Through the Eyes Of" came not just from our freedom to go out there and create, but also the assignment itself. Years later, "Through the Eyes Of" would deeply impact my work as a virtual reality and

Figure 2.4 A collection of mini DV tapes that I shot in high school, now stored in an old suitcase

interactive media director. So much of how we create in interactive media is putting yourself into your audiences' shoes (i.e. "through their eyes") and imagining how they move through and experience the digital world we are sharing.

> **Activity:** Imagine a 360-interactive virtual reality experience through someone or something-else's eyes. What do they see, touch, and feel?

My work in virtual reality first began when I met Nonny de la Peña in the World Building Media Lab at the University of Southern California's School of Cinematic Arts, where I was pursuing an MFA in Film and Television Production. I had taken an interest in World Building as a storytelling practice.

> World Building is a design-thinking concept that creates work story-first. The idea is that if you create a rich story world, and have worked out the details of your world, then it will be strong enough to be told across platforms.

I liked this approach to filmmaking, and it felt aligned with my personal strategy for making work: make the best thing (or tell the best story) with what you have available.

It opens up the playing field of who is able to create work, and how. Considering what media you have access to (e.g. writing, film, social media, games), and how an audience will connect emotionally with the medium. Choosing the best medium also takes into consideration the practical logistics of making work – including funding and access. You do not need to over-spend on your budget and make a feature-length film or a AAA video game to get eyes on your story. Take a look at what is available and get started. If your story becomes platform-flexible, then you have an even greater opportunity to share your voice with the world.

Nonny de la Peña is known as the "Godmother of VR," and also happened to be a PhD in the World Building class where I was the teaching assistant to legendary production designer Alexander McDowell. Nonny embraced the power of presence and embodiment in VR: she asked the question, "Can we tell journalism stories in VR?" At the time, she had just created the pioneering VR experience "Hunger in LA" and was looking to expand her body of work.

I began producing for her, and we created a number of room-scale interactive virtual reality experiences, including "Project Syria," which was selected for the Sundance Film Festival in 2015. This was at the height of the VR excitement, and suddenly, we were traveling all over the world and sharing our VR work. We even installed Project Syria in the tapestries wing in the Victoria and Albert Museum in London. Beyond the hype, what convinced me of the power of virtual reality was watching people take off the VR headsets and be so incredibly connected to the material. All they wanted to do after was discuss the experience they just had.

I believe in making art that considers what opportunities you have access to. I suddenly had a wealth of knowledge regarding how to produce, create, and share virtual reality experiences. I had also built a community of fellow creators and a network of people excited about emerging technology. With this in mind, I knew it was time to try and tell my own story using virtual reality. The whole time I had been traveling with Nonny and sharing our work, there had been something on my mind.

I was still reeling from a recent tragedy in my family. Since childhood, my family had hosted international students in my family – that was our norm. Our family had been hosting a young student named Taro, who had become my younger brother Reed's best friend. Taro took his own life in our house at age 17, in his third year of living with us. This tragedy left me with so many complicated emotions and questions – about suicide, about grief, and about family. Taro had been a true lover of virtual worlds and video games, and it seemed ironic that I was now finding myself in a career telling stories in virtual worlds.

I wondered – could I use VR to tell Taro's story? I had gained knowledge of how to write and produce for the medium through my work with Nonny, and I felt strongly that Taro would have loved virtual reality had he lived to experience it. It felt right. I had my chance when the National Film Board of Canada Digital Studio came on as producers of *Homestay*. With the support of the NFB, I was able to deeply research Taro's story and experiment with forms of VR storytelling. From scenes built in the Unity game engine, to shooting photogrammetry, to drawing in Google Tilt Brush, we took a stab at many different forms of VR storytelling. I worked with illustrator Kaho Yoshida, an artist and animator, who had also experienced a Canadian homestay in high

Figure 2.5 A cherry tree planted for Taro at his high school in Vancouver, BC. It is covered in notes from his classmates

school. At first, I thought *Homestay* would honor his love of video games more directly – it would mimic his favorite game and as you played, you would discover documentary elements of his life in Canada. However, it was not working. I kept hitting walls with the research. I had been interviewing Taro's friends from school, his teachers, and experts in international student and teenage psychology. Nonetheless, I was never able to find any facts. I felt stuck.

I found inspiration when I visited the Japanese Nitobe Memorial Gardens which was five minutes away from the house that we all lived in together. The gardens were built to honor a Japanese diplomat and represent cross-cultural understanding. The attendant at the Nitobe Japanese gardens handed me a map when I arrived, outlining how moving through the garden was like moving through a life cycle, from birth through death. She pointed out on the map how adolescence is the only place in the garden where plants grow out of line.

I decided to root *Homestay* in this space. The virtual world created in *Homestay* is a papercraft version of the Japanese Nitobe Memorial Gardens in Vancouver. Creating a virtual reality world made of "paper" is a reminder of the fragility of our relationships. As you move through the garden, you interact with elements of the garden which unfold and trigger the narrative. You hear more of the narrative, and you physically move through a process of coming to terms with, and understanding, grief. *Homestay* is an audio-driven experience that allows the audience to both touch and listen – I find that this combination of action allows for deep focused attention – in almost like a meditative experience. You commit to entering a new world, and you learn to navigate the space. As you move through the garden, you become more confident in your actions. You learn to reach out and touch the leaves that appear to trigger the audio. However, as you move through the story, this confidence is challenged when you realize that you are not fully in control. Sometimes, a leaf does not trigger the story, frustrating the viewer. This frustration reflects the real experience of understanding suicide – you will never have control or all the answers. As much as you explore and connect with the material – you are in the world alone. My goal with this project is to inspire people to talk honestly with their friends and family about what is going on in their life and to open up conversations about mental health.

One of the most moving experiences with *Homestay* was finally sharing the finished project with my brother Reed while he was on exchange – when it was IDFA in Amsterdam. It was a relief to have him say that I had told the story well and that Taro would have been proud of the project. At times, I felt more isolated than ever making *Homestay*. I felt surrounded by unknowns –

documentary production in VR, facing my own grief every day when working on the project.

I revisited my roots in film and art to make sense of it all. I had so many questions swirling in my mind – Will VR empower us to be more connected? Will it make us even more disconnected from the community and the natural world? Meanwhile, it seemed like everything in the VR industry was moving at top speed – a race to "be the first" drove people to make their work. One of the things I did on my search for VR inspiration was to order the 1996 book "Immersed in Technology" on eBay. It was a book with essays on the projects created at the Banff Center for the Arts during its "Art and Virtual Environments Project." I discovered that artist Lawrence Paul Yuxweluptun had created a project at Banff called "Inherent Rights, Vision Rights" in 1992. Lawrence Paul Yuxweluptun is an internationally recognized First Nations artist of Coast Salish and Okanagan descent, whose paintings and new media works draw from the surrealist movement and Northwest Coast art practices. He uses his projects to talk about the genocide of indigenous people and the destruction of the land – often with humor.

Discovering this VR project and his artist statement was significant. Lawrence was a major figure in my Canadian art history studies as one of the most outspoken voices in contemporary art. On top of that, he had become a friend of mine, yet I had no idea he had created this pioneering work. "Inherent Rights, Vision Rights" places the audience inside of a longhouse where you are visited by spirit creatures. You are yourself, you do not embody anyone else. You are invited into this sacred space by Lawrence, where you observe and create your own emotional connection with what he has created. Lawrence Paul Yuxweluptun paints as a way to exercise his inherent right: his right to freedom. This project tackles what he calls the fear of native people and the lack of understanding of their spirit world:

He says:

"I have been a blackface dancer for 18 years now, and a masked dancer since I was 14. I have been able to draw from these experiences combining them with Western world experiences and technology to make my work. Employing technology that has in the past been used against native people. I created *Inherent Rights, Vision Rights* to show people what is happening to me spiritually. Always, I create art to communicate with others; to let other cultures see things for themselves; to show my world – Indian world, to show them that we do have a spirit, a place to go, so people will understand a West Coast native person."

20 years have passed since *Inherent Rights, Vision Rights* was created, and the same issues still exist. What has changed? To tackle this, Lawrence and I decided to collaborate on a virtual reality experience addressing colonization, climate change, and indigenous civil rights – all within the world of his art. Like in "Inherent Rights, Vision Rights," the audience embodies themselves. However, this time, we decided to challenge our audience more overtly, beyond welcoming them into Yuxweluptun's world.

In *Unceded Territories*, you have the ability to touch and impact the world around you. As you learn to use your hands, you discover the ability to build and create a beautiful surrealist world made up of Yuxweluptun's art style. These actions, which are delightful and addictive, turn ominous as you begin to slowly destroy the world with oil.

> Instead of saving the world and playing the hero (which is the role that many VR audiences are ready to play), you are the destroyer of the world, whether you want to be or not. You are forced to face the impact of your actions and the damage you have created when you are devoured by colonialist snakes.

Cree, Metis Filmmaker Loretta Todd's essay "Aboriginal Narratives in Cyberspace" questions whether VR will rupture existing power relations of the colonizer and colonized OR if it is a disguise for neo-colonialism. These are questions we are grappling with today.

She states:

"There may be other ways to imagine cyberspace, not as a place born of greed, fear, and hunger, but instead as a place of nourishment – a place where people can find their own dreams and not just fantasies of abandon but dreams of humanity."

Is virtual reality an escape, or does it challenge our reality? *Unceded Territories* is not a passive experience. You are the destroyer, forced to examine your actions, even if it makes you uncomfortable. The frustration of embodying the evil Super Predator in *Unceded Territories* plays with the frustration of the audience, much like the frustration in *Homestay*, when you can never quite reach the answers you seek. It is not just stories told in a new world, but also the emotions that we feel as we explore a world that we do not control.

It is the conversations and actions that come after experiencing virtual reality stories that are most important. Does this story connect with audiences? Does it frustrate them? Does it cause the audience to reflect on their own actions? In both *Homestay* and *Unceded Territories*, how people relate to the story elevates the work and gives it value. It is my hope that, after taking the headset off, they will look at the world around them with a new perspective and shift how they see the story *through their eyes*.

BUILDING *THE ARQIVE* AS A DIGITAL INTERACTIVE STORYTELLING PLATFORM

▶ By Cynthia Wang

Figure 2.7 Cynthia Wang

Dr. Cynthia Wang is an Assistant Professor in the Department of Communication Studies at the California State University, Los Angeles. She is interested in the impact of digital communication technologies and social media on social relations, cultural practices, and power dynamics – particularly framed in perspectives of time and temporality. Her work can be found in journals like Social Media + Society and Time & Society. She is the co-editor of the recent Bloomsbury anthology, Indie Games in the Digital Age.

In July 2009, I visited Hong Kong for the first time. My dad had just moved there for work, and I was on summer break from grad school at NYU after finishing a study abroad program in Paris. Incidentally, I had also started being more open with myself about my queerness. To feed my curiosity, I wanted to check out the gay scene, but where to start? First, I tried Google. However, my results were disappointing; I only found an outdated list of Yahoo groups that had not been updated since the turn of the century. Still, without other leads, I clicked on the links to directly check out some of the sites, but I could not actually find a single one when I tried. These sites and spaces were shut down, inaccessible, or there was some secret to getting into which I was not privy.

At this time, a worldwide game called *Geocaching* was rising in popularity. The official website (geocaching.com) provided Global Positioning System co-ordinates of "caches." If you went to that exact location, then you would find a hidden physical container. Geocaching was the start of the rise of location-based "augmented reality" games. I wondered, could consumer platforms that used location-based media help counter the erasure of queer spaces and stories that stymied my journey of self-discovery?

In this essay, I will describe why I created *The arqive* – an LGBTQ[1] storytelling map – and how it elicits vital questions about queer identities, histories, and communities. Built in 2014 as *GlobaltraQs*, *The arqive* is an interactive digital repository of LGBTQ events and stories that present narratives of LGBTQ history. User-generated stories and narratives are visualized as pins on a digital storytelling map, indicating the location where a story occurred. Stories can be anything from historical events (i.e. Stonewall), to personal happenings, to LGBTQ-specific resources provided by local community organizations. Each pin, connected with a story, increases the visibility of LGBTQ experiences around the world.

The arqive is an interactive platform that not only tells well-documented histories, but also enables anyone to tell their own not-so-straight stories as well. Being queer often comes with persistent alienation from one's families and communities of origin, which often cling to heteronormative values. Hence, queer individuals – particularly those who have not yet come out and found their own communities – often disproportionately struggle with social isolation, mental distress, depression, stress, suicide, and other negative emotional impacts (Kelleher, 2009; Higa et al., 2014; Kann, 2016).[2] Digital media has given us the ability to connect across time and space, reconfiguring how we communicate and share knowledge. My hope is that this map of stories opens up and expands digital space for queer community, connection, and solidarity.

The importance of telling our stories

LGBTQ histories and bodies are marked by invisibility and erasure. We are often born and raised in heteronormative families. When we discover our sexualities, the process can feel isolating – especially when we look at our communities and families of origin and do not see ourselves reflected in them. I was born to an immigrant family from Taiwan. Even though I grew up and lived my entire life in the United States, I often feel like I straddle being Chinese/Taiwanese and American without fully belonging in either. My family taught me cultural history at home, and I learned American (i.e. Eurocentric and heteronormative) history at school, but I made it past college before I learned about Stonewall[3].

My challenge in learning LGBTQ history is not unusual. These histories have often been told piecemeal, spread through word-of-mouth, and are not generally taught in schools. Larry Gross (2001),[4] in his discussion of LGBTQ representation in the media, writes about why the invisibility endemic to being queer is a double-edged sword. On one hand, invisibility creates an opportunity for LGBTQ individuals to "pass" as straight, although oftentimes they are coerced into invisibility. On the other hand, social isolation is rooted in this coerced invisibility. Despite a slow increase in civil liberties, LGBTQ individuals and communities are still marginalized within heteronormative societies and cultures. Especially in places that are less open to discussing different sexualities, being queer can sometimes feel like being the only person who has "unacceptable" desires (Farrar, 2019).[5]

In 2012, I took an LGBTQ history class at USC with Alice Echols, where we read George Chauncy's book, *Gay New York*.[6] The book details queer stories and happenings in New York City in the early 1900s. Chauncey includes specific locations and addresses of important queer sites that constituted Gay New York. I thought to myself, would it not be cool if you could walk around a neighborhood in New York City and see that the Chipotle on the street corner that used to be a popular gay bathhouse in the 1920s? The perpetual capitalist cycles of construction and destruction of physical spaces – often in the form of gentrification – erases community histories. Accordingly, queer communities have had to fight for their stories to be recognized and told.

Queer people have been forced to negotiate visibility throughout history. Fran Martin (2010)[7] details how fictional stories of female homoeroticism are spaces for queer expressions of intimacy. She also argues that they act as a reinforcement of heterosexual patriarchal values in East Asian literature and cinema. Martin Meeker (2006)[8] explores media and communication used by queer individuals during the 50s and 60s to both form communities and to cruise. Diana Fisher (2003)[9] relates stories of how individuals from the Russian Gay and Lesbian Group in West Hollywood voluntarily oscillate between visibility and invisibility, being able to codeswitch and pass as straight when needed. In each case, storytelling confronts a tension between queer voices being heard and disappearing to conform with heteronormative society in order to stay safe. This dialectic works on micro and macro levels. As more stories are told, we hope that society becomes safer for individuals to move between visibility and invisibility.

In recent years, LGBTQ individuals have increasingly turned to digital platforms and social media to seek community. Queer history itself has been largely dominated by voices that are cisgender, male, and white, but with the rise of the Internet, there is potential for lowered barriers to publishing and ease of sharing content (Shirky, 2008)[10] to elevate marginalized voices of queer individuals of color, queer women, transgender people, and gender non-binary individuals, among many others. There is potential for networked digital tools to create "spaces of autonomy" (Castells, 2012)[11] that foster social activism and organizing. I do not wish to downplay the corporatization and concentration of power that persists in the use of digital platforms and the internet, nor do I deny that preexisting power dynamics (Dean, 2003; Hindman, 2009)[12] and problematic algorithms (Introna and Nissenbaum, 2000; Noble, 2018)[13] shape what is consumed by digital audiences and what they value. At the same time, *The arqive* creates space for the hope that digital affordances (Baym, 2010; Schrock, 2015)[14] can create spaces of resistance to dominant narratives by connecting marginalized communities across physical distance.

As I mentioned, I was born into an immigrant family and grew up with a transnational mindset. We grew up traveling to Taiwan to visit extended family and friends overseas. For this reason, it was important for me to incorporate a global or international aspect into storytelling. While certain parts of the world become increasingly accepting of LGBTQ individuals and communities, homosexual behaviors are still criminalized elsewhere. LGBTQ individuals live in precarity and isolation, sometimes risking arrest and even their lives should their proclivities be revealed. Communication scholar Walt Fisher (1984)[15] has called humans *homo narrans*, because we construct our values and beliefs through the process of narration. Diverse stories allow us to understand the diversity of queer experiences while creating links of common struggle and connection toward solidarity and support. Storytelling is a way to shift hearts and minds toward inclusion and acceptance.

Creating the arqive

In 2013, I received a small grant from the University of Southern California's Diploma in Innovation program, which allowed me to hire a programmer and a graphics designer. The first version of *The arqive* – which I called *GlobaltraQs* at the time – was thusly born. It launched in 2014 mainly as a proof-of-concept. In the past few years, I presented this project at multiple conferences and speaking engagements. I have been fortunate to be in conversation with organizations like the ONE Archives at USC and the UCLA Library, not to mention more local LGBTQ organizations. I had friends and colleagues who helped seed historical content onto the site. The concept was great, but it lacked actual stories from a diverse set of storytellers.

The initial incarnation of *The arqive* stagnated because building a platform for interactive storytelling was challenging to do alone. There were then three main components of the project: content, publicity, and development. While I was able to solicit content from friends who were working on LGBTQ history, I did not have the technical knowledge to update the site from Google Maps, which was what we built the original site with. Finally, between finishing my dissertation and applying for academic positions, I simply did not have the time nor expertise to devote to marketing this project properly and soliciting stories.

In the fall of 2019, the College of Engineering, Computer Science, and Technology at Cal State LA sponsored *The arqive* as one of its Senior Design Projects for five of their graduating Computer Science seniors. I brought on Zachary Vernon, faculty in the art department at Cal State LA, as a Co-Founder. This was my impetus for creating the new incarnation of this project. Still dubbed "GlobaltraQs" at the beginning of the fall 2019 semester, Vernon brought on a team of three art students who spearheaded the newly designed and rebranded site, *The arqive*. We also worked with a team of six Communication Studies students who assembled a social media and public relations campaign. *The arqive* had its soft launch on May 8, 2020. For us, this process of creating an interactive storytelling platform also becomes a story of interdisciplinary collaboration.

As digital platforms increasingly become spaces of engagement, activism, and solidarity, *The arqive* becomes one of the digital tools accessible to communities around the world to increase the visibility of LGBTQ experiences. The interactiveness and digital nature of the map potentially not only works to decrease social isolation and give LGBTQ individuals a connection to a larger historical consciousness; it also connects activists, organizers, resources, and community spaces around an ethos of solidarity for LGBTQ rights.

Moreover, as *The arqive* generates more content and stories, it is becoming a research tool to consider how online storytelling and social networks create a dialogic space for political and social activism through storytelling.

While *The arqive* is meant to be an interactive storytelling site, we should question who is interacting with stories and why. When it comes to building a digital site for stories of marginalized communities that still struggle for acceptance globally, the interactiveness of the storytelling requires framing, structure, and other considerations. Through the design of *The arqive*, we attempt to address *how* these stories are told and what the potential broader implications are of telling stories to Internet strangers on a digital platform where physical location can be determined. In addition to simply telling stories and allowing the posting of multimedia images, videos, and hyperlinks, readers are also able to interact with posted stories through commenting and liking, thus creating additional levels of interactivity.

The process of physically locating queer stories is particularly important in LGBTQ communities, given the erasure and invisibility of queer spaces. With the proliferation of digital technologies, LGBTQ individuals have been able to use the internet to seek community and decrease social isolation. Being LGBTQ often affords a certain modicum of invisibility, for better or worse (Gross, 2001), including an ability to "pass" as straight, if one so desires. As such – especially in places that are less open to discussing different manifestations of sexualities – it can sometimes feel like one is the only person who has "unacceptable" or "deviant" desires. *The arqive* is designed to lift the veil of invisibility by presenting stories from all over the world, both globally and locally. Our goal is to decrease that sense of social isolation by showing people that they are not alone. They could very well find not-so-straight stories and LGBTQ resources right in their own neighborhood as well as on the other side of the world.

As LGBTQ acceptance is rather patchworked across the globe, locating international and transnational stories comes with consideration about privacy in the design of the site. While LGBTQ individuals in most parts of the Western world are protected against violence through both legislation and popular sentiment, there are many places where harming queer individuals is legal and acceptable. Accordingly, one of our design considerations was how to allow for *approximate* locating on the map. For example, in countries where LGBTQ visibility comes with the risk of bodily harm or death, we do not want to geographically pinpoint locations that would reveal safe spaces for LGBTQ individuals. As such, there are features on *The arqive* where users can post stories anonymously and also pin their story on an inexact location. This allows them to control the visibility and range of their own identities as embodied locations.

There are obvious limitations and considerations that *The arqive* team – or any other effort at designing a space for stories – should address. As much as there is potential for this platform, it will never be a perfectly utopian experience, because queer history cannot be absolved of historical inequalities and colonization through a locative media platform. The stories on the site, at the time of this writing, are almost all in English, including the stories that happen in non-English speaking countries. Moreover, even in 2020, access to digital platforms and the internet is uneven and dependent largely on socioeconomic factors. Still, the existence of such a platform speaks to how the affordances of the Internet create potential spaces to shape the types of voices heard and stories told. *The arqive* is a space for stories, and not only the stories that LGBTQ history has told us. It is up to all of us to write a diverse and inclusive version of our histories.

Therefore, can digital platforms and interactive storytelling sites do the work of community-building and telling LGBTQ stories? The answer is both yes and no, and it depends. Zizi Papacharissi (2018)[16] has said, "The technologies are there to help us along and to network us, but it is our stories that identify us, connect us, or further tear us apart." Digital platforms that afford interactive storytelling have the potential to empower communities in amplifying previously muted voices while allowing them to define how their stories get told. Storytelling is a collective process that requires participation between multiple actors – those who tell stories, who listen, and who pass them on. For queer communities, faced with persistent erasure, marginalization, and isolation, stories are of particular importance and poignancy. Until the heteronormative framing of our society disappears, we have to actively seek out queer stories, spaces, and communities, and work hard to carve spaces for ourselves. Therefore, *The arqive*, while merely a vehicle to facilitate the telling of queer narratives, experiences, and histories, carves out a potentially fruitful space for queer imagining and belonging.

We tell our stories to let others know that we are here. In this time of remote access, video chatting, disembodiment, and discombobulation, our stories are more important than ever. Given the fragile ephemerality of queer stories, as they are passed on through communities, rather than through families and formal education, it is so easy for queer stories to fade away, so we have a duty to keep telling them. I have been asked, often by the more conservative individuals in my personal networks, why I insist on sharing my experiences of being queer, in a way that implies that I should not – that somehow highlighting this "deviant" part of myself is shameful and should remain hidden. My response? If telling my stories can help just one person feel less alone in the world, then that will all be worth it.

Notes

1   "LGBTQ" refers to the entire spectrum of identities that comprise of LBGTQIA + throughout this piece.

2   Kelleher, C. (2009). Minority Stress and Health: Implications for Lesbian, Gay, Bisexual, Transgender, and Questioning (LGBTQ) Young People. *Counseling Psychology Quarterly, 22*(4), 373–379. https://doi.org/10.1080/09515070903334995. Higa, D., Hoppe, M. J., Lindhorst, T., Mincer, S., Beadnell, B., Morrison, D. M., Wells, E. A., Todd, A., & Mountz, S. (2014). Negative and Positive Factors Associated With the Well-Being of Lesbian, Gay, Bisexual, Transgender, Queer, and Questioning (LGBTQ) Youth. *Youth & Society, 46*(5), 663–687. https://doi.org/10.1177/0044118X12449630
    Kann, L., O'Malley Olsen, E., McManus, T., Harris, W. A., Shanklin, S. L., Flint, K. H.,... Zaza, S. (2016). Sexual Identity, Sex of Sexual Contacts, and Health-Related Behaviors Among Students in Grades 9–12 – United States and Selected Sites, 2015. Retrieved from https://www.cdc.gov/mmwr/pdf/ss/ss60e0606.pdf.

3   The Stonewall Riots started on June 28, 1969, when police raided Stonewall in, a gay bar on Christopher Street in New York City, and the patrons fought back. Stonewall is generally noted to be the start of the Gay Liberation Movement, even though it was not the first of such uprisings.

4   Gross, L. P. (2001). *Up from invisibility: Lesbians, gay men, and the media in America.* Columbia University Press.

5   Farrar, M. (2019). *Tackling Loneliness In The LGBTQ + Community.* The Proud Diplomat. Retrieved March 18, 2019, from http://www.theprouddiplomat.com/facts/2018/6/10/tackling-loneliness-in-the-lgbtq-community.

6   Chauncey, George. (1994). *Gay New York: Gender, Urban Culture, and the Making of the Gay Male World 1890–1940.* Basic Books.

7   Martin, Fran. (2010). *Backward Glances: Contemporary Chinese Cultures and the Female Homoerotic Imaginary.* Duke University Press.

8   Meeker, Martin. (2006). *Contacts Desired: Gay and Lesbian Communications and Community, 1940s-1970s.* University of Chicago Press.

9   Fisher, D. (2003). Immigrant Closets: Tactical-Micro-Practices-in-the-Hyphen. *Journal of Homosexuality, 45*(2–4), 171–192. https://doi.org/10.1300/J082v45n02_08.

10 Shirky, C. (2008). *Here Comes Everybody: The Power of Organizing Without Organizations.* The Penguin Press.

11 Castells, Manuel. (2012). *Networks of Outrage and Hope: Social Movements in the Internet Age.* Polity.

12 Dean, J. (2003). Why the Net is not a Public Sphere. *Constellations, 10*(1), 95–112. https://doi.org/10.1111/1467–8675.00315Hindman, M. (2009). *The Myth of Digital Democracy.* Princeton University Press.

13 Introna, L. D., & Nissenbaum, H. (2000). Shaping the Web: Why the Politics of Search Engines Matters. *The Information Society, 16,* 169–185. Noble, Safiya Umoja. (2018). *Algorithms of Oppression: How Search Engines Reinforce Racism.* New York University Press.

14 Baym, N. K. (2010). *Personal Connections in the Digital Age.* Polity.

Schrock, A. R. (2015). *Communicative Affordances of Mobile Media: Portability, Availability, Locatability, and Multimediality.* 18.

15 Fisher, W. R. (1984). Narration as a Human Communication Paradigm. *Communication Monographs, 51.*

16 Papacharissi, Zizi. (2018). *A Networked Self: Identity, Community, and Culture on Social Network Sites.* Routledge. 1.

CHAPTER 3

FINDING SUCCESS

Interactive storytelling as a career is extremely broad in scope. There is a wide variety of ways to thrive in a career in interactive storytelling. Your path to success will include inevitable challenges along the way, especially in the constantly shifting landscape of interactive storytelling. Each setback can be a potential learning moment that can help guide you towards finding your own avenues for success. A career as an interactive storyteller requires one to adapt. Your ability to adapt to change will define your ability to write a happy ending into your own tale of personal career achievement.

Veterans in the field of interactive storytelling know firsthand the value of adaptability in interactive storytelling. Technological advancements have afforded creators exciting new ways to craft and present stories and experiences. Likewise, these new affordances are providing users and audiences with a broad range of entertainment options. In order to find and keep your audience in this broad media landscape, you will need to not only figure out your own niche in the industry, but you will also need to stay educated and inspired to adapt to the new developments in emerging technologies.

While the very thought of trying to find your place in interactive storytelling in an ever-changing world may seem quite intimidating, it is important to recognize that the constantly dynamic nature of the industry means that there are always new opportunities to make your own way. The progress of technological advancements and the utilization of new storytelling strategies alongside our long-held narrative traditions is providing a seemingly infinite realm of possibilities for storytellers. Technological progress in interactive storytelling has never been more exciting.

In this chapter, we will look at some of the ways that successful interactive storytellers have adapted to the constantly changing landscape of interactive storytelling, and we will see how those storytellers have approached new technologies to find success. You will learn about:

- Working with newcomers to create enlightening interactive experiences
- Adapting to changes in the academic setting
- How to approach designing successful immersive experiences
- Challenges of designing large-scale experiences while trying to make a profit
- Working with producers and finding funding for your projects
- Strategies for developing more socially responsible projects
- The significance of utilizing physical spaces alongside new technologies

To begin, let us take a look at some creative applications of interactive storytelling in creating exciting experiences at theme parks.

SIXTY SECONDS YOU NEVER FORGET

Designing a theme park ride

▶ By Michael Rüger

Michael Rüger is the Creative Director at Ravensburger Innovation Lab. He worked for many years as a freelance Creative Director/Producer. He has worked for advertising agencies, theme parks, and toy companies and has received several international industry awards and nominations, like the Toy Innovation Award 2010 (for tiptoi®).

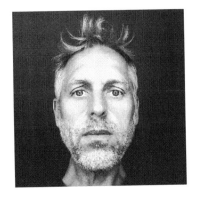

Figure 3.1 Michael Rüger

I started out in product design, later moved into advertising, and learned that it does not matter if your idea is for a theme park, advertisement, a product, or a story on TV. When you come up with an idea, a world, or a story, you have to consider what the best platform is for your audience. Maybe it is only one platform. Maybe I need a big screen. Maybe I need a small screen, because I want to get more intense or more intimate. Maybe it is about interaction – I want to get more involved with the story not only by seeing, listening, and feeling, but also by interacting.

In theme parks, you have another layer. You have to guide the audience. It is not like sitting for two hours to watch a movie or play a game. In guiding the audience through a theme park, you have to pay attention to four aspects. The first is the security aspect; it must be secure. When something happens, you want to be able to quickly bring 200 people from point A to point B. Second, you do not want long, waiting lines. In this regard, Disney is unbelievable. When you enter a line at a Disney park it does not feel like you are waiting in a line. The line is part of the entertainment and the ride. You are not waiting for a ride; you are already on the ride. Even if you have been waiting for 90 minutes, it is fantastic with actors, the interaction, and sounds.

Third, you want to guide the audience in a form of storytelling – a dramaturgy where you want your audience to explore ride A first and then ride B, not the other way around. Or you want to another level of gameplay like the hidden Mickeys in Disney Parks.

Fourth, a park should be built on a theme. For example, in Rick and Morty – an animation series, Rick designed a theme park in a body. Like Rick, you start with the mouth and go down. It does not make sense to start with the stomach and go to the heart. You want your audience to follow the theme. For example, we gave people a 3D camera so that people could take photos. We did this because we wanted them to explore the park. We did not want them going directly to the newest ride. Instead, we gave them a reason to walk around and to explore the scenery.

When you guide someone through an experience, it should not feel like it is guided. It should feel like a natural flow. Keep in mind that your audience has a certain attention span, and everything in the experience is crying for their attention. Every product, story, cinema, and ride says, "Come to me. I am better. I am next. I want you and only you." The audience should not feel like they can get lost in the world but, on the other hand, that they are free to explore.

The theme is the basis of a theme park. When Disney started theme parks, they already had 30 years of film heritage. People knew what to expect from 30 years of storytelling. Disneyland was built on heritage, and the park was an extension of the movies. Look at what resonates with people. What are people doing right now? If they read Harry Potter, then create a Harry Potter ride. Next, within Harry Potter – what will it be about? Maybe it is about flying a broomstick or the floating candles? It is not just about the ride itself. It is about the emotion and the feeling of being in the school. Maybe, it is about the spells. When people exit the park, they can take a unique magic wand home. They will always remember that this is their very own magic wand. They chose it, or maybe it chose them.

> After you have found a theme, you start creating a world. You start with what you already know from this world. Do your research. Then, add fiction to it.

Even if you just mimic reality, that will work too. For example, the Ferrari ride mimics the feeling of a Formula One in a Ferrari. When I go there, I do not want to have the feeling of a spaceship. I want to have the feeling of F1 Ferrari acceleration – no fiction. The only problem with rides based on reality is that sometimes reality is boring. When you are in an F1 car, is 300 or 400 kilometers per hour fast? What is the difference between 300 and 400 kilometers per hour? I have no idea. In a spaceship, when you travel at light-speed, you can add fiction into it. You can add the stars going by. When you add fiction, you add a story into it.

For a theme park ride, you may have only sixty seconds, and those sixty seconds must be unforgettable. People wait in line for an hour for a sixty-second ride. I once spent two weeks at Disney World in Florida in 1991. I can still talk about it and remember everything. Every night, we celebrated a happy new year on Pleasure Island. I remember the Star Tours ride. I remember when I waited in line – rather, it was not waiting – it was actually entering a space harbor. You are not waiting in line; you are waiting in a space harbor to the stars. This was 20 years ago, and I still remember these pictures and emotions. The theme park must touch the heart and brain, and that can be with something small. In Norway, in a theme park for kids, we gave them something they will never forget and that they can take home. For example, a document saying, "You made it!" Or let us say in a Star Wars ride, you get the assignment: "You are now a stormtrooper, a Jedi, or a Sith!" It is not only fiction. It makes it real, and you can take home your badge or lightsaber.

Target group

If you want to create something unforgettable, then you have to know your target group. I need to know what the user already knows. Then, I need to know about their expectations. Sometimes, there is none. What expectations can I add? If someone says that they will never be afraid of a ghost, then what will it take to change their mind?

It also requires balancing all kinds of emotions from the user and the ride technology. Always put the user at the center. Ask people what they would love to experience in space exploration. Is it the lack of gravity? That might be too expensive, and you might have a problem. However, this is the challenge, and challenges are always great. Thus, never forget the target group. When designing stories, toys, products, books, or TV series, a lot of people write for themselves. Maybe it is their family story or some personal issue. I have never worked this way. I have always wanted to do something for the audience. To create for the audience, you need data. Where is your audience coming from? What are they expecting? What is their level of knowledge?

Star Wars is always a great example. At Disney's new theme park, they have an audience that knows everything about Star Wars. If Disney designs one thing wrong – even with one screw in the spaceship – then their audience will get mad, "That screw is not in the movie!" You need to know what the expectation of the audience is. Before you start on something that you want to create, you need to talk to the people that you want to create for. Additionally, you need to have knowledge about what you are creating. You need to know what the problems of the people are, what they want, and what they want to hear. In order to do this, you need to listen to them. Then, you have a picture with data from all kinds of sources – like interviews, surveys, general research – and you know what your audiences expect.

Next, you start forming a universe. I always start with the rules for that universe. These are practical rules and physical rules. The universe is based on physics, sound, and behavior. Is there gravity in this universe? Are there different aspects of size? Maybe, I am an ant in the ride, then the story world must feel huge to me, and even the sound may be different. As an ant, I might not see my environment the same way as humans do. Do I have a different way of communicating? Everything must adhere to what is true to the universe.

When creating a fictional universe, you can come up with anything, but it must be believable and not be "too much." You can kill emotions if you add too much or overdo the fiction. For example, you can kill an emotional scene in a movie with super emotional music. Suddenly, it is cheesy. In the beginning, when you write a concept, you must throw in a lot of stuff and then sort it out. What is really necessary? In the end, less is more. You must remember that the audience also brings their emotions to your ride, the story, or the film. For example, when you ask the audience, "Do you remember this certain scene?" Most people will say yes, but this scene was never in the movie. In reverse, if you give the audience all of the emotions, then it is like a bucket full of water, and it spills over. It is all about balance. If you turn it down and introduce the audience to a well-balanced universe with characters, then they will add their emotions to it. Everybody will add different kinds of emotions – some are individual; some are social. Personal emotions often depend on age groups. A seven-year-old has different emotions than a fifty-year-old. Age forms you; time forms you, and time forms your emotions. When you get older, and suddenly, you get hit by an emotion – you often think, "This is like it was in my childhood." In "Ratatouille," one of the best movies ever, there is a certain scene with the food critic who tastes the ratatouille and suddenly remembers his childhood. Unbelievable. Amazing! Thus, concept creation requires developing an insight, creating a universe, and leveling the emotions.

Leveling and balancing also apply to the production process, because everyone wants to contribute. You have people who want to add new technology, more design, more characters, or more music. It is important for a producer of a TV series, a game, or a ride to remember that less is more.

Prototyping

In prototyping rides, products, or games, you are testing expectations. You are always testing extremes. When testing the extremes, you have to level up or level down until you find that sweet spot of perfection.

For example, when we test something for a new sound system or a toy with sound, you always test something that is super loud. You find out when the sound becomes annoying – when it is annoying for the parents and when it is annoying for the kids. You are never testing the whole concept, but rather only one aspect until you are sure about this aspect. For example, imagine a ride at a rollercoaster where you stand in and not sit. Standing is different, because there is a tipping point. You feel that the ride is totally different when standing. How long can you stand? What is happening to me when I move? It is like being on a plane 80 years ago when there were the double-winged planes, and you stand at the top? It is the same feeling. Maybe, you do not need to design a ride with many loops. Maybe, it is enough to just dip down a bit. These are aspects that you have to test.

The main question is: what is the tipping point/sweet spot where people really believe that they are part of the story? If you provide too much pressure on the body – such as too many loops–then they might miss the whole story. In a roller coaster in the dark like in Space Mountain, for example. you do not need to see anything because you just need to feel it. For a Star Wars ride or a Wreck-It-Ralph ride, you want to see the environment. Thrill could come from the movement of the carriage, the temperature, the sound, or artificial wind. You want to feel what it is liketo live in the place where your main character lives. If the ride is too wild, then the emotion is gone. You fear for your life, while it should be fun and leveled with a little bit of thrill. It is amazing to see that you do not need a shocking moment for the thrill.

VR rides

In new attractions like "The Void" where VR comes in – such as the Ghostbusters or a Marvel VR attraction – the designers rely heavily on the emotions of the user. The user feels like a part of a real-life game. For example, you can go through a dark room, and suddenly, you feel spider webs on your forehead. You know they are only strings, but you feel (and see) these on your eyes and head. It is cold. You believe that you are in a dark cellar, and somewhere there are monsters. Typically, you feel fear. For example, you will look down, and suddenly, you are on a skyscraper looking down into the abyss. That is a cheap thrill. However, a slight difference in temperature or a slight breeze makes you wonder where it comes from. You wonder if there is something behind you breathing. The cinema in your head starts to play tricks, and that is the real thrill.

It is easier to build a physical ride in the real world rather than a ride in a VR experience. In a physical ride, there is so much that we have already learned. If you build a new BMW or a new Porsche, it is easier because you are building on something. You know the physics and have a foundation. You just tweak it by pushing the limits. You hit the gas pedal, and it starts running. In the car industry, every car company, except for Tesla, is doing the same. When you are going into VR, everything is new, and you are relying on new technology. When creating a prototype, it always works, but when you are creating something for a mass market that has to function 24/7 through winter and summer, then you have always tech problems. Let us consider something simple, like the headset, for example. Your audience has different sized heads and some wear glasses. How do you provide technology for different people's needs? Coming up with something new is not easy and not cheap. You have to test-try, fail, do it over again, and stay awake until late at night. That is when you face huge problems, because the technology is so new, but there are a lot of start-ups that want to push the limits. They want to invent something new, because they want to change the world. This is the mentality of most VR companies. You always see a new prototype, and as I said – the prototype always works, but when you have to mass-produce it, use it for the masses, maintain it in masses, then that is a different story. Ultimately, when you experience a lot of VR, you experience a lot of similarities. VR is building on technology that is not finished. You are in a constant state of prototyping. However, in the end, doing something new that has never done before is always more interesting than pushing the limits in something that already exists.

The magic triangle

I always work with a triangle. When I conceptualized the triangle, it was not my invention. There have been different words for it that all refer to what would be a common denominator for advertising, product design, theme parks, and storytelling. The triangle consists of three areas.

The first area is the heritage. I believe that your creation should be based on heritage or tradition. For example, look at the lightsabers from Star Wars. If create a lightsaber and omit the famous sound to it, then it is not a lightsaber. It might be a sword that lights up, but it is not a lightsaber.

What is heritage? The heritage could be a feeling, a sound, or a smell. It could be an event, like the moon landing in 1969. For a lot of people in the 60s, this was an unbelievable event. What is the heritage of something? In the Western world, you may relate to different heritages than people in Asia – or not. You have to find a shared heritage. Also, from the toy industry, we know that the parents are the gateway to the kids. You create and sell a toy by tapping into the heritage of the parents too.

Next, I look for a new aspect to add to it. What is something new or something that has never done before? Otherwise, you are just copying another thing.

The third part is: there must be magic. When you are creating a game or something else and people are wondering, "How did they do it? How does it work?" – this is magic.

> When you have these three qualities – heritage, something new, and magic – you can level them.

For example, I could have an idea that is new, advanced, and pioneering, let us say in VR. You have to overcome a lot of obstacles – when people are walking through an attraction with glasses on, they are sweating. It is a heavy piece of equipment, and they do not really want to wear it. Then, you add heritage. An example is the Ghostbusters VR attraction. Everybody wants to be a Ghostbuster and wants to have a photon pack. Suddenly, your backpack with the VR equipment is not a heavy burden. Instead, it is a photon pack. You have a theme, a story, something people already know, and now, you can play with expectations. This is the heritage of something new. In Harry Potter, the Hogwarts school comes from the traditional British school system. Everybody knows what is going on there. Now, you are adding magic and new aspects to the story. Make sure to balance the triangle well. In an advertising pizza, for example, you could overdo heritage by having an Italian guy delivering the pizza. This pizza does not come from Italy. We all know that.

> Heritage should be something that has happened in our childhood and teenage years, and that allows us to go back in time.

Perhaps, there was a movie character who you always wanted to be, so you bought the merchandise – like from the Star Wars universe. You would love to go back to those years where your fantasies were totally open, and you were not buried between spreadsheets, Excel charts, or business presentations. You were a child and felt safe at home with mom, dad, or grandparents. In the past, everything felt good, even if it was not exactly quite like that.

Balance

The most important thing in creating a world is balance. Talk to people. Do a lot of research. Meet your target group. This does not mean that you have to 100% do what the target group wants. You have to know what the acceptable tipping point is. Based on heritage, can you make people accept something new? For example, consider the iPhone. When the iPhone entered the world, many thought that a touch screen was unacceptable before. Normally, nobody would touch a glass screen, because you leave fingerprints; it is sticky; it breaks. To make it more acceptable, Apple did something fantastic. They created a reason why you should touch the screen. In the first iPhone versions, you could flip over the pages of notes or a book. It is called a skeuomorph. You turn the pages, and you have a reason for touching and sliding across a surface. Without this touch/swipe feature, no one would quite accept touching a glass screen.

This is the heritage – mimicking the action of turning actual pages. In the mind of the users, they were not touching glass, but rather turning pages.

When I go to Disney World, for example, I expect to see the EPCOT center. If there is no EPCOT center, then it is not Disney. I expect a Space Mountain ride, because it is traditional for me. For my kids – they do not know what Space Mountain is – so for them, it is totally different. Instead, they ask where the Harry Potter ride is or whatever the new movie is. In the Marvel movies, there are a lot of holograms – people flying and superpowers. I expect the emotions that I felt from watching the movie in a theme park. By the way, I have been waiting for 40 years to have a West World theme park. The second West World movie (Futureworld) when they ski on Mars – I think it was Mars–that was unbelievable. I hope this finds a way to reality.

TELLING STORIES WITH VIRTUAL REALITY

The empathy machine

▶ By Michael Grotenhoff

Michael Grotenhoff is the Co-Owner of Filmtank and the Interactive Media Foundation, the Producer and Director of international award-winning cross-media projects and TV documentaries – such as netwars/out of CTRL, DELTAS with the virtual reality installation Inside Tumucumaque, and Bauhaus Spirit with the virtual reality dance experience Das Totale Tanz Theater.

The following has been translated from German by Sylke Rene Meyer.

Technological development in virtual reality (VR) is fast. After the first VR hype has passed, the technology is now developing to the second or third generation. Devices become cheaper and more mobile. The technology will be affordable for cultural institutions; mobile viewing devices will be available for larger groups of visitors. For example, augmented reality or AR (i.e. the combination of real images with virtual projections) can be experienced on a mobile phone display. Already, people's information and communication behavior are no longer comparable to that of ten years ago. We should see this challenge as an opportunity to reformulate the role and function of the cultural and scientific institutions in the 21st century. 3D cinema, 360-degree experiences, VR, and AR – these new formats, developments, and groundbreaking innovations have revolutionized our experience.

Looking at VR as an empathy machine, cultural institutions – such as zoos, theaters, concert halls, or museums – may implement immersive experiences and take advantage of the enormous potential to direct the focus and amplify messages. One of the first 360-degree documentaries was commissioned by the United Nations. *Clouds over Sidra*, filmed in a Syrian refugee camp, drew particular attention to the refugee problem and the war in Syria. The documentary was launched in 2015 at the World Economic Forum in Davos and found its way to charity events worldwide. In the end, the United Nations raised $3.8 billion. Every sixth person donated after traveling to the refugee camp with the help of VR glasses.

A few years ago, we decided to expand the scope of our film production company Filmtank, and we began to experiment with cross-media and digital storytelling. This new interactive option lead to new target groups and international partners. We no longer work only with TV studios, but also with partners such as museums, zoos, and publishers. Consequently, we changed our business model and established the Interactive Media Foundation, a non-profit organization, to focus on social topics in areas such as education, technology, and science. Working as a film production company *and* a not-for-profit, we now produce documentary films, interactive applications, games, and interactive installations. For each project, we create big media universes to cover as many aspects of a topic as possible. This way, we can address a wide range of audiences, find business partners internationally, and see how our projects can become more complex and win awards! The following examples may illustrate the wide range of cross-media productions and creative applications.

Take, for example, the *Frogs and Friends* project. The marketing manager of the zoo in the German city Magdeburg had a problem. Let us call it the "flagging" of the zoo's range and communication policy. Everything seems to center on those species that are supposedly attractive to visitors, while the supposedly unattractive species disappear from both the zoo and the planet. Amphibians are a good example. Many of them are endangered species, and, at the same time, extremely underrepresented in zoological collections. Frogs are usually boring for visitors if we display them in terrariums as we did 120 years ago. So would stories, as we have different ways of telling stories today than we did 120 years ago. Thus, we decided to start building a themed universe around amphibians by combining offline and online worlds integrated into the physical exhibitions. To this end, we created an interactive web documentary, a documentary film, games, and several shows at the zoo that feature the wonderful world of amphibians.

Another example is the *Ulm Stories*[1] project. Audience members could immerse themselves through "Birdly," a full-body flight simulator, to fly over the German city of Ulm and to see the city from a bird's perspective. In our VR installation "Dreaming of Flying," the users fly through the city of Ulm in 1890. We also produced this project in cooperation with the city of Ulm and the Ulm cathedral community as an application that surrounds the user with sounds from the Ulm cathedral.

In the *Bauhaus Spirit* project, we created a themed world for the centenary of the legendary Bauhaus school in 2019. At its core, this VR experience is *Das Totale Tanz Theater*. The user can dance with "the innovative spirit" of the

Figure 3.2 Inside Tumucumaque

Bauhaus, the famous "Bauhaus Spirit." In addition, we also produced a documentary feature, a radio drama on the design history of the Bauhaus and situated it in Minecraft™, started "Baukraft" – a building competition for young people in social housing projects.

Inside Tumucumaque is a project that began as a five-part TV documentary series about river deltas. One episode took place in the Amazon Delta in Brazil, where we also produced an interactive VR experience. In the VR experience, *Inside Tumucumaque*, the user experiences what it feels like to be a tarantula in the Amazon and to see the world with the sensory organs of a spider. With the help of ultraviolet color spectra, movements in super slow motion, visualizations of sonar location, and color night views as well as spatial 3D sound, the perception of the animals is interpreted as comprehensible to the human.

Visitors can explore more than 400 hectares of virtual rainforest, consisting of over 7,500 authentic plants, exotic animals, and a varied landscape with waterfalls, rocks, jungle giants, and rivers from the perspective of animals on the ground, in the air, and in the water, during the day and at night. However, we did not want to recreate a "jungle" in a kind of hyper-reality. Instead, we wanted to remind the user that VR cannot compete with the beauty and fragility of nature. Thus, inspired by scientific illustrations from the 19th century, we merged analog painting techniques with digital 3D models. We created all models, textures, animations of plants, and living creatures in collaboration with scientists and worked closely with the Berlin Museum of

Figure 3.3 Michael Grotenhoff

Natural History and the Berlin Botanical Garden. In this collaboration between scientists and media designers, we first had to find a common language to communicate. Scientists are careful to ensure that content is scientifically sound and factually correct. We, storytellers, have dramaturgy, storytelling, and emotionalization in our heads. We want to tell the stories as excitingly and grippingly as possible. These two cultures sometimes clash. We had intensive discussions about how "artistically free" scientific findings can be interpreted. How do you show, for example, the color spectrum of an arrow poison frog that can also see at night? How do I implement the sonar perception of a vampire bat scientifically correctly, yet make it also fun to fly through the treetops? We had to go through more design iterations than expected and coordinate the communication between scientists, designers, designers, and programmers. However, the result was extremely satisfying for everyone involved.

> Design thinking and iterative work allowed us, through testing and prototyping, to find the best possible form to artistically transfer scientific

knowledge. The user can slip into roles that they would otherwise never be able to take on, and thus, VR serves as an empathy machine.

Note

1 Ulm is the hometown of the 19th-century flight pioneer and inventor Albrecht Berblinger.

SPACE AS INTERACTIVE STORY

▶ By Yvette Granata

Dr. Yvette Granata is a media artist, production designer, and media scholar. She is an Assistant Professor of Digital Media Production at the University of Michigan in the Department of Film, Television, and Media and the Digital Studies Institute.

Figure 3.4 Yvette Granata

Interactive stories are not only actions that occur in time between people and objects, they also happen in space. A space itself, or a setting, can tell a story – even when this is unseen. The 1928 silent film, *The Passion of Joan of Arc* by Theodor Dreyer, takes place during the 15th century and is set in Rouen, a medieval French town. The film is famous for the extreme close-up shots of the actors' faces. What is less known, however, is that the film set of *The Passion of Joan of Arc* was the largest and most expensive film set ever created at the time of making the film. Production designers Herman Warm and Jean Hugo rebuilt the town of Rouen as one large interconnected structure – a massive, foreboding film set. The tall angles of the buildings overwhelmed the actors and engulfed them into a medieval reality. Only segments of the film set were ever seen on screen, however, because Dreyer focused the camera close up on the emotional state of the actors – particularly, on Renée Jeanne Falconetti's face for most of the film. Why did the filmmakers build such a massive and detailed film set of a 15th-century French town if only the actors and film crew would see it? Dreyer explained that the film set of the city was not meant for the screen but for the actors; it enabled the actors to give the beautiful and convincing performances that they did. In other words, as the actors interacted with the film set, the film set was reflected in the actors' performance. The evocative experience of the towering walls and the meandering paths of the foreboding medieval walkways haunt us through the actors' eyes.

Before I began working with interactive media arts, I spent many years working in film production, spending most of my time as an art director, set decorator, and production designer. The process and practice of production design have informed my interactive media practice in many ways. However, I will focus on one aspect in this chapter: space itself and how it tells an interactive story.

In doing production design for a film, one designs for actors and for a camera around lights, dolly rails, and with an entire film crew in mind. The film set is a closed space that is inaccessible to the public and contained in the private space of an industry. All of the traces of the construction of the film set are erased by the camera's tendency not to break the fourth wall (i.e. for the camera's presence to be ignored) and by the conventions of editing techniques. The camerawork and editing techniques ultimately put together a fluid experience on the screen for the audience to view linearly on screen. The film erases the space and equipment behind the scenes and hides those on the set behind the camera. As a production designer, the film set was, for me, always an immersive and interactive design experience made for the people involved in making the film – for the actors, the director, and the crew. They are surrounded by the film set and interact with the props, the objects, the constructed rooms, the shadows that fall across the floor – as if within an alternate reality game or immersive reality experience.

> Now as an interactive media artist, I try to think of the audience in the same way that I think of the actors on a film set. The actors and the audience have their own creativity that they bring with them and that they utilize while they explore a setting. Rather than a linear storyline, I give the audience a spatial experience and the freedom to roam around and explore a space.

I allow the audience to invent the details of the narrative with their own experience. Their presence in the space is what fills in the storyline. In my piece, *The Wurlitzer* (2015–2018), I created an interactive sound application at the site of the old Wurlitzer factory in Buffalo, New York. The factory had formerly produced popular musical instruments – such as pianos, organs, keyboards, and jukeboxes – for over a hundred years, but it has been shut down since the 1970s. Using the old factory as a setting, I wanted to tell the history of the musical instruments and to bring the musical objects – now absent from the site – back into action, albeit digitally. The Wurlitzer app brings the musical instruments back to their site of production by playing the sounds that they make as the audience listens to the app on their phone as they walk around the factory. Each piece of the history of the various instruments is geolocated at different points around the perimeter of the factory, and, as the audience explores the site, they hear different mixes of the instruments playing at different points along the perimeter.

> Unlike a film that unfolds on a screen in time, a spatialized interactive media piece cannot direct the audience exactly how they should explore a site at every step of the way. With a film, there is no choice but to view the next scene, as it has been placed by the editor. With a spatial site, the audience *becomes* the editor of their experience.

It is, therefore, important to create interactive spatial experiences without trying to overly control the order of events or overtly planning each step for how an audience must interact within a space. Leaving room for multiple approaches to a site is important. This is, however, more difficult than it sounds. There is a sweet spot somewhere between directing an audience every step of the way and giving an audience a simple course of directions. After testing the first version of my Wurlitzer app, in which I had laid out absolutely no directions for the audience, I watched a colleague of mine listening to the app in the parking lot standing in one spot but never walking around the site. This is because an audience of spatialized interactive media needs *some* directions, but not too many. The first iteration of my app had *too little* direction.

In the second iteration of the app, I created an introduction screen that opens when the app initializes, and it contains simple, open-ended directions for the audience: "Walk left or walk right. Listen to the sounds of the Wurlitzer instruments. If you stand in the same place for a long time, then the sounds will repeat. To hear different sounds, keeping walking around the building. Explore in any direction that you like. Walk at your own pace." I never again had to instruct visitors on what to do, nor did I have to guide audience members around the site. With a set of simple instructions, each visitor can use the app to create their own version of the sound mix by walking where they choose and at different pacing. As long as they know how the app functions and where the site is, with a few simple directions, the possibilities are endless.

What is missing from within a space – the ghosts of what used to be there – often makes a powerful experience when coupled with audience interaction. This in fact is the premise of a "haunted house" attraction. A space has a story to tell, but it is best told via the actions and reactions of the audience members exploring the site. The mixture of space and history is a mixture of what is present and absent, and it can produce a plethora of rich experiences – both in physical space and in the digital realm. While a historical site, such as the one in the above example of the former factory, has its own story to tell or its own things that haunt us – as much of history does – the principle of letting the audience roam freely in a site can also apply to digital spatial sites as well. For example, with 360 and VR, the audience or "the visitor" has the control of editing their experience via the headset and controller. A VR creator can place things all around the visitor for the visitor to find, without telling the visitor where to look at all times or where to go. Sometimes, the absence of things will direct an audience member to look around, to think to themselves that "There must be something more here to find!" In this way, it is often useful to not only think of what to put in a space, but also to think about what to leave out.

What other ways can the audience discover things in digital spaces? How can a digital space haunt the audience in interesting ways? There are many ways to approach making interactive digital spatial stories. One may think firstly of the possibilities of interactions. I, instead, think of the possibilities of the spatial and proceed from there: up, down, left, right, above, below.

> There are possibilities for interactions and discoveries in all directions within a digital space. The collection of details, colors, lights, shadows, the proximity and density of objects, the angles, and edges – these all add up to produce an evocative experience or "mood."

Sometimes, the mood is enough to provoke the audience to further explore a part of the space and to contribute their interpretations of a spatial experience. Sometimes, a long hallway sparks curiosity. A shadowy door sparks anticipation. A set of colorful lights pulses in the distance, prompting the visitor to seek it out. Sometimes, I find a reference for a color scheme – a sci-fi paperback book cover from the 1980s, an ad for a sofa from the 1960s, a contemporary painting, a Google image search for hats – any of these might be the inspiration for a particular color scheme. I pick three main colors and two secondary colors, and I build things around this color scheme. I search through 3D model libraries and create a list of evocative objects: a palm tree, a pink toaster, a watch, a stack of ice cubes. Sometimes, the list of objects inspires a landscape. Sometimes, it does not. There is no wrong way to begin.

Sometimes, it is useful to think of an "event" to create a digital space for or around it, rather than to think of how to create a space for a story. For example, in his architectural drawings in *The Manhattan Transcripts,* Bernard Tchumi draws what he calls "transcripts" of architectural "moments."[1] Each transcript is an architectural design that comes from imagining a fictional event, where the architecture is based on the concept of an unconventional moment. Whereas, the norms of architecture connect with the functional purpose of a space over a long period of time – such as a church design, school, or office – Tchumi's transcripts are based on events that one does not purposely design spaces for but those that happen in life anyways: a murder, a heist, or an accident. The transcripts are spaces that "transcribe" the imagined event into a form. It is an interpretation of a moment that could occur in reality, similar to an imagined event in a film, but without a scripted story and without directing actors in the way that a film does to mimic events. The event will be filled in by the audience.

Can you think of a space to create for a possible event? Can you think of a shape that anticipates an action? Close your eyes and imagine a very long tunnel. Rather than jumping to think about what is at the end of the tunnel, think about the details of the tunnel and what it looks like. What is it made of? Are there lights? Are there windows? Are there shadows? What color is it? Look up, down, left, right. Turn around in it. How much space do you have? Is it narrow? Is it wide? Can you touch the walls? What do they feel like? Are they cold or warm? Are there pictures on the wall? Do you hear sounds? What has happened in this space in the past? What else do you see?

What is a great space for a story to happen in? How can the audience interact with your space? An interactive spatial story can be created with 3D VR software, such as Unity; it can be an installation in a gallery; it can be an app that is geolocated at a particular historical site; it can be a haunted house. Regardless of the medium or material with which you build your space, the same principles can be used across all of them. If you think of the space itself as a site to interact with, and if you give some directions to your audience but not too many, then you can create multiple ways for a story to unfold. Try it out. Create an interactive piece with the idea that the visitors will be free to roam and wander through the space. They will fill in the story – if you let them.

Note

1 http://www.tschumi.com/projects/18/

REAL MONEY IN IMMERSIVE EXPERIENCES

▶ By Coline Delbaere

Coline Delbaere is a graduate of Political Sciences. She is specializing in cultural expertise, has produced many immersive VR theater pieces at DV group (Paris). She is currently the Producer of Immersive Experiences and Touring Exhibitions at Phi Centre (Montréal). She is also a member of the "Digital Experiences" Commission of the "Centre National du Cinema" (Paris).

The following has been translated from French by Sylke Rene Meyer.

Figure 3.7 Coline Delbaere

More and more, cultural enterprises are now working on the development and production of original content. The marketing and distribution of these immersive experiences are at the crossroads of art and new technology. The relationship between an image and the narrative process has irreversibly transformed. This transformation affects technological research and the economics of storytelling, and it challenges our culture. Some even claim that the use of machines to create art introduces a break in the history of art (Ferenczi, 2007).

At all times, the creation process maintains a close relationship with technology. However, technology rarely exceeds the status of being a tool and has very little influence on the creative act. In recent years, not only have the boundaries of artistic activity widened, thus giving developers, engineers, and creators the opportunity to redefine the means of doing the work; they have also redefined the purpose and the status of creation as being the result of the research work they carried out. The arrival of immersive experiences brings new knowledge, know-how, and codes to reinvent modes of creation and dissemination. In this context, the relationship between the work and its audiences is also a new experiment. The previous nonexistence of economic models of these immersive works has directly influenced the construction of audiences.

The word "immersive" has been used to describe all kinds of things. While the effectiveness of the term in marketing has diminished from overuse, its importance as a conceptual principle – both within and outside of the entertainment industry – cannot be underestimated. According to the annual report of the Immersive Design Summit in 2019, the words most regularly used to describe an immersive work are "interactive, intimate, experiential, storytelling, and participatory." The industry must constantly remain vigilant to meet the expectations of users along those lines to find a sustainable economy.

> ## Therefore, the industry seeks:
>
> 1. New ways to engage and keep visitors coming back by providing experiences that audiences cannot experience at home
> 2. Social experiences that are highly interactive with a deep level of personalization
> 3. Franchises of a recognizable brand name (i.e. intellectual properties) that can help to overcome potential public apprehensions about the technology or the price of access to its experiences

Many companies dedicate their independent production activities to the creation of immersive works. Most often, they collaborate with authors and directors from different backgrounds, searching for fresh writing, forms, and audiences.

Domestic markets alone are not sufficient. Investors have to develop for an international market with production devices that – if not innovative – have to be at least inventive, putting technical expertise in the service of new forms of storytelling. For example, the VR play, *Alice* by Marie Jourdren and Mathias Chelebourg, which I worked on in 2017, was the outcome of several years of experimentation with VR that lead to a hybrid of artistic creation and technological innovation. It was a real paradigm shift. For our Parisian studio, the idea was to give freedom to the public and to make sure that a spectator can become an active actor in a virtual universe that responds to his/her behavior and his/her reactions. Ultimately, despite a very complex technological setup, highlighting the spectator status allowed for a new experience. The project also met the three conditions previously listed in order to convince a curious and growing audience. This type of immersive work requires a lot of energy, inventiveness, and funding. However, no economic model specific to this immersive experience existed before the creation of this work. Consequently, the question of the economic profitability of these new formats, and more particularly of the deployment of personalized immersive experiences, was the subject of an important part of my reflection in the production process.

Some entertainment projects such as *STAR WARS™:Secret of the Empire by THE VOID* were used in 13 places (ten in the United States and three in Canada), selling tickets between $30 and $40 per visitor and accommodating up to 12 visitors per time slot. However, this mode of programming-franchised projects remains very rare. Immersive experiences in out-of-home entertainment focus on the Asia-Pacific markets. Since 2019, these markets have had the biggest number of users and, therefore, present a territory where distributors must succeed. While many centers in this region previously offered relatively "low-end" content and have not, in fact, met consumer expectations, there is now talk of being able to offer "premium" experiences to audiences in the key countries in this region. We are seeing an increase in the number of centers that operate with mobile VR systems. This type of interactive, participatory work works well in these new markets. While producers and distributors in the Asia-Pacific region are often oriented towards forms of gaming – with the main trends being in eSports – in the North American and European territories, the creation of original content dominates.

Types of immersive experiences

The technology-based industry had already invested more than $1 billion in 2017. Globally, the VR and AR sector – together known as XR – are sectors that we perceive today as being divided into entertainment markets based on location-based entertainment (LBE) and/or household equipment. From here, three main economic models are linked to the dissemination of immersive works:

- Platform models like Netflix, Hulu, Amazon – these are the primary delivery model for VR works. Spectators pay little for the works available for viewing, and the cost of consumer equipment remains quite low. The global AR/VR headset market is growing, and the estimated at $6.3 billion in 2019 is expected to increase to $23.1 billion in 2023: a value that will be divided equally between virtual and AR devices, while the latter will represent only a quarter of the units sold. For platforms such as Steam VR or Oculus, the commission rate is 30% of the sale. Other more gaming-oriented platforms – such as Epic Game Launcher – have lower commission rates at 12%.

- Location-based models – these are models oriented towards arcade, gaming, and attached operations of the MK2 VR or IMAX VR type. This model is encouraging, since many venues have already been created around the world. However, it is still difficult to envision a short-term return on investments (ROIs). The location-based VR experience (LBVRE) market was valued at $1.2 billion in 2018, while the XR residential device market was valued at $1.8 billion in 2018 – creating a combined market of $3 billion. XR markets include significant contributions from video games, movies, television, live events, and marketing – all of which are part of the Immersive Entertainment Industry. The LBVRE market expects to grow and reach $8.09 billion in 2022. More generally, the number of places whose activities link to the programming of this type of LBE content in VR (including shopping centers) is expected to continue to grow until it reaches 45,000 locations in 2022.

- Finally, the live performance/exhibition model – based on a ticketing system, the creator sells fairly high-priced tickets at between $20 and $150 per ticket for longer experiences or group exhibitions. Currently, only this model would allow for short-term ROIs. Venues dedicated to analog immersions are gaining popularity around the world. As of 2018–2019, there are already more than 5,000 spaces worldwide, and we expect to see more coming up in 2020. Indeed, the audience's interest in these places proves that today's audiences are constantly looking for new cultural and leisure outings.

The analog model

Installations that allow the spectator to have an experience that they will not be able to have at home are based on a few simple affirmations: history repeats itself; disruptive technologies have always taken time to reach the consumer market; each technological breakthrough follows the same pattern. Cinema, telephone, or video games all started as a new practice outside of the home before equipping the home, and only then did they transition to the mobility stage. It would, therefore, be through LBE that the immersive experience would really reach the mass market and eventually find viable economic models. Independent producers of immersive experiences are often inspired by forms of immersive theater – like *Sleep No More* by Punchdrunk, Meow Wolf in Santa Fe with 750,000 annual visitors, the Atelier des Lumières in Paris, or the TeamLab exhibition in Tokyo – that demonstrate that immersive productions have already found their audience.

Some producers – like myself – aim to participate in the creation of new forms of storytelling by offering an unmatched level of immersion and personalization. These are, for example, simulation systems allowing spectators to evolve in a virtual setting while interacting physically and in real-time with characters. In 2018, when our VR play, *Alice,* was released, we were certain that our new format – which we called Immersive VR Theater – would be a revolution in the entertainment landscape. However, *Alice* could only accommodate one spectator per performance, and we failed to create a viable business model. The objective of this creation was, first of all, to demonstrate the relevance of an art form that centers on a new active position of the spectator. One of our subsequent projects aimed to tell stories to a large audience in an unprecedented sensation of immersion: *The Horrifically Real Virtuality,* a work of immersive VR theater by Marie Jourdren, allowed spectators to evolve in a virtual setting while interacting physically and in real-time with characters and material objects. First presented at festivals, the project was subsequently commissioned for a longer term at the Phi Center in Montréal. The one-hour experience was presented eight times a day and six days a week for two months, and it accommodated 3,920 spectators. With an added scenography and a bar surrounding the work, we even extended the experience before and after each show. Although we did not make big money, we could at least brag about not losing any more than we invested, and we generated interesting data. The breakdown of the revenues revealed that the occupancy rate was 57% during the week (but who would go to the theater on Tuesday at 10 a.m.?) and 91% during the evenings and weekends. Also, 51% – more than half of the spectators – had witnessed a VR experience only once before, and for 25% of the spectators, it was their first experience. Thus, I feel that we were on the right track in believing that the theatrical form of this show convinced a new type of public that was perhaps less frightened by the technological aspects of the work.

At the very heart of these multi-user experiences is a form of storytelling that allows for immersion through emotions and personalization. As opposed to the passivity of spectators in exhibition shows, these forms create a social experience and maximize revenues. The combination of video games, cinema, physical scenography, and theater brings together different narrative fields and responds to a real need for decompartmentalization.

Following these principles, I started to work on projects such as *The Roaming* by Mathieu Pradat: an immersive experience in free-roaming for a group of eight people to interact in a new universe with real objects, pre-rendered characters, and an actor that enters the story world via motion capture. Using the theater walk model, our system of flow management accommodated eight spectators per chapter every ten minutes, and thus held up to 32 spectators simultaneously.

The scenic, interactive, and innovative experience takes the form of a journey through four distinct spaces. It combines real and virtual objects and offers strong sensory immersion. Users move barefoot through a swamp, on a thorny

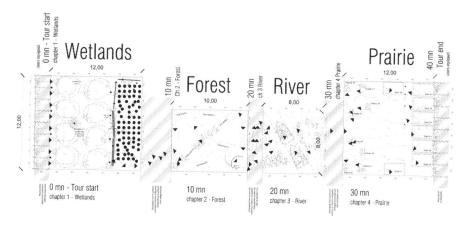

Figure 3.5 Floor Plan of The Roaming

path, along a river, and across a meadow. In each of the spaces, the user is guided by a mysterious glow pointing to elements of the physical setting: a tree branch, a mask, a magic door, or a boat. The narration reveals itself through the physical progression of the user. Spectators can, thus, comfortably settle into the experience until they completely surrender to the narrative by becoming more and more active in it. Currently, at the Phi Center, I am collaborating with the studio Felix & Paul on a new immersive exhibition in a physical scenography space of 10,000 square feet, allowing to welcome up to 150 spectators per hour of operation.

Production checklist

Producers are responsible for establishing various distribution strategies. Starting with the development phase of the projects, they have to consider the technological and scenographic investments necessary for the operations. This will prevent distributors from having to reinvest in the project in order to achieve an otherwise profitable business model. One of the objectives of these new emerging projects is the development of a distribution pipeline. What is needed is the multiplication of market players and international players with real know-how. Currently, in location-based models, distributors typically agree to distribute the work for visibility, education, and profitability. Then, they market the work worldwide exclusively for a period of three to five years. For the makers and franchises, the margin remains low.

The profitability of experiences calculates for each square meter used per experience and operating time. If we account for the time spent in an experiment with around $0.50–$1/minute and sell tickets of $5–$40 per experience, then the revenues generated by the works struggle to exceed an income beyond $200 to $400+ per square meter – assuming that the occupancy rates rarely exceed 50%. With the necessary costs for rental space, human resources, operator training, software and licenses, maintenance costs, and net revenue per producer to share, the makers' net income is pretty low. Content producers and distributors must, therefore, succeed in exhibiting their content on a large scale to increase income.

The experiences need to be open to the public for a certain number of days per week and for longer periods (most of the time, more than six weeks) to break even with the costs of installing and uninstalling. Projects must have the capacity to accommodate several spectators per time slot, sell fairly high-priced tickets, and maximize the occupancy rate. To allow for an ROI, content

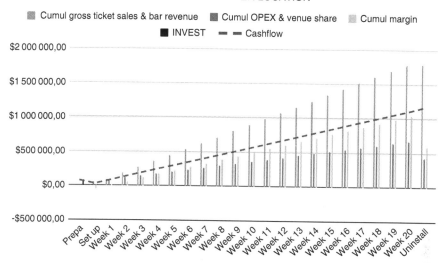

Figure 3.6 Results of Figures Linked to the First Use of a Location-Based Experience

producers need to recoup the OPEX (i.e. operation expenses) of the venues that include all of the costs related to the operation (e.g. transport, installation, wages, maintenance, removal, possible rental costs of the place, etc.), as well as marketing costs, the license fee charged by the producer, and, quite often, a percentage on the door that is most often between 10% and 15%.

> New formats age quite quickly; hence, the project will need to be able to reach its break-even point after only a few sales. By charging a license fee to the various places of distribution, the distributor and the producers will receive some income share, thus ensuring a regular and consistent return. This distribution model allows for some capital gain at a predictable frequency.

Also, although costly for producers, the selection of immersive projects by category A festivals have contributed to the legitimization of the medium.

Today, enjoying a first exhibition during one of these festivals is still highly useful, making it possible to arouse the interest of the press in order to facilitate the operations of the sale of the projects. Finally, for distributors, the challenge is to create a catalog made up of certain immersive projects – including 360 videos, scenographic installations, content for domes, or collective exhibitions to offer as a package.

We know that the VR market is in its beginnings. Today, they are only a few viable circuits for the export of works. However, on the other hand, this freedom gives creators the opportunity to improvise and advance without nets. Emerging beyond any categorization, new productions ask to be democratized and spark at new hybridization zones. Research and creative practices can no longer enclose themselves in a protective cocoon from the management of immediate deadlines but shall rather foster the ambition to implement policies for the long run. The sociology of art and the sociology of work are already monitoring the development of creative work. I wonder if it would be possible to shed more light on these "little theaters" of operations and negotiations that are the subject of immersive content creation processes. Not only can these negotiations take place between both actors and objects, but also between creators for whom this cooperation can prove to be complex and promising.

ADD PLAY TO YOUR DAY! PUTTING ON A PLAYSHOP

▶ By Yvette Murrell

Yvette Murrell is a Power, Voice, and Choice Coach, the Co-Founder and Connector of the former Playback Milwaukee Theatre Company, and has multifaceted, cross-sector career accomplishments in expressive arts, business, and education. Currently, she is enjoying full-bellied laughter and dreaming life sweet beyond her imagination in the woods of the Pacific Northwest. She revels in the distinct roles of twin, mother, facilitator, artivist, writer, and alchemist.

Figure 3.8 Yvette Murrell

A playshop is an experience where the Playback artists and theater practitioners hold space for community members to come and experiment with different elements of Playback theater. One of the most asked questions before people come to the playshop is "what is a playshop?" Well, it is not a workshop. It really is time to play. They usually think it is for kids, but adults need to play, too. We have all forgotten how to play. Children already know how to play. What's fun and even courageous is that adults get to remember how to play, and they can actually play together in a playshop. In the former Playback Milwaukee Theater Company, we worked with schools (elementary schools, high schools and colleges), community centers, businesses, small organizations, non-profits, people in our networks, churches--all kinds of folks. We worked with everybody from everywhere. First, an invitation was sent out to the community, and then, people showed up. People never knew what they'd signed themselves up for and they never quite knew what to expect.

Participants were only prepared to be open to telling stories with movement. Participants were informed they would create a small community together; they did not know the full scope of Playback. Participants would arrive, be individually greeted and welcomed to the space by the Playback players (actors). The players would usually start with doing simple warm-ups and physical exercises. These include primary forms, and improvisational body poses to get an idea of how it works. Participants are always invited to take excellent care of themselves by not doing something that doesn't feel good to the body. The most important thing is to relax and be creative in the safe container we created for full self-expression. We addressed most questions within the basic structure we provided, and still, there is often a lot of welcomed wonder and curiosity. The "I don't know" of a participant is the best place to begin a playshop.

Warms-ups are really wake-ups; we are waking up our individual and the collective body. Some of the warm-ups we do are merely shaking parts of our body. We shake it all out. We start by shaking our hands and legs for a count of five, counting to five -- "one, two, three, four, five" -- shaking your right hand, left hand, right leg, and then left leg. Then shaking the head, your seat, "one, two, three, four, five," and then shaking everything including and re-leasing a nonsensical sound from the mouth, "blehhh," - attempting all at one time. This exercise is a simple somatic comrade-building warm-up, mainly because you can't do that in a group without feeling your own body, looking at someone, and laughing!.

Take an exercise like mirroring or a core exercise like "random walking." These serve to gather energy created by the players and participants and move it into and throughout the room. People walk randomly in the play space, in random walking, and walk toward the most immense, open space they can see. Over a short time, the participants will realize it creates a bottleneck in certain areas and quickly adjust and find a different location with more space. Continuing until the conductor says, "freeze," everybody freezes in place. The conductor shouts, "random walking" again, and the participants continue the sequence of walking randomly toward big spaces and freezing when the conductor calls for it. The conductor then guides the players and participants to walk under certain random conditions like swimming underwater, like you're being chased, or like you've won the lottery. In between these, the conductor will guide the people back to regular random walking until they must freeze again. Creating frenzied, silly, anxious, and easeful energy in the space, the conductor guides the group through various emotions and situations they might en-counter while "playing back" or (acting out) a story in the formal pedagogy of Playback theater. This activity's conductor always ends the group on positive emotion, so players and participants can have a place to land that feels good in their bodies.

Guided questions, led by the conductor, will prompt, or what we call "seed," the room with stories. The conductor will invite the participants to bring to mind a story they might share this afternoon. The conductor says, "You don't have to share it, but if you were going to tell a story, what story might you tell?" Each person is invited to pair up with someone and share the story they might tell. They are given a couple of minutes to talk with someone (perhaps someone they have not met before) and exchange stories. The group is encouraged to talk amongst themselves until they hear the African drum playing. The conductor reads the room and signals the musician when it is time to play the drum. Now, participants recall their stories. The ones they want to tell and the stories have been seeded in the space.

Three different elements help Playback come together cohesively, the expressive arts, the social context in which we live, and ritual. These three elements come together to provide a container for the Playback performance to happen holistically. Continuing to build on the expressive arts, social context, and ritual, we have participants do the Mandala exercise, where all five members of a formed group are silent. They stand in a circle facing each other. When one person moves, everybody copies their same gesture. Everybody is moving at the same time and moving in those gestures. As someone else changes that gesture, they all go with the new posture. The group finds their rhythm together in whatever forms they are doing. The Playback players are strategically placed, so they blend in a few unusual movements expanding a bit beyond people's usual comfort zones. They help participants safely go outside of the box with their bodies. Through this exercise, the group focuses on each other. They gain an energetic feel for one another and listen generously to each other. These are all skills they will use when they practice playback forms and performance. The Mandala exercise is another building block that playshop participants will learn and practice to do playback forms together.

After several other exercises and intentional games, the group is now more cohesive and is ready to do the Playback form called fluid sculpture. The fluid sculpture is a fundamental and straightforward form, yet it invites participants and players to embody an emotion or some aspect of what the (story)teller is sharing. At the start, five participants are selected to be players, and we invite the new group of players to get comfortable with their group moving together. Seated upstage while listening to the teller, after the story is complete, they stand in a line, shoulder-to-shoulder, facing the audience, so they attune themselves to the story and have a felt sense of each other. Instinctively and collectively, the players get a sense of who is ready to move.

Players are expanding peripheral vision and the ability to feel the energy. Whoever feels inclined moves first. They walk neutrally toward the audience down to centerstage -about two or three feet in front of the other players. They start to make a sound and a gesture. They repeat the sound and motion like a "whoop, whoop, whoop," The player keeps going with their sound and gesture. After a couple of beats, the next person enters the play space and starts doing their own sound and gesture, and they continue until the next player comes forth, and then another one, all with their own different sounds and motions (each relevant to a moment/emotion in the tellers story). "Wonk, wonk, wonk." Now you have simultaneous cacophony and symphony going at once, "Whoop, wonk, whoop, wonk." The last player comes out, and they move in very quickly so that all of these pieces come together. Now this whole fluid sculpture, with a sound element and movement happening all together, just as in the beginning, using their peripheral vision and now collective instinct, they find they're ending together.

They freeze to a roaring round of tremendous applause from the rest of the participants. The players receive lots of verbal affirmation -- usually "That was fantastic!" or "Great job!" The players remain in their spots, all neutral positions, to receive their applause and praise. Then, in unison (as they were previously instructed), they turn around to the left, walk back to their starting positions, and turn again to their left and sit. They are now ready to begin again -- prepared for what is next! The ritual of having the players turn around and walk back together in a straight line to the place where they began upstage and turning around again is a significant collective somatic gesture for Playback theater players (actors). It is a powerfully symbolic, yet practical gesture, and it keeps rhythm or beat for the performance. The audience has now received an offering (like a fluid sculpture) from the players, and in a slow rhythm of stage reset, we give closure to the story told. As the players walk back, they clear their minds letting go of what just happened so they can become really receptive to what is next. They let go of all the residue as they return to their starting positions upstage. When they turn around again, they are ready for the next story from the audience. We call that "de-rolling." It is an essential practice in the art of playback theatre.

These timed elements and rhythms are part of the ritual aspect, helping the audience and playback players feel that we are unique and perhaps sacred. What we have done is changed the pace of how things move. Through these ritualistic elements, we shift the rhythm, pace, and space of the gathering. As observers, we can see and feel the collective breathing shifts in place, and as this happens, people become much more relaxed and inhabit shared liminal space. There is an in-between time distinct from the movement at our regular, busy pace, yet we are also not in a complete sleep or disengaged state. Players and participants are in someplace that is a limen or threshold together. We create a ritual experience by changing the pace, rhythm, and other aspects of shared time and place together.

If there are five people in a randomly formed group, four playshop guests and one playback player, or three playshop guests and two playback players. We intermingle seasoned playback players with guests to help guide the energetics in the room and ground each group to safely explore the edges of the unknown together. The players help give shape to the group in which they are located.

The conductor's role as a bridge between the players and the audience holds a crucial place in playshops and performances. The conductor does a lot to help set the tone and tenor of the groupings and incite wondering, curiosity, trust, and build the muscle of imagination. Most of the people entering the playshop have differing levels of self-consciousness around embodied movement, dramatic interaction with others, and play. In the short forms of the playshop, the conductor gently guides participants through skill-building exercises like fluid sculptures and mandala exercises. Adeptly, moving the group through warm-up exercises using their voice and gentle commands, randomly moves the participants into groups of five (the number needed for a playback for performance) to give all consenting participants a chance to play.

There are many elements of a Playback performance that we won't touch on here. The former Playback Milwaukee Theater Company consisted of many unique aspects as the only all Black (African American) playback ensemble in the US at that time (to my knowledge). We utilized a musician and a visual artist in our performances, but true to the playback structure, art form, and life: we told stories. We heard stories. We do not usually get to witness stories. It is such a valuable thing to have your story offered back to you and witness and express in the community the gift embedded in this creative form.

> We tell stories. We hear stories. We do not usually get to witness stories. It is such a valuable thing to be able to have your story offered back to you and witnessed and expressed in community is the gift embedded in this creative form. Playback is more than an expressive art; it amplifies the capacity for healing through being seen. Everyone in a playshop,

> whether they tell a story or not, has seen something of themselves in each story. They have seen something of themselves in the person who is witnessing their own story.

Playback is more than an expressive art; it amplifies the capacity for healing through being seen. Everyone in a playshop, whether they tell a story or not, has seen something of themselves in each story. They have seen something of themselves in the person who is witnessing their own story. The storyteller is often moved and deeply grateful. We create this precious moment for stories to be captured and gifted. We practice deep listening. We play each other's stories, which means we are building and weaving a very tight web of capacity to listen deeply to each other, to hold each other, and to experience nuance and ambiguity as a collective. We invite people into a container of themselves and the community when they come to a playshop. Participants show up, it looks really magical, and we put a tremendous amount of work into this process, and its rewards are returned to us in folds too numerous to count.

CHAPTER 4

GETTING AHEAD

Sylke Rene Meyer and Gustavo Aldana

Technological progress has and will continue to open up the world of possibilities in interactive storytelling. As the world becomes increasingly interconnected and as technology becomes more intertwined with human development, interactive storytelling takes on even more significance. Through the combination of old and new storytelling techniques, narratives are written and presented across a broader variety of platforms and technologies than ever before. As we experience these exciting developments and adapt to new forms and methods, it is essential to acknowledge the potential impact that interactive storytelling has on the development of culture.

The practice of transmedia concept design came into being as the synthesis of various forms of distribution such as print, TV, radio, Internet, mobile communications, games, and virtual reality (VR), as well as various narrative fields like art, journalism, advertising, public relations, film, theater, and so forth. The idea of transmedia is closely connected with the concept of the story world and story world design. The difference between a story and a story world is that the former is based on time and linearity, and the latter on space and user-interaction. In other words, a story is authored and has a beginning, a middle, and an end; while a story world is a narrative universe that may contain films, games, cartoons, blogs, and so forth that are characterized by similar patterns and a shared topic. In this sense, the term "transmedia" was first introduced by the game theorist, Henry Jenkins, in 2003 in the MIT Technology Review and later explored more deeply in his book, *Convergence Culture* – in which Jenkins defined transmedia as storytelling that unfolds on several media platforms and where each text contributes in a unique way to a unified communicative whole: the story world. Since then, transmedia storytelling – in a variety of approaches – is used in the marketing, entertainment, and advertising industries as a must-have tool for consumer engagement. As the number of distribution platforms is continuously increasing, new ways to deliver information to the consumer emerge. All of this led to the emergence of the phenomenon of cross-media – where the same media product moves from one platform to another while retaining essentially the same amount of information yet engaging the consumer/user in new ways.

This chapter details some of the ways that new transmedia approaches to interactive storytelling can be used to maximize social impact. In an increasingly chaotic world full of disinformation and distraction, it is more important than ever to utilize creative talent to benefit, and maybe even edify, audiences. As a successful interactive storyteller, you will have the opportunity to craft multimedia projects that have a lasting impact.

As you read this chapter, take note of the multitude of approaches and attitudes that professionals are using to craft their own impactful works. The freedom of interactive storytelling is a blessing in the sense that you are provided with the opportunity to reach users on multiple and varied platforms. From gamers, theater enthusiasts, to casual web users, interactive storytelling can be and has been used to present narratives that have the potential to reach all kinds of users. In your professional career, you will have the chance to tell stories to many people in the world. The power of interactive storytelling allows you to create works that help not only you, but also your audiences to participate in creating a more peaceful and loving world.

In this chapter, you will learn about some of the ways that industry professionals and the artists in the world of interactive storytelling have used their talents for the good of society. We will gain valuable insight regarding:

- Things to keep in mind as you begin designing your projects
- Transmedia applications in the field of science and education
- The use of video games as educational tools
- The benefits of using interactive storytelling as an educational tool
- How video games can be used as an alternative mode for teaching history
- The ways that educational projects can help teach creators
- How to tactfully approach controversial subject matter
- Methods for implementing transmedia approaches while maintaining the integrity of your subjects

We will begin by reading about some of the approaches and strategies that you can use to help in your quest for artistic independence and the freedom to craft your message.

SIX DEGREES OF FREEDOM

▶ Liz Rosenthal

Liz Rosenthal is known as a leading expert in immersive and interactive storytelling. She is the Programmer of Immersive Content for the Venice International Film Festival, Executive Producer of CreativeXR – a unique Immersive Content Accelerator Programme, and the Founder and CEO of trailblazing innovation organization, Power to the Pixel. Liz is regularly invited to speak and mentor at major international events.

Figure 4.1 Liz Rosenthal

I started in independent film and was running the UK office of Next Wave Films, a company of "The Independent Film Channel." We were very well known for helping first/second-time feature directors to get their films financed, finished, and then sold. We financed 13 feature films, and I learned a lot about the sales and marketing of films. They were winning awards at Sundance and other big festivals. The independent film business was pretty dysfunctional even back then – this was at the end of the 90s. However, we sold our films. We were one of the first companies that started financing feature films shot on video, and then we got known for using the internet to build a community around independent films.

I became enthusiastic about how the internet and interactivity would change the way that audiences would engage with storytelling. Power to the Pixel: The Cross-Media Forum was a forum that I ran in association with BFI London Film Festival for ten years, which included the first project finance market for interactive projects, a conference, and a think tank around developing and financing these projects. I also ran an incubator lab called the "Pixel Lab," where we helped to develop over a hundred projects in interactive and immersive media. Therefore, I was right in between new creative practices for interactive and immersive media and was also looking at new business ecosystems. If you want to be culturally relevant, and if you want to evolve your practice as an artist or businessperson, then you have to be very aware of evolving audience behavior, technology, and business strategies. I am now the Executive Producer of CreativeXR – an accelerator program that supports creative teams in the UK by developing projects using immersive technology and new ways to reach audiences on immersive platforms.

How do you develop VR experiences?

If you are out there, fascinated with the possibilities of VR technology, and want to create immersive experiences, then it is essential to spend time getting to know this totally new format by trying out as much VR as possible. This is a radically new medium – one that is more psychologically powerful than any that has previously existed and that will radically transform the way we communicate, learn, design, and understand our real world. It will take us to places that are impossible to visit, enable us to inhabit the body of any avatar, and see the world from different perspectives. When working with evolving technology, keeping track of how new tools evolve and what they are capable are is essential for aspiring and experienced producers and creators. Joining a development incubator or an accelerator program is always a good way to develop projects. For example, CreativeXR, the program run by Arts Council England and Digital Catapult that I helped design and executive produce, is an end-to-end development and finance program. We select 20 projects, support them with £20,000 per project finance for a prototype, and offer business, strategic, and technical support with a wide range of mentors. They are subsequently introduced to our global network of potential financiers and distributors.

Programs such as CreativeXR, the Venice Biennale's VR College, and Kaleidoscope are great resources to producers who would be unable to tap into what is state of the art in a rapidly evolving production, technical, and business ecosystem. There are also many free resources – WhatsApp groups, online forums, and podcasts with invaluable insights that are shared by the XR community. One of the leaders in the field is Kent Bye, a journalist, philosopher, and oral historian whose podcast – *Voices of VR* – features interviews with thousands of artists, technologists, curators, and specialists in the field.

At the beginning of the development process, it is important to be aware of how the format is developing. It is tempting to focus solely on experimentation with form and technology, but my advice is to be focused on the user and audience and how they will experience your work. Try and develop a strategic plan on how to resource and distribute your project as well as consider who you need as partners and collaborators.

Flat-screen media is an established form. We understand how it is produced and distributed. It has a format and licensing model that has evolved for over a hundred years. Immersive media is changing so fast that most financiers and people in the field often find it hard to conceive of a new project when it is described on paper. Once you are past working on the initial creative concept, I always advise prototyping an idea for the team to develop a production process, to check user experience, and also to inform potential financiers and distributors. I am always involved in the whole ecosystem and like to keep very much on top of what companies are financing, what technology/hardware companies need, what the trends are, who are the new players in distribution, and how they can be connected in the development process. It is important to be holistic when you are working with something new. With no established production process and business ecosystem, it enables you to be agile and adapt to a rapidly changing scene.

Many of the projects that we have selected at Venice or for CreativeXR are totally new formats that mix practices from performing arts, games design, cinema, and visual arts that mix fiction and non-fiction elements. For example, *The Key* by Celine Tricart, which won our Grand Jury Prize at Venice in 2019, is an impact project funded by the Oculus's VR for Good Program that demonstrated a whole new format for documentary social impact projects. The user steps into a physical installation accompanied by an actor and is then placed into a virtual allegory created in CGI in a games engine in-headset that combines with documentary still images. The project also has a version that is for headset only and was launched recently on Oculus Quest.

Until this year, many in the immersive XR content business have been focused on exhibiting their works in location-based entertainment venues (LBE) since the consumer headset market has been slower than expected, and often, the types of equipment needed for fully embodied multiplayer experiences are too complex for at-home setups. With the increased emphasis on the use of technology in the home, immersive content business is going to have to rely more on at home and mobile formats. The last months have seen an acceleration of social VR platforms, virtual production technology, and new entertainment forms where participants can experience something together in a virtual space. For example, the largest ever cross-reality event took place in 2020 in Helsinki, where a Mayday concert took place in a virtual version of Helsinki, 12% of the population attended, and 150,000 created their own avatars.

12 Sectors

In the development process of a project, you have to map out how you are going to describe the user experience. In the film, a script and a storyboard are the blueprints for a film – these are some of the important elements used to sell the idea to financiers and also to communicate an idea to talent and crew. How do you find a language to describe that you are in a space that is not flat, where you participate, where you have an agency as a viewer? Can you storyboard it? Are you doing live-action? Is it interactive? What do you want people to do? How is the user's presence designed into the experience? How do you go into the experience? How do you get out of it? Is it multiplayer? There are multiple types of experiences that you can create with immersive technologies, and there is no single standard way of presenting these – as in film or TV. Each project is bespoke, and you – as a creator – have to find the best method to communicate it.

Creating successful immersive formats requires a whole new combination of skillsets.

Understanding real-time performance, interactive design, game mechanics, and coding and spatial design is essential. I have observed that, often, the people who pioneer new formats that require understanding new technologies tend to come from a technology and postproduction background. However, it is rather important to bring the skillsets of experienced writers, theater and TV directors, and performers together with these technologists. Building a balanced team is often one of the biggest challenges, as there are few artists and practitioners from traditional arts and media backgrounds who have an understanding of this format.

The next challenge is training producers in this new area who have skillsets in production workflow and delivery, and then producers who understand the IP development side and the new business ecosystem of financiers and distributors. There is a need for more programs that train these particular skillsets.

I have mapped out 12 different sectors that have been involved in financing immersive projects. I would say that the main ones are government subsidies, hardware, and software companies. You will find varying opportunities dependent on where you are based. For example, in Europe, Canada, Australia where there is a tradition of state interventions for the arts and media, many of the film and arts funds are now funding immersive content. France, Canada, Germany, and the UK have significant government funding and tax credit mechanisms. We are also starting to see a significant amount of work from countries like Taiwan and Korea. In the US, it is a mixture of headset manufacturers and software companies who have content divisions within their business but are often focused on financing Hollywood Studio Evergreen IP. China will be a huge market, as the government is intent on the territory adopting VR – especially in the education sector and with the launch of 5G networks there and in Korea, there will be big opportunities for immersive content.

Beyond the creative industries and entertainment, the enterprise sector is the area where VR has been the most successful. It may not be in the hands of the majority of consumers for a few years, but it has a successful resumé beyond gaming and entertainment in several fields. In medicine and healthcare, there are huge developments in its use. For example, in psychology, it has been used to treat war veterans for overcoming post-traumatic stress disorder (PTSD) and as an anti-anxiety and cognitive-behavioral tool. It is being used in several trials for pain relief by paraplegics wanting to feel a sense of flight and by doctors performing intricate surgeries. Architects, interiors designers, urban planners, and product designers are starting to see the benefits of designing and prototyping headsets. In the automotive industry, it has been used as a mechanism to prototype almost every vehicle fabricated in the last few years. Simulation in VR, where you need to train people in areas that are dangerous, expensive, or impossible to access, are transforming many industries. Even the pharmaceuticals industry has started to design drugs with scientists in virtual spaces, building up molecules of different substances. There has been an acceleration of virtual world platforms and collaborative working solutions for businesses, conferences, and events.

2018 and 2019 saw the rise of location-based multiplayer fully embodied experiences in a variety of different venues. High-end shopping malls such as Westfield are the venues for some of the most sophisticated examples, such as

The Void or *Dreamscape* – a VR company invested in by Steven Spielberg and Walter Parkes where multiple people enter sophisticated virtual story worlds as fully embodied avatars, or *Zero Latency* – an Australian company who is one of the most success LBE companies which mostly feature shooter games.

There have been stunning examples emerging from the art world. Marshmallow Laserfeast's *We Live in an Ocean of Air,* an environmental VR installation, was a major hit at the Saatchi Gallery in London, where breath technology allows you to see your real-time breath along with five other spectators who experience a forest simulation with you.

Then, there are immersive theater works where actors embodied as avatars enter the virtual world along with you. For example, *The Horrifically Real Virtuality* premiered at Venice Film Festival in 2018 and went on to do a three-month run at The Phi Center in Montréal.[1] The project, created by DV Group in France, takes six viewers into the b-movie world of Edward and Bela Lugosi, and, as fully embodied humanoids, you go into another dimension with actors embodied in roles.

AI and Machine Learning are starting to be incorporated into virtual experiences, creating a more seamless and personalized experience where characters. For example, they can react to your movements, or the visuals develop depending on your verbal reactions. For example, in *Wolves in the Walls* by Fable Studios that is based on the Neil Gaiman book that won an Emmy in 2019, you interact with the main character – Lucy, and she will personalize her reactions back to you, including the positioning, the gesture, and eye movement. It is the beginning of people starting to design virtual humans and characters. Another project, *Bonfire* by leading VR animation Studio Baobab, successfully blended AI and handcrafted animation. People are also using Alexa and Siri in voice-activated experiences. *A Life in Flowers,* which we premiered in Venice in 2019, is an interactive VR experience and fine art installation powered by the participant's own voice. The project combines the work of renowned botanical sculptor, Azuma Makoto, with veteran VR creator, Armando Kirwin. Once inside the virtual environment, they will explore the harmony between flowers and human life during a conversation with Azuma achieved using advanced artificial intelligence technology. As the conversation progresses, a unique bouquet of flowers will form based on each participant's life.

For VR, the best way of categorizing work initially is to separate it into works that are created for three degrees of freedom and six degrees of freedom. In three degrees of freedom, the user is in a sphere: there is limited interaction, and you cannot change the distance of your eye, so your agency as a viewer is where you look. These can be shot in live-action 360 video or created in CGI. In six degrees of freedom experiences, the user can move around the world, interact with it, and be embodied within it as a participant.

Anybody can shoot with 360 cameras, but it is quite hard to make high-quality work with these. Despite the fact that the industry has said that 360 will be a thing of the past very quickly, we are still receiving rather high-quality 360 live-action works for our Venice selection. The majority of projects will be built in game engines. In our VR program in Venice, we have all kinds of experiences – from things that are 360 videos with three degrees of freedom experiences where you can just sit on a chair and experience, or you have got things in six degrees of freedom where you are in a headset and moving around inside a world alone, or there are installations where you and others can enter a virtual world as an avatar who is sometimes encountering performers who you can interact with and are embodied as avatars. VR venues can be in art galleries, museums, theme parks, VR arcades, or installations in shopping malls or other venues.

In VR, you enter a virtual world where you are entirely dislocated from the real world, whereas with augmented reality, or AR, 2D digital information is layered over our physical world on a mobile or tablet screen. The most famous example is *Pokemon Go*. AR has mostly been used by advertisers and retailers. High-quality storytelling worlds have been scarce due to the limitations of the devices and user experience. We are all waiting in anticipation for consumer-ready smart glasses for experiencing mixed reality and allowing you to interact with three-dimensional (3D) holographic objects superimposed into the real physical world. These smart glasses can scan the room and place things in the room. It is actually understanding the space with six degrees of freedom devices. The only devices presently on the market are the enterprise-focused HoloLens and Magic Leap, which are expensive and complex to use. There are several consumer models that will launch later in the year – like Unreal, a Chinese company launching a device with a $500 price tag in November. Apple announced that they will release their smart glasses in 2023. The Apple ecosystem is more developed than anything else, because they have a complete ecosystem of software, hardware, and chip manufacturing. The other devices use Qualcomm chips and the software and hardware are manufactured by different companies which hamper the ability to iterate fast.

Because VR is a new medium, in terms of diversity, it is especially important to ask the question of who is telling the story and what is our lens or filter on the world. There is a strong community of amazing women across the world who are the leading figures in the VR world. Because this is a new sector, conversations around diversity and inclusion have happened early on. This does not mean that the VR world is entirely balanced! The technology sector is infamous for lack of diversity and for being a hostile environment for women and minorities. However, in the VR creative sector, where there are no established business ecosystems and power structures, it is sometimes easier to move forward for those who are often excluded. At the Pixel Lab and Pixel Market, we often had a majority of women participants, and at the Venice Film Festival, our selection in 2018 featured almost 50% female directors – which was a major feat for the sector. We are in a new medium that is grappling with incredibly serious issues around data privacy – AI and capturing biometric data. People who are in an innovation sphere often get excited about the "new," and they do not necessarily concentrate on the ethical. VR is set to be the most powerful medium ever created, where artists will have a canvas to create fantastical and powerful interpretations of our world and existence. However, we need to be aware of the many ethical issues that this exciting new format presents at an early stage in order to prevent the fictional dystopias that we know so well from becoming reality.

Note

1 See also in Chapter 3: Coline Debaere, "Real Money in Immersive Experiences."

THROUGH THE DARKEST OF TIMES

Making a digital game about the historical resistance against the Nazis

▶ Jörg Friedrich

Jörg Friedrich is a Game Designer from Berlin and is the Co-Founder of Paintbucket Games – an independent game studio that made the historical resistance sim Through the Darkest of Times. Before he founded his own studio, Jörg worked for 15 years in creatively influential roles in big production games like SpecOps: The Line, Dead Island 2, and Drakensang.

Figure 4.3   Jörg Friedrich

Through the Darkest of Times is a game that takes place in Third Reich Berlin: the player leads a civilian resistance group in resisting the Nazis, helping the persecuted, educating the people, and weakening the regime while evading being captured by the Gestapo. It is also an experiment: a game that wants to entertain and excite its players and, at the same time, contribute to commemoration.

Following Jesse Schell's game design classic, *The Art of Game Design: A Book of Lenses*, every game is made of four basic elements: Aesthetics, Narrative, Mechanics, and Technology.

Aesthetics refers to the game's appearance – its looks and sounds. The game narrative contains plot and setting, while the mechanics describe the rules of the game and how much interactivity there is for the player within the limitations of the physical and technical make-up of the game. These basic elements are our key ingredients. To create a game about the historical civilian resistance, we used:

• Tales of terror and bravery
• Aesthetics of avant-garde and suppression

- Rules of resistance and fear
- Technology for all

Tales of terror and bravery

Individual memories

Civilian resistance fighters in Germany during the Nazi regime were regular people with families and normal jobs, who saw what was going on in the world, and decided that they had to do something. They went underground and risked their lives to stop an inhumane regime. The game's heroes are these resistance fighters. This is the player's own avatar, as well as the other members' of the group. To design these characters, we needed to understand their real-world role models. We needed to find out:

"When did someone make the decision to risk their life to fight an inhumane regime?
Is it despair or hope that drives them?
Pride? Anger?
How do they keep up their courage?
Is there something that connects them?"

When we reviewed literature about civilian resistance groups, we were mainly interested in firsthand experiences and documents – such as interviews, letters, and reports of relatives and friends. Luckily, there is a lot of material we could look at, especially in Berlin.

We found the blog of the journalist Nora Hespers, the granddaughter of re-sistance fighter Theo Hespers, who was active in Cologne and was murdered by the Nazis in 1938. Nora was publishing the diaries of her grandfather. We reached out to her, and she liked the project so much that she decided to help us. We studied collections of interviews with Berlin resistance fighters that were printed in small numbers in which they talked about their feelings, about their anger at the regime and the people who fell for it, including their neighbors, co-workers, or relatives.

They spoke about their hope for change; they talked about how they hoped that the world would come and help them eventually, and they spoke of their despair when they had to realize that no one would come to their rescue and that they were alone. Did we find an answer to our question – what motivated these people to fight? We found that there was more than one answer; there were many! The answers as to why someone would risk their lives to fight an inhumane regime were as diverse as the civilian resistance groups themselves. Many were political of course, including democrats, socialists, communists, and conservatives who despised what the new regime did. These people abhorred it so much that they felt they had to do something. Some were spiritual or believed in a higher goal, a higher cause: a cause that would not need to be religious – although many were Christian as well. Some were humanists. They believed in humanity and were convinced that humans were able to build a better world and that this would happen sooner or later. The Nazis were just a temporary delay on humanity's path to a brighter future.

Of course, there were people who were affected by the discriminations of the Nazis, and some were angry at the regime because it had taken away their culture. Berlin, in the 1920s, had been a place of progressive lifestyle – a place for clubs and parties, experimental music, and art. The Nazis ended this.

A question that we were asked ourselves a lot was, "Can you play as Sophie Scholl?" – or any other famous resistance fighter. This is where you have the clearest difference between a game and a movie. If *Through the Darkest of Times* would have been a movie, it might have just retold the biography of one of the many civilian resistance groups – like the Red Orchestra, for example. However, *Through the Darkest of Times* is a game, and we wanted to use the strengths afforded by games. Therefore, what about individuals?

During our research, we had collected all of these individual memories and wondered how we would implement these into the game. One way would be to let players play as one specific historical character and limit the player's decisions in a way that the outcome would match the biography of that person. This, of course, would have significantly limited player freedom, so we decided against it.

Another option would have been to let players play as a specific person but to allow them to make whatever decision they liked. This was better, but it did not feel right to let players change the biography of these people who really existed. Somehow, this potential alteration feels okay for collective memories, like those of a state, but not for individuals – especially individuals who had often suffered as brutally as the ones we are talking about in this case.

> In the end, we went with fictional characters, and later, we even included procedurally generated characters. Rather than reproducing the exact events and memories of existing people, we tried to build mechanics and dynamics that would lead to situations that were similar and then recall the appropriate event.

For example: From the diary of Theo Hespers, we learned that when a resistance fighter got caught by the Gestapo and was interrogated and tortured, they gave them names and actions of resistance fighters who were already dead or that the Gestapo knew already about. Accordingly, we added this as a mechanic in interrogations.

Saskia von Brockdorff, the daughter of a member of the underground resistance group Red Orchestra (Rote Kapelle), told us about a letter that her mother wrote to her when she was five years old, and her mother was imprisoned and knew that she would have to die soon. This is a heartbreaking story, but instead of literally retelling it, we simulated that members of your group could have children and that the group mentions these children and talks about how terrible it is if someone dies who has children. The events for the group moaning about a mother who dies and leaving her child are individually written, but they appear in the game following specific rules and mechanics, creating a unique narrative situation that cannot be predicted.

Collective memories
Individual memories are at the core of *Through the Darkest of Times'* narrative, but these are always interwoven with the historical timeline and the collective memory – such as events like the Reichstag Fire or the Nazis boycotting the Jewish shops. Players cannot stop the Nazis in the games, but they can participate in these historical events that most people only know from history books and not from a personal experience.

These experiences will differ depending on who you play in the game. For example, if you play a Communist, then you will get arrested during the night of the Reichstag Fire that was fabricated by the Nazis to persecute their political opponents. If your character is Jewish, then you would lose your job and suffer from other forms of discrimination up to the point where you need to give up your identity, leave the country, or be murdered.

The eyewitness principle

Due to the nature of the topic, we knew that the game would center on some of the most horrible crimes in human history. It is impossible to fully grasp the scope of the Shoa. Thus, as game designers trying to translate the holocaust into an interactive experience, we could only fail at this objective. Our approach came out of discussions with history educators: how do you convey the worst events in history to an audience by neither trivializing the horror nor traumatizing the audience? They told us that what worked better than shocking footage or dry books was working with eyewitnesses who came to classrooms and explained their experiences. They inspired us to use virtual eyewitnesses. Instead of having players go through a traumatic situation in the first person, they meet characters who had to suffer through the worst and tell players about it. These eyewitness accounts in the game are based on the true stories of survivors. We did not build an "interactive Auschwitz scene"; instead, the player had an interactive dialog with an Auschwitz survivor and learned about what happened there.

Aesthetics of avant-garde and oppression

From Weimar avant-garde to Riefenstahl

When in 1918 the Western world as we knew it collapsed, monarchs abdicated, and Germany became a republic; revolutionary movements started all over Europe, and new ways of thinking spread not only in politics, but also in art and design. Magnus Hirschfeld's Institute of Sexology pioneered the study of transsexuality. The suffrage movement succeeded, and women fought for equal voting rights. The legendary Berlin nightlife featured international musicians playing jazz and swing. Artists and painters like George Grosz, Otto Dix, Käthe Kollwitz, writers like Berthold Brecht, Kurt Tucholsky, Erich Kästner, and actresses like Marlene Dietrich were the stars of the so-called "Roaring Twenties" in Berlin. They were socialists: critical, modern, fresh, and sometimes sexy and decadent, and they processed the trauma and horrors of the Great War in a broken, emotional, direct, and touching style – German Expressionism. The Art of the Weimar Republic was born.

When Hitler and the Nazis got into power, all of this was banned as un-German or as so-called "degenerate art" (German: Entartete Kunst). The Nazis enforced a fantasy-Teutonic-Greek-Roman historicism in writing, art, and architecture.

Sculptors, filmmakers, and architects like Arno Breker, Leni Riefenstahl, and Albert Speer were eager to create the new look and feel of Nazi Germany – the "Third Reich." Germans were portrayed as white heroic "übermenschen" (superhumans), while Jews, people of color, and Slavic peoples were defamed as inferior humans.

Developing an art style that the Nazis would have banned

One of the most popular genres in literature at that time was the so-called "Fronterlebnis," or front-line-experience literature. The genre pictures war as a spiritual experience. Books with titles like *Storm of Steel, Storms of Fire and Blood,* or *Total Mobilization* tell the myth of heroic soldiers. Today, violent video game narratives use similar patterns – featuring male heroes and lonesome warriors who must make tough decisions and solve all problems by using violence. The notion of the "heroic men" who are experiencing the "Fronterlebnis" mirrored fascist aesthetics that are, at the same, aesthetics that we can find today in action movies and video games. In making a game about civilians that risk their lives to fight the Nazis, the last thing that we wanted was to reproduce fascist aesthetics. Instead, we aimed for visuals and sounds that our resistance fighters would have loved, and the Nazis would have banned. As references, we used expressionist artists of the era: a German art book for children from 1924 mixed with more contemporary graphic novel art like Art Spiegelman's MAUS comics, *Berlin 1931*, a graphic novel painted in the way of German Expressionism, or *Waltz with Bashir*, an animated movie about the war in Lebanon in 1982.

Starting with the procedural characters

One of the first things that we did was to create the character generation menu. In this case, we did two things in parallel: developing a system to create characters with different attributes and faces and defining the first look of the game. Quite quickly, the first corner points were shaping out. We decided to tone the game in a monochrome tint but to keep the option of using color to highlight special occasions, which allowed us to lead the player's attention.

Figure 4.2 Through the Darkest of Times

Having the character generator as an example, we realized that keeping the faces of our resistance fighters in black and white but colorizing their eyes creates an intense relationship between the player and their avatar. The second idea was to do the graphics in a rough, bold, and blocky way – like woodcut or linocut prints – and to create a bold and distinct picture with a handcrafted appeal. The reduction of the color palette to black-white-red also quotes the graphic design and poster art of the 1920s and 1930s.

Using historical scenes as a base, but stage design as a role model for environment and backgrounds

For every scene that we created, we spent a good amount of time on historical research. Even though we were going for an abstract and simplified look, we made sure to get the details right wherever possible by using the original locations of the scenes. We were also collecting plenty of historical references for architecture, typography, or uniform details. While we barely used all of these references for a game scene, we think these helped us to create a believable tone and added plenty of time-specific details to scenes. When we began to combine the procedural characters and the background environments into a full panel, we realized that they needed room to breathe and unfold their impressions. Inspired by the stage designs of theater plays from the 1920s used by directors like Bertolt Brecht and John Heartfield, we built similar setups for our digital stages. Rather than trying to rebuild realistic environments, we built digital stages with reduced sets to give players an idea of place and location. Thus, the visual style resembles paper cuts or shadow puppetry, where you see the outline of a story and fill the gaps with your imagination.

The sound of the resistance

The sound of *Through the Darkest of Times* is built on three pillars – sound design, music in the narrative sequences, and music in the headquarters – where you manage the strategic planning of the resistance fighters.

The minimalist visual novel-style animated images in combination with players reading the text were what defined the requirements for the sound design. We continue the paper cut-like style in the audio to draw you into the scenery, but we always add a weirdness that underlines the nightmare feeling of most scenes.

The game is made up of four chapters, and each features a specific period of time. It begins with Hitler becoming chancellor and ends right after the war. During the narrative scenes, the main goal of the music is to depict historical events and to set the mood. We wanted to keep the narrative music simple and direct so people could empathize with it, and we felt that the music should not contain synthesizers. These were very real and horrible events to depict, and we wanted them to feel real. Our sound designer used instrumentation as a tool for differentiating the four chapters from each other and evoking specific moods. Using "real" instruments has the advantage of people recognizing them. It gives players the chance to have them connect instantly to a sound that they know and to have them be irritated by little alterations to that sound.

In the first chapter of the game, a prepared piano was used for exactly that reason. The sound of a standard piano is noncontroversial; everybody knows it and feels comfortable with that sound. However, the sound of a prepared piano can be anything from very weird to scary; it perfectly embodies the growing horrors that people experienced while Nazism grew stronger.

Chapter 2 centers on the Olympic Games in 1936 and features music that is more pompous in instrumentation to accentuate the hype for the festivities with an increasing threat to everyone who was not conforming to Nazi politics.

In Chapter 3, with the beginning of the war, we incorporated Schönberg-like music to allude to the spirit of "entartete" (degenerate) music banned by the Nazis. The narrative music for the final chapter closes the circle and comes back to a more familiar and usual piano sound, but the music is, by choice, not dynamic; instead, it laconically meanders along, illustrating the helplessness felt when facing a world that is destroyed by a horrible war.

Apart from the music in the narrative scenes, we also used contemporary music of that time in the game. The idea was to have a radio playing in your resistance group's headquarters. That way, we would have a lot of variety in the game and also another slice of "normal" life – even when times are desperate, people will listen to music that makes them feel good, and this gave us the option to include a broadband selection. We found a band who was playing the kind of swing music typical for Berlin in the 1920s to record a soundtrack for the game, featuring music that our resistance fighters would have loved to listen to.

Rules of resistance and fear

Mix of rules and narrative
We wanted *Through the Darkest of Times* to have a strong focus on narrative, but we also wanted to create a thrilling strategy game. We wanted the game to enable a player's choices. This way, players had the freedom to write their stories of resistance. In the gameplay, however, players tend to forget the narrative and only play for the score. To break through the player's strategic mindset, we added narrative sequences that play like an interactive comic book. We ask players to make tough decisions that often have no right or wrong answer but only a bad or worse outcome. For example, if you have an event where players can help out a member of their group with money, then the choice is only important if money has a role in the game and could be spent on something else too.

Difficulty as part of the theme
We knew that the game had to be difficult – that it needed to be hard to survive until the end of the war to reflect the theme of the game. This meant that players would often not reach the last chapter. Decisions needed gravitas – choices needed to be tough, which is why we wanted permadeath – which means if your character is caught in the game, then there is no way of going back and fixing your error. Instead, you have to live with the consequences, and if the character should die, then the game ends, and you would need to start again with a different character. To make this acceptable, the game needed to offer enough variety, and since most narrative parts have to do with the character you play, the members that you have in your group, and the

supporters you meet – these were the parts that needed to be different if you played again. This is why all of the characters – the player character, the group members, and the supporters – are procedurally generated by the game, and they are different each time you play, which gives you a different base for your resistance story even though the historical timeline stays the same.

Non-player characters are people too

You play the leader of a resistance group, but for us, it was important to show that the members of your group are not units who you can just boss around. They are civilians, not soldiers; people with families and with jobs. They voluntarily risk their lives to fight an inhumane regime. If they do not like your directions, then they will leave or lose faith in the cause. We also wanted to show that these people were not born as resistance fighters but that they were often interesting and creative people. Before the Nazis came to power, they enjoyed life, made art – and suddenly, all these of these things were gone. We wanted to create Non-Player Characters who could talk to the players and build relationships with them but still had their own agenda, their individual political views, and quirks – elements that can lead to internal conflicts that make the life of a resistance group even harder.

Breaking game design rules to make a game about being oppressed

Good game design keeps players always in control of a game. However, when your game is about being a civilian who is opposing an authoritarian regime and society, then you put people in a situation of powerlessness. Good game design has fair rules, but when you play as a person being at the mercy of an inhumane regime, then the game must be unfair. Good game design measures the player's success, but, in our context, "winning" and "losing" are meaningless.

If you managed to fight the regime for several years and saved dozens of people, but now your group dissolves because its members are scared of death – does that mean you lost?

Providing a feeling of closure instead of winning or losing

Ending a game of *Through the Darkest of Times* with a "You lost – Try again!" or even a "You won!" screen felt wrong. We needed to find a way to provide a feeling of closure without the classical winning or losing, and what we came up with was an epilogue. Wherever the game ends – by the end of the war, when the group dissolves, when everybody gets arrested, or when the player character dies – the game generates an epilogue based on the members that you had in your group and the decisions you made during the game. In this epilogue, you learn what happens to every group member after you "have left" them. Maybe one member dies in the war; another one is deported and killed by the Nazis, or another one survives in exile and comes back later to live a fruitful life. This way, rather than telling players that they lost, the game says: "The story of your resistance group – that story you wrote and created has ended here."

Technology for all

Every graphic we made for the game was painted as a bitmap in Photoshop, converted to paths in Adobe Illustrator, and saved in vector graphics format Scalable Vector Graphics (SVG). Vector graphics are resolution-independent and had two benefits for us. They are resolution independent, and they scale freely without any loss in quality, so the graphics will always look sharp, and they are "cheap" – meaning they can run on affordable hardware.

We wanted *Through the Darkest of Times* to be accessible for people who usually do not play a lot of video games and do not own a high-powered computer nor a game console. By using vector graphics and simple effects, the game can run on low-specification computers, and we could release a version for mobile phones to reach people without access to computers too. The game's controls and the rules are designed in such a way that anyone who has played a board game and used a website before should be able to play it. As a result, many people have access to travel back to the "Darkest of Times" in Germany 87 years ago and take back a lesson to apply to our troubled present.

STOP, COLLABORATE, AND LISTEN

▶ Zachary Vernon

What does "interactive" mean *to you*? Think about that for a second and write your answer below.

_____ -

_____

_____ -

_____

_____ -

_____

_____

_____

When you have got something down, go on ahead to the next page. No rush.

The literal definition of interactivity from the Merriam Webster Dictionary is "mutual or reciprocal action or influence," but that only goes so far. For many, the word "interactive" conjures up visuals of digital surfaces and interfaces – of action and response. For some, it is a back-and-forth power play between creator and participant resulting in the creation of some form of dialog. Interactive storytelling can mean a lot of different things depending on your background and experiences. Though regardless of definition, media, or content, the heart of interactivity is and always will be the people involved. Like me – the author of this chapter, and you – dear reader.

Stories are shared experiences that transcend the boundaries of time and space, and every story, no matter the medium, becomes partly interactive through the telling and receiving of it. As the old adage goes, "it takes two to tango." In any story – designated as interactive or not – there must exist at least two entities: a storyteller and an audience. Whether the story manifests itself in a book like this, a video game, a wayfinding system, or an ensemble cast performance, it originated from a person (or persons): the storyteller. On the other hand, without an audience, without people to receive the content, the story finds no end or meaning; it dies with its creator. The reception of and response to the story is itself an integral part of the interaction. Therefore, how do we best shape those stories for our audiences? How do we invite people to be a part of them and truly mutually interact with the content and, by proxy, with us? In the words of the great bard, Vanilla Ice, "Stop, Collaborate, and Listen." The act of collaboration, both with your co-creators and your audience, is the key to creating more immersive, engaging, and impactful stories.

How did you feel when my writing directly talked to you and asked you to participate at the very beginning of this chapter? Do books normally do that? Are we collaborating right now? In a sense, yes. Collaboration requires three things to work effectively: group activity, mutual respect, and a common goal. Currently, we have two of those three: group activity (the telling and receiving of this story) and mutual respect (I hope). However, what about our common goal? To answer that question, we must ask another: what do you want to get out of reading this book? You picked it up for a reason, so… what was it? My goal, for this chapter at least, is to provide a glimpse into what I have found successful in my career as a designer of interactive stories and experiences in order to help others find success in theirs. Does that match up with your goal?

When embarking on a collaborative project, it is paramount to establish early on that common purpose. Ask yourself and your team, "What is the point of this project – what are we doing, for whom, and why?" Charles Kettering, famed inventor and the head of research for General Motors, said, "A problem well stated is a problem half solved." Clearly communicating your intent – both internally among your co-creators as well as externally with your audience – creates a mechanism by which you can quickly evaluate all ideas, interactions, and outcomes. Does an idea serve the overall purpose? If yes, then it is worth exploring; if no, then there is no need to waste your time. Likewise, understanding your audience's goals can help you provide a smoother experience by assisting them in their endeavors. Setting clear expectations for a form of interaction from the start reduces the possibility of your audience having a negative experience – which is a core tenet of User-Experience (UX) Design. Take a mobile app, for example; what is the app supposed to do or achieve? Is it to help you find love? Lose weight? Pass the time as you avoid making eye contact with people in line? Whatever it is, anyone should be able to understand that purpose right from the start so they do not waste their time and end up with negative feelings toward your project. You would not want to walk into a movie advertised to be a horror/thriller and find that the movie turns out to be a rom-com. You would hit up Rotten Tomatoes immediately after to write up a scathing review. The same goes for any interactive story. Communicating intent – whether that is through promotion ahead of time or direct instruction during – removes ambiguity and confusion, leading to a more positive experience for all.

Setting clear expectations at the start also allows you to better anticipate the needs and wants of your audience and provide experiences and interactions to accommodate them. Good storytelling guides potential actions and responses from the audience through careful research, planning, and a fair bit of empathy and understanding, but collaboration allows for and adapts to unexpected responses as well. In my experience as a designer who has worked on inter-actions in both the physical and digital realms, I have found that my work is often more effective when I communicate *with* others rather than *to* them. The more I involve the audience in the telling of the message (or story), the more effective that communication becomes. At the beginning of this chapter, I invited you to input your own thinking and words into the book. Hopefully, that provided an opportunity for you to interact on a deeper thought-level with the content rather than just being a passive observer of my words.

One way you can apply this co-creation strategy is to think of your purpose as a prompt in an improvisational exercise that includes you, the content of your story, and your audience. My personal favorite improv exercise is "Yes, and…" In this exercise, everything that is said or done by any participant becomes a part of the story – no naysaying or take-backs allowed. For example, say you are creating a video game. You have the overarching story (e.g. local citizen finds magic item tied to a prophecy) and a purpose (e.g. fulfill the prophecy). As you are building out interactions for the player to experience, invite others to help brainstorm all of the things that your audience could possibly do on their way through the plot. See if you can include one person's desire to save a prince as well as another's cooking challenge idea. Maybe the two could work together; perhaps you must cook a meal so sumptuous that it awakens the prince from a deep slumber. The point of the exercise is to force yourself to accept things as they are and to find ways to continue the story with the new content. There can be no "wrong" answer or idea. The entire concept of "Yes, and…" hinges on respecting everyone's contributions as valid and useful while also trying to further the story. The best improv actors (and storytellers) are able to adapt their stories depending on the reactions of others – especially the audience – because they understand that those others are also a part of the storytelling. In turn, the audience becomes more engaged with the content, because they have a personal stake in it. Their perspective is not only ac-knowledged and validated but woven into the experience itself.

As a real-world example, I once worked with a non-profit called Art Alliance Austin that wanted to highlight all of the beauty and "art" of the city of Austin,

Texas through color. With collaborators from the non-profit, an app development company, and my design team, we created an app called "City Swatch." The app allowed the people of Austin to take pictures of various art pieces, scenery, and whatever else tickled their fancy in order to create a color swatch library for the city of Austin. The app-making process was highly collaborative, as each contributor to the project had their own perspectives and skills to bring to the table. As for the audience, besides offensive content, we did not disallow any interpretations of that prompt from contributors. We said yes to their content, and then showed them other people's interpretations. By allowing the audience to contribute and interact with the content in their own way, we created a deeper appreciation for and level of engagement with the non-profit organization.

This is not to say that you should give up any and all autonomy or control over the interactions you create by inviting others to contribute. You still have a goal to accomplish, after all. You can create collaborative stories that have flexibility to them, allowances for unexpected outcomes or pathways, and guideposts to help wayward participants back on the path. Collaborative interactions give the audience a clear direction to go in pursuit of a specific goal but allow for some meandering here and there at their whim. Human beings are complex, multifaceted creatures with multiple desires, wants, and needs happening all at the same time. Recognizing and providing space for those alternative purposes or goals will help make the audience feel like the story is catered directly for them – that they are indeed the protagonist. Perhaps, the aforementioned cooking challenge to save the prince is not related to the main plot but could be a helpful side-quest that provides resources or an alliance to assist in the endgame. Many different types of interactive stories have a means of allowing exploration but also simple ways to get back on track. Museums have individual audio tours for self-guided tours, but they also have maps and wayfinding to ensure that the wanderers can accomplish their own goals. Websites have site navigation to allow the audience to jump around easily while they search for content they care about. The purpose of providing these different methods and paths of interaction is to allow the user/audience to create their own story and experience based on their wants and needs. The purpose is not diluted or derailed through these actions; on the contrary, it is enhanced and broadened. Respecting the audience's autonomy is one way to foster mutual respect.

Speaking of respect, taking into account that different people are, in fact, different – especially in their backgrounds, experiences, and abilities – is fundamental to collaboration. Truly, collaborative stories accommodate those differences without needlessly calling attention to them. For example, making allowances for someone with a physical disability to access the story in their own way without singling them out or separating them from the main experience allows participation and autonomy without ostracization. When approached from a collaborative mindset, more universal access is not only useful for the person with the disability, but for others as well. Case in point, closed-captioning on videos with sound not only helps deaf or hard-of-hearing people, but also those who do not speak the language or people who are in a loud environment and cannot hear the video over the din. Recognizing, understanding, and accommodating the vast array of abilities and needs of an audience is difficult and may seem overwhelming, but if we take collaboration a step further by involving the audience in the creation of the story, then it becomes a lot easier.

Involving the audience in the telling of the story can happen at different stages of the project and allows you to see new opportunities, possible pain points, and how your work might be or is currently used out in the world – often with surprisingly varied results. Practices like co-design or participatory design invite the audience into the creation of the message/story from the very beginning. This is especially important in community-oriented projects where you need buy-in from the people who will be ultimately affected. By including the audience in the initial stages of creation and development, you head off a lot of issues of what is wanted/needed and what is not by fully understanding and establishing a common goal. You also have the opportunity to see completely new directions to pursue based on firsthand interaction. Primary research techniques like user-testing and interviewing also help to establish a rapport between the storyteller and audience during the development stage. Bringing in your target audience to try out a prototype of your interaction is the best way to test your assumptions against the reality of use and gauge responses. Even after the project is launched, data collection methods like analytics and surveys can help provide clarity and direction for refinements, future iterations, and new projects. By creating, implementing, and responding to feedback loops, you invite higher levels of collaboration and engagement with your story. The more people there are involved in the making, the more they are invested in its success.

Speaking of success, have you started seeing ways how you can implement a more collaborative spirit to your projects? Do you have a more concrete interpretation of what "interactive" means to you? What other questions do you still have? I suggest writing them down here and then referring back to them as you read the rest of this book to see if you can find the answers elsewhere. If not, you can always grab a friend and collaborate.

What other questions do you have? Write them here:

_____ -
_____

_____ -
_____

_____ -
_____

_____ -
_____

_____ -
_____

_____ -
_____

_____ -
_____

Zachary Vernon is an educator, designer, and storyteller with an international background in branding and advertising. His work now focuses on the intersections of community engagement, storytelling, and social design at the local, national, and global levels. Zachary is an Assistant Professor in the Department of Art at California State University Los Angeles.

Figure 4.4 Zachary Vernon

BUILDING A TRANSMEDIA WORLD INSPIRED BY SCIENCE

▶ Amanda Tasse

Dr. Amanda Tasse designs multi-platform immersive and ambient storytelling experiences for VR/AR, mixed reality, film, animation, apps, and games – often in collaboration with scientists. She received her PhD in Media Arts + Practice from the USC School of Cinematic Arts and is an Assistant Professor of Emerging Media at the Occidental College.

Figure 4.6 Amanda Tasse

MIRAWORLD is a transmedia world of collaborative and interactive media arts projects that I built around a theme from science, and the name of a boutique media arts production company I run – inspired by similar working themes as the original MIRAWORLD project. This essay explores themes and processes of interactive storytelling that were involved in creating the original MIRAWORLD project, with special emphasis on the design process for the art-game *Miralab*.

In Spanish, Mira translates as "sight" or "view." Mira also relates to its English sound-alike word, "mirror." A world refers to a bound space and ecosystem. In its broadest sense, a MIRAWORLD is a creative space and ecosystem connected through a diverse collective vision or methods for seeing that reflect the real world. In this case, it is a comprehensive transmedia world housing multiple emergent views bound together by thematic exploration. Transmedia refers to a story or other project that emerges across multiple media in such a way that each medium contributes something unique to the greater whole. Though often associated with storytelling, a transmedia approach to media production and distribution can be applied to many different types of content and contexts.

With MIRAWORLD, I applied a transmedia approach to the development of a comprehensive world built around a theme from science to explore how transmedia might support an art-driven approach to informal learning and science communication. In this process – which I call transmedia poetic science – integral elements of a scientific prompt are explored and communicated through multifaceted formats and channels, thus providing many access points for audience engagement across a spectrum of hard science to poetic science. Each format maximizes its own affordances for the highest impact while encouraging exploration across multiple formats.

Creating MIRAWORLD was an exercise in world-building, a term that emerged primarily from the science fiction genre in which the experience of discovering, exploring, and interacting with fantastical worlds is a central component of the experience.

> The process of world-building is a system for creating rules and behaviors for fictitious worlds that arise from the science, technology, social structure, geography, economics, and politics governing them, which then inform the characters, conflicts, and plotlines. Though science fiction often explores worlds beyond earth, science continues to explore and reveal unknown and less easily accessible worlds on earth, such as difficult to reach underwater worlds or microscopic universes.

The thematic inspiration for MIRAWORLD is inspired by the real-world lifecycle of the immortal jellyfish – sometimes called the "Benjamin Button Jellyfish" – because it grows from embryo to adult and then, when it gets hurt, reverts back to an embryo instead of dying. MIRAWORLD aims to reveal and make the world of the immortal jellyfish and its unique lifecycle accessible and available on multiple levels as a model for world-building that includes both fact and fiction: its real-world habitat, its imagined microscopic perspective at different phases of its lifecycle, and the world of the scientist's investigation of it.

MIRAWORLD offers an experimental approach to developing an emergent transmedia world bound together and generated based on a theme from science, rather than being based upon a shared narrative story world. Inspired and informed by the structure and otherworldly lifecycle of *Turritopsis dohrnii*, the MIRAWORLD team/s conceived a comprehensive media arts world with tentacles, permutations, and cycles across media, perspectives, and disciplinary palettes.

Though MIRAWORLD is not a conventional story system, it is useful to deploy metaphors from storytelling to describe how the world was designed. This transmedia world is built around the story of its main protagonist – the

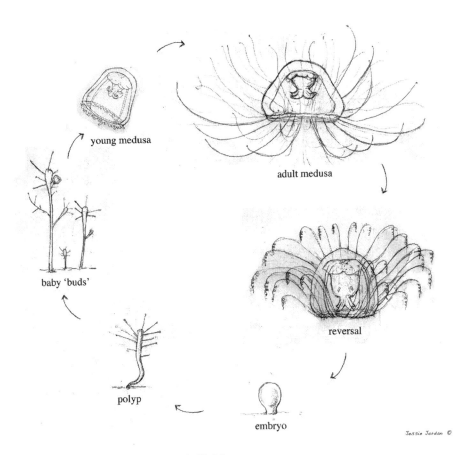

young medusa

adult medusa

baby 'buds'

reversal

polyp

embryo

Jessie Jordan ©

Figure 4.5 Turritopsis dohrnii Lifecycle Sketch

immortal jellyfish – with the lifecycle as the primary structural theme and plot for the world. Viewers and players who interact with this MIRAWORLD become its extended participant actors – scientists, detectives, and enthusiasts. These elements – the jellyfish and its relationship with its surrounding eco-systems – are the basic story, structure, and content source for world-building.

Systems design theory often draws from preexisting models in the natural world, which can be similarly useful for transmedia. For MIRAWORLD, the immortal jellyfish's unique and remarkable lifecycle acts as an apt and poetic metaphor for the cyclical and morphing quality of a transmedia ecosystem and the creative development process itself as it gestates and takes form across varying media. An open transmedia system can evolve through varying life-cycles and build up a colony of works that are genetically linked. Never in a fixed state, it continually evolves and devolves. Similarly, MIRAWORLD morphs into multifaceted variations, reflecting amyriad of means for ex-ploration as participants play with the information in the world which sometimes responds and reflects back to the user.

With MIRAWORLD, my goal was to experiment with transmedia primarily as a methodological approach for discovering and communicating popular science. I explored scientific, artistic, and narrative prompts and guidelines through the lens of varying media with a free reign so that I could see what arose within these open, generative, and emergent systems. As each team discovered the science through the lens of their own particular practice, be it engineering or design, they invoked their own curiosity as a guide. With each project – video game Miralab, short film MIRA, data visualizations MiraFlux and MiraViz, and multiple forms of writing – I sought to create a context whereby individuals could discover their own sense of wonder about this species and its implications for their own worldview.

Miralab, one of the projects that emerged out of MIRAWORLD, is an ex-perimental puzzle-based exploration game that immerses players into the un-derwater world of the jellyfish as it cycles through its lifecycle. I will dive more deeply into the design process for Miralab and its relationship to MIRAW-ORLD to more fully explore world-building, transmedia, interactive design, informal science learning, and environmental storytelling.

Environmental storytelling refers to an unfolding, layered experience that is navigated spatially rather than via linear time. Elements of the story are triggered via the environment or are told using spatial cues. The player's story of trajectory through the world emerges not only as major events are experienced, but also through the navigation of connections between spaces and events and through the ways and means in which they are linked.

When spaces and events can be revisited and experienced in new ways, additional layers of meaning emerge. Similarly, in transmedia worlds, meaningful discovery and play happen not only within individual media artifacts and events, but also in navigating the spaces between the parts of the larger transmedia world. Experimenting with the surroundings – both within the game world and within the larger transmedia world – is active problem solving and story/meaning-making.

In Miralab, we juxtaposed puzzles, which were a more concentrated and constrained experience, with areas of open play exploration. A player guides an immortal jellyfish through an underwater world while surviving and solving simple puzzles that teach them about the creatures, plants, and properties of the jellyfish's underwater ecosystems in a non-didactic way.

Through solving puzzles, players learn about how the world of the jellyfish works, as well as other strategies for surviving as a fragile creature. Each of these learned affordances provides knowledge for navigating the open-sandbox play environments, which we wanted players to discover like a bioluminescent playground and to play like an orchestra. Both the puzzle system and the open-world zones encourage self-discovery of the system – a story that unfolds and emerges through series of choices, consequences, linkages between them, and also through ambient affective experience that is less based on activity. Though most players as assessed through play-testing interviews did not describe themselves as scientists, they nonetheless engage with motivating qualities inherent to the scientific process: curiosity and a desire to examine the world and decipheringnature as an elaborate puzzle of relationships.

As mentioned, in Spanish, "Mira" translates as "sight" or "view." A lab is a place to experiment, discover, explore, be curious, try things out, and play. As such, I envisioned Miralab as a space for the development team to discover the jellyfish and its environment through the lens of their own disciplines as a "seeing laboratory." So long as the game did not contradict, undermine, or stray too significantly from real-world science, imaginations could run wild. In this way, the science could find its own new lifecycle in this hybrid co-creation between imagination and marine biology study.

We hoped to sneak science in – through the translation of our own curiosity and fascination – to inspire similar curiosity so that a player might want to learn more about the creatures or ecosystem on their own rather than to present scientific information in a didactic way. We provided an opportunity for players to be immersed within this world and to ask their own questions about it. As a result, both the making and playing of the game was an educational process for both learning about science and considering how to creatively and technically communicate the peculiar, dynamic, and fascinating experience of the jellyfish and its lifecycle.

As the MIRAWORLD mentor, I encouraged ongoing learning by sharing knowledge and resources including online databases, scientific literature, marine biology textbooks, art books, and scientific illustration guides. I encouraged students to teach one another about what they had learned and to integrate this knowledge into development throughout. I arranged interviews and tours of science labs with immortal jellyfish and marine biology experts, behind-the-scenes tours at aquariums and science centers, and snorkeling at a Catalina Island marine preserve. These field trips and interactions were intended to provide a multisensory experience of the live species and research lab environment to students, to demonstrate how interdisciplinary connections can be developed, and to encourage inspiration beyond the classroom.

Participants studied scientific information in traditional textbook ways, such as learning about the lifecycle, transdifferentiation, and the ecosystem make-up. However, as non-scientists, they were often most inspired by how scientific information connected with their own discipline. For example, the artists fell in love with the visual, auditory, textural, behavioral, and philosophical possibilities that the underwater world and species suggested. Engineers also considered graphics, but many got most excited by species behavior and by considering complex webs of relationships as puzzles and systems design.

The process of relating, reframing, and integrating learning into students' favored disciplines reinforced connections, familiarity, and closeness when they could tangibly see how the original source material related to and was, therefore, relevant to their practice. Though some were fascinated by the science for its own sake, the majority were most excited when they combined it with creative application and problem solving related to a playable outcome. Through digesting and translating the material to integrate it into their own discipline, students actively make it relevant to themselves and resonate with it. This creative rediscovery and translation can be useful for introducing subjects to audiences that might otherwise feel alienated.

Throughout Miralab, the immortal jellyfish evolves and devolves through two stages of its lifecycle. Depending on whether they are in a microscopic embryo or an adult phase, players solve puzzles in different ways, and the visual look and feel of the world morphs simultaneously. During the embryonic phase, the game world is rendered with primitive outlines, using a custom-built edge shader to communicate the feeling of being in a simpler stage of development. The player rolls around on the reef floor collecting food particles (red spheres) by moving over them, setting off a visual and sonic cascade. With each particle consumed, the player evolves from embryo to full jellyfish medusa. First, the embryo grows in scale to the world. Then, the world appears less primitive. It gets brighter and the edge shader morphs to a fully 3D-rendered universe. At this stage, when near the vicinity of a polyp, the embryo will start transforming into a fully formed medusa jellyfish.

We intended to communicate the feeling of being immersed in a living underwater ecosystem that grows and dies according to its own vitality system – a component inspired by the project engineers. For example, as the game progresses, modular kelp grow and sway in the water. As the player releases food particles from pillow anemone, they multiply and grow while quivering with movement.

We designed a generative sound system using interactive sound authoring tool, FMOD, in the game engine Unity. Within the open-world areas, each flora or fauna has its own sounds that morph based on their size, quantity, and distance from the player. As players swim past objects, they evoke a cascade of sounds, playing an aquatic kelp forest orchestra, which in and of itself can be a compelling immersive visual and sonic experience.

To achieve the feeling of being underwater, we iterated extensively on graphics and player controls. Instead of a photorealistic look, I developed a style I call Aquatic Retro Futurism – a cross between a low-polygon retro aesthetic inspired by early 1990s graphics, the movie *Tron* (1982), and a futuristic sci-fi style which we achieved through a combination of custom shaders, textures, and modeling.

Underwater jellyfish player controls were extremely challenging to develop. Our engineers worked with principles similar to 360-degree flying controls but had to make the movements feel organic rather than mechanical and to undulate in less controlled ways. At the same time, we did not want the player to feel too frustrated or overwhelmed by the difficulty of controlling the jellyfish, since they had to solve puzzles that required somewhat precise navigation. In flying games, players can more easily situate themselves with horizon lines and variations between sky and ground, which is not possible in an unfamiliar underwater world. To decrease player frustration based on play-testing feedback, we made the jellyfish more precise and controlled in its movement than an actual jellyfish would be. However, carefully guiding a fragile, undulating, and difficult-to-control jellyfish through an environment could easily be a compelling game in and of itself!

Non-Player Characters were designed based on living species appropriate to *Turritopsis dohrnii's* natural habitat – such as yellow boxfish, keel-tail needlefish, and carnivorous cup coral. The gameplay design and engineering of the artificial intelligence behavioral patterns were based on ecosystem relationships and species attributes.

We mapped out the jellyfish's habitat to be within the lagoon of an atoll – a circular barrier reef formed at the top of a sunken volcano. After first navigating a corridor as an embryo, the adult jellyfish ventures into a vibrant, open-world kelp forest ecosystem and reef. From there, they are carried into a tunnel-like current that gives them a "fly-over" establishing tour of the game world before pulling them through a sea sponge tunnel into a distant hub crater, deeper into a cavernous reef, introducing them to a darker "underground" puzzle level. From there, the gameplayalternates between puzzle zones followed by connective currents and open-world sandbox areas which build upon learned abilities in the puzzles. The player attempts to navigate through this otherworldly environment, surviving as a fragile creature. It is ultimately reunited with its colony of clone-like relatives in a magical bioluminescent world that becomes increasingly luminescent and psychedelic. In designing the world for Miralab, we used the world-building strategy of "overdesign" – a production design process whereby more props and details are designed and built for the environment than necessarily depicted on screen. World-building scholar, Derek Johnson, describes overdesign as effective, because it contributes to the sense that the world extends far beyond what could be contained in a single format or on-screen narrative depiction and, therefore, makes it seem as if the world actually exists as a real place.

For Miralab, we embraced overdesign as an engaging process of researching science and imagining how to make it resonate through play. We created a vast catalog of detailed information about the ecosystem, custom concept designs, and gameplay ideas. Through quick initial iteration of concepts via storyboards, simple mind maps, drawings, whiteboard sketches, clay sculptures, pipe cleaner dimensional diagrams, Pinterest boards, and Googledocs, we pruned our ideas to be implemented while preserving our learning and appreciation for the wild chaos of an actual ecosystem. Our intention was to populate a centralized MIRAWORLD database with these "unimplemented" designs alongside further information on the underlying science.

In addition to overdesign, we designed texture – elements that provide a deeper understanding of the world whether or not they advance the narrative in a direct way (Johnson). As details of audiovisual features, stylistic elements, technological affordances, historical context, and narratives of interaction are increasingly built into an environment. It is more likely that the environment itself will be treated and perceived as an active and alive character. Through overdesigning and integrating as much texture as possible, we hoped to make players aware of the existence of a fantastical and fascinating real world that is stranger than fiction and extends far beyond our gameplay environment and to become curious about exploring it – both across the MIRAWORLD universe and in the actual world of science.

INTERACTIVE STORYTELLING: FROM ANALOG TO DIGITAL

A review of contemporary case studies

▶ Carman Ng

Dr. Carman Ng is Postdoctoral Fellow affiliated with Universität Bremen and Freie Universität Berlin. A former Fulbright scholar, she researches digital games and affects, with a focus on game design for empathy and mental health. She has participated in the Hong Kong community theater as a performer, writer, and techie.

Figure 4.7 Carman Ng

This essay interweaves observations from my experiences on stage and off, as well as my journey as a budding scholar navigating the disciplines of game studies, multimodality (which studies how expressive resources combine to communicate), and affective sciences (which examines how nonconscious feelings mobilize thought and action). Anchoring this essay is a central interest in understanding how digital media and emerging technologies create designed, embodied experiences with transformative possibilities. In the subsequent sections, readers first find a discussion of imaginaries and experimentation. I consider the changing motifs and innovations in the medium's content and form, focused on the interconnections among digital games, affective computing, and human-robot interactions. The second section proceeds from the vantage point of theater productions, discussing the analog-digital combinations in staging experimental works and implementation challenges in general. This guides readers to the third section on networked resistance, which approaches the cultural and technological ramifications of interactive storytelling. Throughout the essay, I refer to selected digital games, theater productions, and "hybridized media" as illustrative examples.

On imaginaries | experimentation

Storytelling incubates feelings, creativity, imagination, and change. This perennial practice unfolds across conversation, literature, film, theater, graphic narratives, digital games, VR/AR experiences, "hybridized media," and a myriad of forms of expression. My focus lies in the intersections among affective, technological, and cultural lines of digital games as an increasingly dominant cultural form. In particular, I attend to the imaginaries of human-technology interactions that digital games gesture toward and how these visions shape the design of and experimentation through emergent technologies. To elaborate on these dynamics, it is helpful to consider two digital games: *Nevermind*[1] and *Detroit: Become Human.*[2] *Nevermind,* a psychological thriller/adventure game, is the first title featuring biofeedback sensitivity to support a narrative focus on trauma recovery through the processing of traumatic events and emotional regulation. Examining *Nevermind* offers a glimpse into how motivated game design can harness both interactive storytelling and gameplay mechanics to implement particular principles and foci of therapeutic practices, contributing to emotional awareness and resilience.[3] The narrative breadth of the game extends to such motifs as PTSD, substance abuse, suicide, and LGBTQ identity. As a "neuroprober," the player navigates a client's psyche (in the form of surrealist landscapes), collects, and organizes ten memory photos into a coherent narrative of a traumatic event that is crucial to the client's life. Common across all cases, the player distinguishes "true" from "false" events – which the client has subconsciously constructed for coping. Applying affective computing technology, the game detects players' stress levels from such signals as micro facial expressions and heart rate and modulates gameplay difficulty accordingly. This creates an immersive, embodied, and personal gameplay experience – illustrating the growing possibilities of game design to tackle complex and stigmatized phenomena, such as mental health and trauma.

Detroit offers a recent portrayal within a lineage of science fiction media on affective bonding among humans and machines – bearing relevance as debates on artificial intelligence, algorithms, and robot ethics abound. A central pleasure of the game is that each choice that a player makes can irrevocably change the narrative across 32 chapters – with the cruciality of choice, variables, and possibilities mapped in an interactive script commonly stretched across 4,000–5,000 pages.[4] The gameplay progress represents the choices that players enact as three androids. Each seeks freedom, equal rights, and identity in a world where robots are seen every day as caretakers, laborers, lovers, law enforcers, and, to some, sources of social issues and unemployment. In *Detroit,* players engage with the longstanding imaginary of androids capable of sentience and empathy and are, thus, subjects of autonomy.

These two examples foreground possibilities of using technologies and popular cultural artifacts to deepen understanding of socially important issues and immersion. Digital games have long pushed the boundaries of interactive storytelling by harnessing the spatial properties specific to digital environments. As Janet Murray[5] observes, digital environments represent navigable space that one moves through. Space in digital games is organized nonlinearly in response to gameplay actions – unlike linear depiction in such media as novels, films, and television. Game designers, as "narrative architects," realize environmental storytelling in four ways: evoking, enacting, embedding, and/or enabling emergent narratives.[6] Especially relevant to the games discussed are the modes of enacting and embedding. In both titles, players enact narrative events through exploring and interacting with objects in the game worlds. These interactions help solve particular puzzles and unlock further gameplay options, leading to deeper layers of the narrative. In *Nevermind*, for instance, players unlock a safe with the combination of "milk," "gun," and "sorrow," introducing the micronarratives of strained family relationships and suicide in a client's life story. Solving the mystery of androids increasingly turning deviant in *Detroit*, on the other hand, requires players to collect and decipher clues. These narrative fragments, from a design perspective, are embedded in the game world as an information space; their discoveries constitute the emergence of the story.

In the current transmedia ecology, digital games and interactive experiences interweave aesthetics across media. Recent examples such as the independent game, *Gorogoa*[7], evidence rich possibilities of experimenting with features previously considered as specific to either comics or games. Its jigsaw puzzle mechanic evokes acrostic poetry and the analog qualities of playing with a Rubik's cube, heightening the game's nostalgic aura as players explore the impact of encountering a mythical creature on the protagonist's lifetime. On a similarly important note, the hand-drawn graphics developed over more than five years highlights a creative process and commitment crucial to any forms of experimentation.

This historical moment sees wider possibilities in interactive storytelling and interaction with the world, made possible by new technologies. Across works of electronic literature, gesture-based installation, *Breathing Room*,[8] where player movement guides the procedural generation of frames and utterances of a tree's story and Meta AR headsets that emphasize intuitive use and embodied actions,[9] we find a unifying motif. Namely, we find a deepened focus on embodiment in the designs and discourses of technologies. In this case, complementary input can be drawn from discussing the realms of culture and networked artistic practices.

On horizontal power structure

Through seven years of partaking in independent, semi-professional theater productions and dabbling in experimental theater, I have observed an intermingling of analog and digital elements that underlie and enable performances. These connections particularly feature in areas of experimentation and production culture, critically shaping performances with a multimedia orientation. In my former role as writer and committee member of Shingha Theater (Hong Kong), digital tools enable performances that push medial boundaries and draw creative input across borders. For instance, collaborations with the Taiwan-based group, "The Useful Idiots", involved filming, narrative design, theater, sound art, and dialog to create video art in theatrical performances for political commentary. The aesthetics might be raw in contrast with the works of established companies. These, nonetheless, convey messages that vividly engage one's sensorium and thought, imbued with a politically engaged artistic vision of youthful velocity. The (collective) sincerity underlying in both communities of theater and digital games is a persistent allure as I delve into these worlds.

Challenges abound in staging quality theater productions as independent organizations. Of key importance is to secure funding and infrastructure for continuous, creative efforts. This calls for acumen in navigating systems of art and commerce. In Hong Kong, this translates as the need to deftly anticipate or engage with visions and parameters of funding bodies (e.g. the Hong Kong Arts Development Council) and liaising with government agencies and relevant enterprises (such as the Hong Kong Leisure and Cultural Services Department) to secure economical venues for rehearsals and performances. These pragmatic steps are invariably part of any creative pursuits, signaling tensions in resource and different evaluations of artistic and commercial activities.

Participating in independent theater clarified for me that what undergirds any sustained, artistic endeavors is a culture comprised of individuals aspiring for a shared vision. They carry forward generous contributions of time and effort, despite the historical tensions and contemporary challenges that envelop artistic projects. It is important to acknowledge the values of such a horizontal organization of artistic and critical energies within a mainly vertical, societal hierarchy. The co-emergence, collaborations, communication networks, and competitions that organically unfold among theater troupes are fundamental to the growth and diversity of the field regarding content, participants, and outreach programs. All efforts, ideally, are dedicated to developing a creative community; a unifying vision to voice the seldom-heard, kaleidoscopic ideas and feelings of the human condition.

On networked resistance

This section condenses the three threads discussed above and considers techno-logically enhanced means for interactive storytelling with a sociopolitical focus.

> Technological progress without criticality slips into fetishism, the signs of which are seen in multiple spheres of the digital contemporary. The prolifera-tion of Massive Open Online Courses, digital apps, and gamification in contexts from business, health-care, to the military, for example, indicate a common frame on digital games and media that has drawn cautionary notes.

Political and pedagogical issues are being rewritten as technologically solvable, leading to a misguided embrace of technical skills and new technologies as automatically transformative to learning.[10] Viewing these issues through pol-itics, Jodi Dean [11] discusses the reductionistic problem/solution approach that animates technological fetishism and how networked media and ease of in-formation access construe a "fantasy of participation," which enables a secure belief in one's role as an informed and engaged citizen, without considering any potential shortcomings and accountability.

Against this backdrop, inspiring my transdisciplinary endeavor is the continual expansion of moral imagination through digital games and media. *Metal Gear*

Solid V: The Phantom Pain,[12] the latest installment of a world-renowned Japanese stealth game series which originated in 1987, offers a galvanizing example of using networked gameplay to amplify the series' anti-war message. The final, secret mission of *MGSV* was playable only when all of the players on the same regional server disarmed their nuclear weapons. In the game, players assume the role of a soldier who, disillusioned from the Cold War and patriotism, attempts to build a military force unbound to nations nor ideologies. In consolidating one's military base, players find themselves ensnared in the vicious cycles of the war economy, where nuclear armament turns into a pragmatic necessity among other ethically thorny choices. Rather than promoting a sympathetic view of nuclear warfare, the open-world, the war-themed game illustrates the series' penchant for subverting the military entertainment complex from within. To tackle dynamics between complicity and control, *MGSV* situates players in an experience that interweaves narrative nuance, simulation, and complex affects that are not commonly engaged in mainstream games. These affects include discomfort, helplessness, alienation, gratification, nostalgia, and more. In this affective landscape, players confront fiction, facts, and the image of a nuclear-free future within the interstices of determinism, uncertainty, and free will that form narratives on alternate histories and speculative futures.[13] The final mission offers a critical space where players worldwide test and imagine the possibility of social courage and collective action on a global scale.

In a period when digital media and networks are ubiquitous, digital games introduce a productive vector to rethink experimentation, analog/digital links, and our roles, responsibilities, and contributions to social change. There is virtue in pondering the spaces and meaning-making practices opened up by digital games and technologies for, through, and adjacent to interactive storytelling. In aesthetic programming, for instance, Winnie Soon uses the generative and collaborative dimensions of coding practice to critique internet censorship/erasure, automation, algorithmic infrastructure that underwrite our experiences and resistance. This manifests as critical works on the geopolitics of images in the Tiananmen Square Protest[14] and critical feminist practice, which integrates human and nonhuman voices to examine queerness and computer programming.[15] Examples discussed so far exemplify how interactive storytelling flows beyond individual media artifacts and performances. Its elements, processes, and impact extend across bodies, technologies, and real and virtual worlds. The importance of approaching interactive storytelling as a critical practice cannot be overstated.

On the future

Storytelling persists across epochs and particularly resonates in our times of planetary and political tumult. Organized on the four pivots of imaginaries, experimentation, horizontal power structure, and networked resistance, this essay illustrates complementarities among digital games, theater, and an expanding range of mediated experiences to further discussion on the prevalence and potential of interactive storytelling. To encounter the ubiquity and cultural weight of digital media and networks, I propose the twinned concepts of capaciousness and dishabituation as critical alternatives. As new media scholar Wendy Chun[16] observes, we should assess why and how networks are seen as valid givens in our current social formation and, as such, preclude further explanations. Interactive storytelling likewise benefits from a differentiating view. By capaciousness, like Katherine Hayles'[17] longstanding inquiry of both literary and computation facets of electronic literature, I emphasize a systematic understanding of interactive storytelling in terms of materiality (both analog and digital processes), embodiment, practice, and cultural implications. Observing such artifacts as *Notes on Blindness VR*[18] and *Building Stories*,[19] one finds a difference in the platform yet convergence toward embodied experiences. Both explore ways of combining expressive resources. The former interweaves visuals, sound, music, and a limited degree of interactivity as a meditation on the experience of going blind. The latter challenges the definition of graphic novels by emphasizing tactile and spatial dimensions of reading and experiencing, in piecing together a story distributed across 14 printed works in a boxed set. Such "hybridized media" will percolate our societies as technologies advance and the demand for innovative forms of interactive storytelling rises, calling for deeper engagement from designers, educators, and consumers alike.

Countering a culture where quick solutions and user-friendly technologies are prized, dishabituation introduces a critical distance for appraising naturalized ways of design, use, and engagement with media. From affective gaming – interactive narratives, embodiment-centric interface design, networked gameplay to artistic codework – these phenomena illustrate how motivated the use of digital games and technologies can impact aesthetic and sociopolitical arenas. While research, design, technologies, art, and experiences interact, elements of ambiguity and unknowns remain and are often absorbed in the obscure umbrella term "hybridity." Approaching research and design with a critical playfulness potentially provides a stronger foothold, fostering further inquiries into the dynamics among meaning, embodiment, immersion, and ways of being in consonance with the ebb and flow of the digital present. As novel experiences of interactive storytelling expectedly expand, it is perhaps time to pause and ponder how to bring nuance into each experience, to deepen understanding of the world. Furthermore, underlying the analog and digital processes across media, theater, and artistic practices are, at times, uncalculated generosity guided by a search for community, belonging, and reimagination toward richer experiences.

Notes

1 Flying Mollusk (2016). *Nevermind.* Steam.
2 Cage, D. (Director), & Wasselin, S. (Designer). (2018). *Detroit: Become Human.* Quantic Dream.
3 Ng, C. (2019). Affecting reality: Intersecting games, trauma, and imaginaries. *APRJA – Machine Feeling*, 8.1.
4 Cage, D. (2018). How video games turn players into storytellers. *TED Talks.* https://www.ted.com/talks/david_cage_how_video_games_turn_players_into_storytellers.
5 Murray, J. (2012). Inventing *the Medium: Principles of interaction design as a cultural practice.* The MIT Press.———. (1997). Hamlet on the Holodeck: The future of narrative in cyberspace. Free Press.
6 Jenkins, H. (2003). "Game design as narrative architecture." In N. Wardrip-Fruin & P. Harrigan (Eds.), *First person: New media as story, performance, and game* (pp. 118–130). The MIT Press.
7 Roberts, J. (Designer). (2017). *Gorogoa.* Annapurna Interactive.
8 Loyer, E. (2014). Breathing *Room* [Gesture-based literary art].
9 Gribetz, M. (2016). A glimpse of the future through an augmented reality headset. *TED Talks.* https://www.ted.com/talks/meron_gribetz_a_glimpse_of_the_future_through_an_augmented_reality_headset.
10 Chun, W. H. K. (2013, Jan 9). "The dark side of digital humanities – Part 1," *Center for 21ˢᵗ Century Studies.* http://www.c21uwm.com/2013/01/09/the-dark-side-of-the-digital-humanities-part-1/.
11 Dean, J. (2009). *Democracy and other neoliberal fantasies: Communicative capitalism and left politics.* Duke University Press.
12 Kojima, H. (Director and designer). (2015). *Metal Gear Solid V: The Phantom Pain.* Kojima Productions / Konami.
13 Singles, K. (2013). *Alternate history: Playing with contingency and necessity.* De Gruyter.
14 Soon, W. (2018–19). *Unerasable Images* [Video documentary/installation/software installation]. http://siusoon.net/unerasable-images/.
15 Soon, W. (2017). *Vocable Code* [Installation/online]. http://siusoon.net/vocable-code/.

16 Chun, W. H. K. (2016). Updating *to remain the same: Habitual new media*. The MIT Press.

17 Hayles, K. N. (2008). Electronic *literature: New horizons for the literary*. University of Notre Dame Press.

18 Middleton, P., & Spinney, J. (Directors). (2016). *Notes on Blindness: Into Darkness*. ARTE France, Archer's Mark, Ex Hihilo, & AudioGraming.

19 Ware, C. (2012). Building *Stories*. Pantheon Books.

CHAPTER 5

STARTING AGAIN

Sylke Rene Meyer and Gustavo Aldana

Throughout this journey, we have learned about the many forms that interactive storytelling can take, as well as some of the ways that these projects can have entertainment value along with an educational value. The multitude of technological innovations in combination with more traditional forms of interactive storytelling gives creators a lot of freedom, and it will be up to you to decide what to do with that freedom. As we have read, the possibilities are endless.

The previous chapter featured professionals who have utilized their careers in impactful ways to benefit their audiences. You read about some of the methods and considerations that are considered in manifesting projects that can help educate both users and creators in a variety of fields, such as history and science. As you read these inspiring stories, you may come to the realization that a lot of important work has already been done in interactive storytelling, and you may wonder where you will fit in and be able to have an impact of your own.

This chapter is about embracing the new developments in interactive storytelling as new beginnings. The utilization of emerging technologies in combination with the evolution of audiences means that the world of interactive storytelling is in a perennial state of rebirth. With every new beginning comes opportunities, and, as you read through this chapter, you will learn about some of the ideas that industry professionals have already implemented to confront social issues and use the power of interactive storytelling for good. The use of new technological advancements to tell modern narratives means that, as an interactive storyteller, you are not relegated to sticking with what is traditional: you have the freedom to start again and make something truly new.

We will be looking at some of the ways that modern interactive storytelling has been implemented to address social issues. In this chapter, we will learn about:

- Alternative approaches to the construction of narratives
- New ways to use video games as a storytelling format
- How to use interactive storytelling for political messaging
- Ways to approach your practice while being socially conscious
- Creative methods for combining multiple art practices with interactive storytelling
- How to implement social and political activism into your work
- Things to keep in mind as you imagine your own novel approach to interactive storytelling

Let us start by reading about how interactive storytelling can be used to challenge the traditional notion of narratives in video games.

FLATGAMES
Videogame Zinesters and their Autobiographical Story Worlds

▶ Lee Tusman

Figure 5.1 Lee Tusman

Lee Tusman (he/him) is an artist, programmer, and educator interested in the application of the radical ethos of collectives and DIY culture to the creation of, aesthetics, and open-source distribution methods of digital culture. He is an Assistant Professor of New Media and Computer Science at Purchase College.
—

Personal narrative time

I have never felt entirely at home in one artistic community. It seems that my generation of artists who embrace the ethos of DIY ("Do It Yourself") culture makes their work in many different modalities. Professionally, I have worn the hats of a curator, artist, musician, educator, organizer, and programmer. I do not think that I am unique in this! Digital artists today are necessarily multidisciplinary, bringing together our diverse interests and skills within a totality of activities, hobbies, interests, and cultural and ethnic backgrounds – among all of the other facets of our identities.

Making a video game has not always been an obvious way to explore and show the many aspects of ourselves as individual artists and creators. Indeed, the allure of blockbuster video games is their fully realized fantasy world-building, complex physics and mechanics, blaring sound effects, and high visual production value. As with the creation of a Hollywood movie, there is much management and teamwork. From *Grand Theft Auto* to *Mario,* the coding and art creation for blockbuster games require elaborate plans and multistep production processes.

In sharp contrast to this corporate, industrialized workflow, I am an active participant in game-making and DIY artist communities both online and "in real life" (IRL). These communities are a unique intersection of DIY culture and digital media practices, making space for new radical forms of inter-disciplinary creation. I am an organizer at Babycastles, a New York-based art space and collective that plays a key role in fostering and amplifying diverse voices in videogame culture IRL. It is home to a unique underground of artist game makers that I am proud to support and be a part of. Online, there are many places to find this expanded underground game community – including websites like Glorious Trainwrecks and Itch.io.

In this essay, I will describe the birth of the nascent genre known as flatgames, what makes a flatgame unique, and the community of makers that are based around this genre. Similar to DIY publishing formats like the zine, flatgames are about empowering the creator to quickly create and distribute their work. The experience of playing a flatgame often features personal narratives, digi-tized handmade art, and a game mechanic that emphasizes movement through these different elements as interactive storytelling. At the conclusion of this essay, I have provided a list of tools and resources that you can use to make your own flatgame. Creating a flatgame brings you into dialog with a whole community of game makers, one that I hope to welcome you into!

Flatgames: a manifesto

The term "flatgame" was first coined by artist, designer, and game maker Llaura McGee in response to the negative feedback that she received for her game *The Isle is Full of Noises*, which she submitted to Indiecade – an inter-national juried festival of independent games in 2016. The negative feedback from judges included several people who said that *The Isle* was not a game. At that point, she decided that it was important to state the choices she made in creating the game were considered, and she thought that coining a term for the genre would help set that intention.

The Isle is Full of Noises is a short game. It opens on an abstract black back-ground pierced with a wavy green line that is soon replaced with a 2D scene of digitally sketched elements consisting of ocean waves, dots and lines of rain, and a simple sketch of a boat. The player navigates through these items which cycle through animations akin to an animated gif, along the sea and through thick rain across a background that proceeds at first from dark blue and neon green to thick gooey pink, then navy blue and green again. The colors contrast deeply, showing a storm-tossed world. Sentences float in the sky, written in a basic font, moving into view as you navigate further to the right. These sentences, as if ripped from a poet's memoir, describe an earlier era in the creator's life. "I had to prove myself every day, commit more, sacrifice more. Everyone depended on me. I was not a loser." Together, navigating through the drawings and texts integrated into the scene, the effect is of one navigating a chapter in a visual novel – one made of the combination of soundtrack and drawings contributing to the feel of a singular creator's unique style and vision.

> In response to these criticisms, McGee used the term "flatgame" to highlight that her game's design considerations were intentional, and she laid out design constraints in a Twitter thread penned a "flatgame manifesto":
>
> - Games inspired by or that recreate real events and places
> - Art made physically in less than an hour
> - No sound effects; only a single soundtrack
> - No mechanics, including collisions, except for movement and animation
> - Release it

She also gave these constraints to her students for a game class that she was teaching and, shortly after, expanded on the idea in a flatgame game jam that was held online – where participants submitted their own flatgames. From the rules, which are designed around making it easier to create a complete game, McGee wrote, "[Flatgames] are focused on presenting a game as the rawest and immediate combination of movement, art, and sound … [they] should be inspired by or recreate real events and places. Feel free to exaggerate/reinterpret and fictionalize."

It may be helpful to think of flatgames in a lineage with sitting around a campfire and listening to a friend tell a story, as akin to an extravagant puppet show, or a playable visual novel. In a flatgame, the player controls a character that can move around this flat world. The player's avatar stays focused in the center of the screen, which follows the player's movement. There can be characters to visit – or small scenes, buildings, or other objects like food – but these do not move around the screen, though they can be animated like looping gifs. Most flatgames have a background soundtrack loop. The story or narrative is told through a combination of pictures and text on the screen. All of this is structural and gives a sense of the elements of the game, but it does not give a sense of the feel of the game. Like McGee's game, most flatgames tell small personal stories with an emotional context. They can feel like a page torn from a diary or a condensed life story. Others are more abstract.

McGee describes flatgames as "games inspired by real-life places or moments about moving through a handmade space, usually with no collision or game mechanics except for movement and a single piece of audio." These simple constraints unlock a form for creating personal games as stories.

Indie Games: Flatgames as Zines Community

The indie game movement has always valued community over corporations, rapid ideation over pitch decks, simplified workflows, smaller teams, and personal storytelling. However, even within the indie game community, one of the barriers of entries to creating games is overcoming your own or others' perceptions and potentially policing the boundaries of what is a game.

Indeed, even in the indie game community, one can feel caught in the middle of competing factions. On one side are those beholden to the genre's most stereo-typical conventions of first-person shooters – killing enemies, collecting points, checking off sidequests, and solving abstract puzzles. On the other border is a faction of cultural naysayers that separate culture into distinct high-art/low-art categorization or even the distinction of genres as capable of creating art or not.

If a typical indie game is somewhat equivalent to an independent film, with attendant gatekeepers, then the flatgame community is more like a Zine.

In the emerging community of creators, a flatgame is a fast way to go from idea to execution. They can be casually created in an afternoon. The primary function of a flatgame is to turn the complex process of game creation into something as simple as telling a story.

Art Game designer and historian Anna Anthropy describes a new diverse community of game makers in her book and manifesto, *Rise of the Videogame Zinesters*. She tracks the increase of tools that simplify game creation and the use of the web as a platform for distribution of single artist-made games and compares the medium of games to the older DIY form of the *zine*.

> "I like the idea of games as zines: as transmissions of ideas and culture from person to person, as personal artifacts instead of impersonal creations... What I want from videogames is for creation to be open to everyone, not just to publishers and programmers. I want games to be personal and meaningful, not just pulp for an established audience. I want game creation to be decentralized. I want open access to the creative act for everyone. I want games as zines."

Zines – or self-published, handmade, and photocopied folded magazines – exist in a world of a do-it-yourself culture where anyone with a passion can create a magazine of photographs, writing, printmaking, illustration, criticism, or experimental form. Considering games in the form of digital zines means that we can take both an expansive and informal approach to their consideration. Like zines, because they can be so quick to make, flatgames reward improvisation and working without preplanning the elements. They emphasize creating things by hand, getting them into the machine, and placing them in their environment. Moving things around and changing things out should be a fast process.

As Anna Anthropy notes, the zine is defined both by its materiality and its address to a specific community. Its materiality suggests urgency, speed of transmission and movement, the ability to distribute information quickly amongst a community, and the capacity to be mass-produced quickly on a black and white printer at home. It does not belie the potential complexity of the subject matter of a zine. From samizdat publishing to radical or queer zines, the zine can cover infinitely complex and provocative material that may not find a home in other publishing methods. Likewise, flatgames allow for the deskilling and bypassing of gatekeepers.

Anthropy's *Rise of the Videogame Zinesters* was meant not just as a provocation, but also as a call to arms for creating the [game] world that she and many others want to see exist – one that deprioritizes the archetype of the default male protagonist in favor of a world made for "freaks, normals, amateurs, artists, dreamers, dropouts, queers, housewives, and people like you." In the years since publication, Anthropy's prefigurative dreaming has turned into a thriving online community of experimental game creators, pursuing their own game creation in just this manner of game-making as digital zinesterism.

The Isle, like many flatgames, was published on an Itch.io page. Itch.io, launched in 2013, is a website that serves as a central space for creators to host games for free, cost, or donation and is a site for players to find games of interest. Visual novels, text adventure games, tools for artmaking as well as immersive 3D worlds all share space together. It serves hundreds of thousands of projects and is a home for thousands of DIY and experimental game creators – making releasing creative games to the world a pain-free process. Flatgame makers on Itch.io are one of many communities that could be said to occupy the margins of games/not-games. Their unconventional approach to game worlds as storytelling vehicles helps move the conversation forward faster than the capitalist-driven communities around AAA games. It is here that we – as creators – can bend convention, discover novel forms, and tell new stories that speak to our present moment reflected in new forms of the day.

Flatgames: Narrative Space and Storytelling

During an online workshop for Babycastles art space, game creator Francisco Rojo described one potential metaphor for building a game:

> "…When you are making a game, and you are trying to figure out how to structure your game, then you should think of your game like a house. Furthermore, if your game has a house with rooms… then you have a bedroom, another bedroom, living room, a kitchen…"

I like this concept of a videogame in the form of a house, as well as the scale implied by it. Generally, I think a flatgame can be thought of as a small, built-out space more like a house rather than a fully developed city or fantasy world. For this reason, flatgames are often used to tell small autobiographical stories. To wit, my 2020 flatgame, *Where I Lived*, takes the aforementioned concept of a game as a house literally. I drew, in pen and crayon, ten of my previous houses or apartments where I have lived throughout my itinerant life and scanned these from my sketchbook. Autobiographical diary text is scanned in from my notebook and placed in the scene as well. The main character is a self-portrait that I created as a piece of embroidery as a child that I have scanned, added simple animation, and placed in the scene. In *Where I Lived*, one gets a window into parts of my life. The crayon drawings and informal diary notes contribute to a player's feeling of intimacy with my story.

As opposed to other 2D game genres such as a platformer game like the original Nintendo *Mario* franchise or RPG games like *Zelda*, a flatgame has simpler mechanics. The player controls a character and is able to move them in the four cardinal directions.

In McGee's initial manifesto, one tenet was the idea of creating your art rapidly, ideally in less than an hour. From this constraint, the tradition to use hand-drawn elements in a flatgame was born. In *From Tool to Community to Style: The Influence of Software Tools on Game Development Communities and Aesthetics*, scholar Emilie Reed says, "Flatgames draw from casual forms of writing (like journaling) and drawing (like sketching) as their source, resulting in a visual style that bears more explicit marks of its process than other technological forms do at first glance." Creators extend the handmade nature further by including audio narration or audio field recording as the backing soundtrack.

Game maker Stephen Gillmurphy says flatgames have "a tendency to place elements independently around the screen which creates the feeling of a flat, depthless plane, [separated] both from a perspective and from the idea of a singular coherent viewing position implicit in perspective." Gillmurphy describes flatgames as a thematic split between what we perceive as traditional videogame tropes and personal matters. Though flatgames make use of traditional movement mechanics, they choose not to focus on elaborating these movement mechanics and instead focus on what Gillmurphy describes as their "overexpressive content," these aforementioned "personal matters:"

> "[What] the flatgames suggest is a movement from our idea of the site of a videogame, the site where the videogame happens, from somewhere deep inside a console or CPU onto the screen itself, [to] where our eye meets and tries to process the objects before it turns into some coherent relationship."

As with any genre, the flatgame has generated certain conventions. Often, the games are made up of photos, drawings, or other objects that the player walks around and explores. It is common to have text, and this text might recount a story such as a particular episode in the game maker's life. In the background is a simple song soundtrack or possibly a voiceover. Beyond that, it can be easier to list what a flatgame does not have: there are no points; there are no interactions, in the sense that you do not need to press a button to advance a dialog; there is nothing to collect and no specific end goal. Like its 3D cousin, the walking simulator game, a flatgame is a virtual space for exploration. In a flatgame, usually, the only point is to experience a short story.

If flatgame is a genre that emphasizes storytelling, then we can consider flatgame creators to be storytellers. Because they lack an objective or end-goal and are casual story experiences, they diverge significantly from the way most games in the videogame industry rely on interaction and game mechanics to advance a story or plot. In their intimate way of communicating, flatgames are intended for a smaller audience of peers. In lieu of interactions that affect an avatar's health, flatgames use text to share one's emotional state throughout the story.

Flatgame resource list

Flatgames exist in the pantheon of beginner-friendly tools and forms for rapidly developing a game concept. There are dozens of tools for making games and digital interactive art – from complete programming languages, physics, and collision libraries, to tiny programs for making top-down 2D gameworlds or ASCII art, for example. While a flatgame is not a single specific tool so much as a mini-genre, due to its productive constraints, it shares similar goals with other beginner-friendly frameworks such as branching narrative games, often called "Choose Your Own Adventure" stories.

At this point, I am going to list a few resources that I have found helpful in creating flatgames. While this is not an exhaustive list, it represents the key concepts of flatgame creation. Regardless of what tool you use to make a game, there is a community of people that are looking forward to seeing what you create!

Itch.io: community/library of flatgames
Flatgames are minimally resource-intensive, which allows them to be published online easily so that games can be played and explored in a browser without requiring downloading or special hardware. Due to the ease in publishing flatgames online, there is a wide community of players, creators, and practitioners. Typing *flatgame* into the search on online game-distribution platform Itch.io, for example, results in numerous examples.

Unity: game engine

Since flatgames are a genre and not a specific tool, they can be created in a number of different ways. In keeping with its beginner-friendly ethos, there are a number of starter methods. One of the most common approaches is to use templates for the Unity game engine. Unity is a game engine for building 2D and 3D games as well as software tools. Several templates have been created by flatgame inventor Llaura McGee. McGee worked together with game developer Siobhan Gibson, and together, they have created the tutorial *The First-Timers' Guide to Making a Flatgame!* with numerous hand-drawn characters and assets as well as a hand-drawn zine (what else?!) to walk you through the process. I have also created a flatgame tutorial series using Unity that is publicly available on YouTube.

Flatpack: android application

One of the most intuitive and hands-on programs for creating a flatgame is Flatpack by game creator Mark Wonacott. Flatpack is a flatgame maker application for Android phones and tablets. It aims to be an intuitive mobile-friendly program and makes ready use of your phone's camera so that you can take pictures of objects or people, trace them out, and add and resize them in your gameworld. When you are finished, you can save and export your game as a zipped folder of HTML files which you can upload to Itch.io to distribute your game or place on your own personal website.

p5.flatgame: javascript framework

Beyond these two options are my own p5.flatgame template which works with the p5.js library: "a JavaScript library for creative coding, with a focus on making coding accessible and inclusive for artists, designers, educators, beginners, and anyone else," and a forthcoming flatgame maker Unity plugin developed by McGee. Eventually, I would like to make a website that integrates this flatgame creation template and allows a user to create a work entirely in the browser.

Works mentioned

Anthropy, Anna. *Rise of the Videogame Zinesters: How Freaks, Normals, Amateurs, Artists, Dreamers, Drop-Outs, Queers, Housewives, and People like You Are Taking Back an Art Form.* New York, N.Y., Seven Stories Press, 2012.

Babycastles. "Babycastles Academy: Intro to Godot." *YouTube*, 17 May 2020, www.youtube.com/watch?v=BWCOrxb3se4&t=3151s. Accessed 13 June 2020. Workshop instructor: Francisco Rojo.

dreamfeel. "The Isle Is Full Of Noises." *Itch.Io*, dreamfeel.itch.io/the-isle. Software.

dreamfeel, llaura, and Breogán Hackett. "FLATGAME Annual 2016 Game Jam." *Itch.Io*, 5 Jan. 2016, itch.io/jam/flatgame-annual-2016. Updated: January 27, 2016.

Gibson, Siobhan. "The First-Timers' Guide to Making a Flatgame!" *Itch.Io*, flatgame.itch.io/first-timers-tutorial. Accessed 13 June 2020.

Gillmurphy, Stephen. "Flat Pak." *My Friend Pokey*, Tumblr, 13 April 2018, myfriendpokey.tumblr.com/post/172890836170/flat-pak. Accessed 13 June 2020.

——. "Output Lag." *My Friend Pokey*, Tumblr, 17 May 2017, myfriendpokey.tumblr.com/post/160775928835/output-lag. Accessed 13 June 2020.

Indie Games In The Digital Age. edited by M.J. Clarke and Cynthia Wang, S.L., Bloomsbury Academic Usa, 16 Apr. 2020. From tool to community to style: The influence of software tools on game development communities and aesthetics, Emilie Reed.

McGee, Llaura. *Flatgame Manifesto 2017*, 2017. Class lecture slideshow. From email correspondence.

——. "Questions About Flatgames." received by Lee Tusman, 27 May 2020.

Tusman, Lee. "Where I Lived." *Itch.Io*, Mar. 2020, notapipe.itch.io/where-i-lived. Accessed 13 June 2020. Software.

Wonnacott, Mark. "Flatpack." *Itch.Io*, 20 May 2017, candle.itch.io/flatpack. Accessed 13 June 2020. Software.

QUEER TIME, PRODUCTIVITY, AND FAILURE IN INTERACTIVE MEDIA

▶ Lark Alder

Figure 5.4 Lark Alder

Lark Alder is an artist and educator who uses interactive digital media to shape speculative worlds and critical design objects. Lark holds an MFA from UC Berkeley, a BA from Harvard University, and teaches digital media art at the San José State University.

What does it mean to "queer" games and interactive art? In academic contexts, the verb "to queer" has expanded beyond a deconstruction of gender and sexuality to a broader dismantling of normative systems of power and privilege. In this respect, queer video games might explore alternative relations to winning or losing as a way to question capitalist drives for success and financial gain. Queer storylines might subvert normative frameworks for chronological markers of productivity and success. Queer technologies construct critical relations to tools and context by turning utility on its head: embracing inefficiency and failure or repurposing technological applications to suit – rather than exploit – the needs of marginalized groups.

The bulk of the media and technology that we use and consume is marked by through-lines of narratives that reinforce systems of dominance and control. How can we as artists and designers "queer" our creations to challenge these systems? The following are a series of loosely connected ruminations and examples of how artists work to escape the confines of these systems – exit strategies where queer dominant narratives offer (at least a temporary) respite where we might find ourselves presented with other options, logics, and ways-of-being. They are gestures that are meant to inspire people looking to use interactive media as a way to break the stories that have broken us: to create anti-narratives that call into question the logic of narrative itself as a product of invisibilized systems of normativity and power. Specifically, these gestures are meant to make room for the alienated through non-standard concepts of time, productivity, and failure and to consider what storytelling means in a digital age.

Drawing on queer theory and disability studies, these are mere snapshots of much larger bodies of scholarly research offered as prompts for people looking to engage with interactive media through a critical and creative lens. The artists that I will mention are almost all from the United States and Canada – many are people I have come across at art shows and conferences. Because of this, the sampling of artists is local in scope. This, by no means, is meant to erase work that is being done in other parts of the world – the cultural perspective offered is admittingly North American-centric.

I will be speaking of stories in the loosest sense, instances where meaning is conjured rather than outlined. They can be as simple as gestures that form a mood or metaphor, mere scraps of the cohesive whole that we often expect of narrative form: typical story arcs with a beginning, middle, and end; series of cause and effect relations that unfold in progression; anything that moves towards a final resting place whose aim is to leave the audience with a sense of satisfaction and closure. To exit dominant narratives is to challenge these expectations.

The words to follow are winding, associative, and end abruptly. This text itself acts against the impulse to control and contain.

Whether it be linear or nonlinear, storytelling is a time-based medium, and time means different things to different people. For queer/trans people, time may not have the same milestones that mark the lives of their cis-gendered straight counterparts. As Jack Halberstam states in his text, *In a Queer Time and Place*: "Queer uses of time and space develop, at least in part, in opposition to institutions of family, heterosexuality, and reproduction."[1] This is not to say that all LGBTQ+people are in opposition to these institutions, but many – especially those who identify as "queer" as a politicized, oppositional stance to normativity – are less likely to fit cultural norms for when and how people should become sexual, what these relationships look like, and ultimately, the ways they result in typical reproductive family units. It is partly because of this disruption to the nuclear family – the atomic unit of capitalist and re-productive labor – that Foucault argued that LGBTQ+people can be seen as a threat to the perceived fabric of society. Thus, "queer time" can be seen as an opposition to "straight time:" the normative framework for productivity and success which Elizabeth Freeman refers to as chrononormativity, "the use of time to organize individual human bodies toward maximum productivity."[2]

In the context of storytelling, innumerable story arcs follow quests for true love, biological reproduction, and landmarks of economic success to set expectations for how time unfurls in a lifetime. These force-fed narratives offer little nourishment as we reach towards unattainable goals, especially for those people whose existence, by definition, is outside the norm. Without belaboring this point, I encourage you to invent radical narratives that challenge these cultural imaginaries as fixed realities.

These markers of achievement also map on to logical systems in interactive media. Many end-goals and point-based systems in video games reinforce neoliberal promises of health, wealth, and happiness. In Halberstam's *Queer Art of Failure*[3], he makes the argument that people dissatisfied with a social context might actually want to fail. For example, an anticapitalist might not want to accumulate wealth so that they can develop other relations into money or possessions. In relation to games, queer failure asks us to explore possibilities beyond capitalist reward systems for skill and dexterity and awards for militarized violence. Rather than trying to "win" a game, what possibility opens up when you purposefully lose or when there are reward systems that do not reinforce narratives that exclude alienated groups?

Queer games scholars have also worked in challenging the broad perception that games are, by definition, "fun." Jesper Juul explores the notion that it is in fact failing – not winning – that drives player engagement.[4] In their conceptualization of no-fun, Bonnie (Bo) Ruberg challenges us to embrace negative affect in games: "Turning our attention to the seemingly unpleasant allows us to uncover underexplored modes of experience – both as players and queer subjects in the world."[5]

In so many ways, art and fiction have long staked a claim in territories of sadness, loss, tragedy, and failure, but digital media is married to concepts of fun or accomplishment. In general, when we click the mouse, we expect rewards – for example, a task completed, a link opened. Functionality is hardbaked into the very definition of technology itself, and technological progress is synonymous with being faster, more efficient, and "better" for humanity. To explore failure in technology allows us to question the "who" in "humanity" that technology makes life better for. Praba Pilar's incisive critical theory and projects such as *NO!!!BOT*[6] are searing critiques of this "Cult of the Techno-Logic" and its violent, globalized impact on marginalized communities across borders, race, and class. Through performances, electronic/digital installations, writing, and various forms of public engagement, she exposes the tech industry's complicity in various forms of corporal exploitation through raw, experimental, and demented repurposing of technological apparatus.

Back to the subject of time. As Halberstam points out, contemporary queer time is shaped by the devastation of the AIDS epidemic in the late 20th century – an era when life became precious, and the urgency to exist in the present here-and-now lodged itself in queer subculture and way of life. For those who were ill, socially isolated, and facing (what was at that time) a near-certain death, time froze or left them hanging. For survivors and the generations to follow, the loss of life from the AIDS crisis resulted in a loss of generational continuity and assurance of a stable future.

Anna Anthropy's game, *Queers in Love at the End of the World* (2013), is a poignant probe into feelings of impending doom and obstacles to queer intimacy and lasting connection. The hypertext Twine game grants the player ten seconds to kiss, hold, and express your love for your girlfriend before the timer runs out. Echoing "no future" trends in queer theory by scholars such as Lee Edelman, the use of time in Anthropy's game seems to embrace the catastrophic; there is something pleasurable in the frantic clicking to find intimacy before the timer runs out.

José Esteban Muñoz provides a counterbalance to this turn towards negative affect in queer theory. In his seminal book, *Cruising Utopia*, he states, "Queerness is essentially about the rejection of a here and now and an insistence on potentiality and concrete possibility for another world."[7] According to Muñoz, queerness resides on the horizon – it is something that we are always reaching towards.

Even more profoundly, it is what queer, trans, and nonbinary people embody in their everyday existence. If queerness resides in the future, then queer lives and bodies are, themselves, time-travelers. Note that I use the language "queer, trans, and non-binary," terms currently preferred for gender expression in the year 2020. I use "queer" loosely, as some trans people might not identify as queer, and nonbinary people are sometimes excluded from trans narratives. By the time you are reading this article, this language might change. Because queerness is always reimagining itself, this perpetual movement forward is reflected in rapidly evolving language which itself becomes a technology for navigating LGBTQ+ identities.

We can also approach a queering of time as an upending of the perception that the passing of time is a stable and fixed experience. At the time and place that this is written – in the United States in the spring of 2020 during the first wave of the COVID-19 pandemic – the stalling of the economy and slowing of life during shelter-in-place and lockdown measures are bending many people's sense of time and dissolving any sense of a stable future. This is further amplified by the mass civil unrest with the Black Lives Matter movement and revolutionary calls to end policing and legacies of violence against black and brown bodies. We currently have no idea how this pandemic and social movement will affect a (now even more) uncertain future, but this moment in history will likely stand out as a bizarre experience of time unlike any other.

In regard to shelter-in-place mandates and staggering rates of unemployment, many are experiencing a slowing of time, as they spend months on end in their homes without the structure of their daily routines of work, school, errands, and socializing. As an artistic gesture towards feelings of immobilization, Tamiko Thiel created the augmented reality artwork, *Suspended Spring* (2020)[8] – where cascades of digital cherry blossom petals descend slowly around the viewer's physical environment: "I wanted to express the feeling that I had of being in a cocoon, watching spring swirl around me without really being able to participate in it."

In parallel but very different situations, other people deemed essential workers might be experiencing time as accelerated, as they face long hours and/or anxiety from high-risk workplaces. Across the board, the shared, albeit unequal, experience of this pandemic is resulting in new perspectives and subjective relationships to time on a massive scale.

With the absence of time as a presumed universal standard, there is one less common, measurable landmark in our consensus reality. This comes as no surprise for differently abled[9] people whose sense of time is based on the experience of navigating day-to-day occurrence with a disability. For people who are differently disabled, crip time[10] refers to the slowing of time when common acts – like taking a shower or eating a meal – might take hours rather than minutes, and the timing of these tasks is determined by one's dependency on others to help complete them. Furthermore, for people who are

Figure 5.2 Screenshot of Augmented Reality Cherry Blossoms from Bedroom Ceiling, *Suspended Spring*, Tamiko Thiel

neuro-socially disabled, time might accelerate or slow drastically due to their mental state.

As an exploration of time as it relates to themes of queerness, disability, and labor, Kara Stone's game *Ritual of the Moon*[11] is played for five minutes a day over 28 consecutive days. The game is played from the perspective of a witch exiled to the moon as a pronunciation of fear and persecution of feminine power. Each day the game is played, you (as the witch) perform a series of ritualistic tasks. You gaze at the Earth from the perspective of the moon, tend to an altar, and make gestures to connect constellations in the sky. At the end of each session, as you watch a comet slowly progressing towards planet Earth, you make the decision whether or not to save the planet, allow it to be destroyed, or destroy yourself.

The duration of the game as a daily 28-day practice speaks to the grueling experience of living in a society that is both punishing and exiling – one where alienated groups have only the options to repair that which is broken, work to dismantle it, or self-destruct. It is also a ritual of self-care and connection – both for the player and the artists themselves. Stone and her collaborators, Rekha Ramachandran and Julia Gingrich, created the art for the game over a span of years using embroidery, paper folding, and other craft-based practices to generate all of the visuals for the piece. In her article, *Time and Reparative Game Design: Queerness, Disability, and Affect,* Stone critiques ableist constructs of productivity in art-making. Building on queer theorist Eve Sedgewick's idea of reparative reading and in dialog with slow-tech movements in feminist art and technology spaces, Stone calls for a reparative art practice: one that resists the drive for completion and allows for experiences of disability, otherness, and the never-ending process of healing.

"I am so used to making things in a hypomanic state – work work work, exhaust myself, then be done – but the pace has to be different for this game, because it is about a different pace. It is about daily dedication in small bits over long periods of time. It is about being confused, stuck, suicidal. It is about meditating for five minutes a day, because, over time, that creates a ritual that sustains us."[12]

In considering how concepts of temporality have evolved across centuries, our relationship to time is closely tied to productivity, accelerating alongside the emergence of machines to facilitate industrialization, colonial expansion, and capitalist economies. The need for synchronized schedules for railroads and the stock market are the catalysts for standardized time. The factory whistle measures the value of labor as the passing of time. Now, with the double-pronged economy of the internet as surveillance capitalism (i.e. mining and selling of our personal data) and attention economy (i.e. monetizing websites by virtue of how much time we spend on them and, therefore, their value to advertisers), time is sold through our attention and patterns in our behavior over time.

Many artists working critically at the intersection of art and technology tackle issues of surveillance and data privacy. One project that can be read as a "queering" of these technologies is Hasan Elahi's epic practice of sousveillance, a form of self-directed surveillance. A year after the 9/11 attacks, Elahi became a target of FBI surveillance after a bogus tip named him as a potential terrorist. The FBI subjected him to months of interrogations and lie-detector tests, and Elahi, a global traveler, was frequently detained.[13]

Instead of letting himself be the target of FBI surveillance, Elahi became the agent of his own data-trail through the act of sousveillance. He turned surveillance on its head by flooding the FBI with self-collected data, taking countless photos of his everyday life and sending them to the FBI. "'You have data?' he asked, 'Well I've got data too. By putting everything out there, the government's data no longer means very much.'"[14] He sent them emails letting the FBI know his travel plans and created a website TrackingTranscience.net

Figure 5.3 Screenshot of the Witch Directing the Comet, Ritual of the Moon

that (still) shows his exact whereabouts via Google satellite images. Having now accumulated over 15 years of snapshots, the *Tracking Transcience*[15] net-art website also leads the viewer to browse collections of related images sorted by subject matter, most likely through image recognition algorithms. Though the sorted collections on the website are not of people but rather objects or places (e.g. parking lots and toilets that he has visited), the classification evokes the racial and gender bias inherent to the algorithms themselves, as now "officially" evidenced in a 2019 study by the National Institute of Standards and Technology.[16]

In addition to using self-reported data to reveal insidious mechanisms of surveillance, many artists also explore the performative nature of sousveillance in our engagement with social media. In Amelia Ullman's famed Instagram project *Excellences & Perfections,*[17] she created multiple Instagram accounts that both mock the culture of Instagram personas while also using them as platforms for provocative performances that trace the unfolding of identity and crisis over time.

The truth is, we are all in a process of interactive storytelling based on our compulsory engagement with digital technology. Beyond the self-posted content of social media and Web 2.0, our data is constantly mined through apps, websites, smart appliances, security/traffic cameras, etc. In contrast to analog eras, the digital age archives our actions and creates algorithmic narratives beyond our understanding or control. The cumulative script of our own lives is traced through digital footprints that are invisible to us – storytelling is now beyond our control.

Notes

1 Halberstam, Jack. *In a Queer Time and Place: Transgender Bodies, Subcultural Lives.* New York: New York University Press, 2005.
2 Freeman, Elizabeth. *Time Binds: Queer Temporalities, Queer Histories.* Duke University Press, 2010.
3 Halberstam, Jack. *Queer Art of Failure.* Duke University Press, 2011.
4 Juul, Jesper. *The Art of Failure: An Essay on the Pain of Playing Video Games.* MIT Press, 2013.
5 Ruberg, B. "No Fun: The Queer Potential of Video Games that Annoy, Anger, Disappoint, Sadden, and Hurt." *QED: A Journal in GLBTQ Worldmaking,* Vol. 2, No. 2, 2015, pp. 108–124.
6 Pilar, Praba. "The NOBOT." https://www.prabapilar.com/nobot
7 Muñoz, José Esteban. *Cruising Utopia: The Then and There of Queer Futurity.* NYU Press, 2009.
8 Thiel, Tamiko. "Suspended Spring." http://tamikothiel.com/suspendedspring/.
9 Language around disability is nuanced and dependent on people's personal preferences. I am using the terms differently-abled, disabled, physically, or neuro-socially disabled, though people with disabilities might choose other identifications and there are many types of disabilities.
10 McRuer, Robert. *Crip Times: Disability, Globalization, and Resistance.* New York University Press, 2018.
11 Stone, Kara. "Ritual of the Moon" https://ritualofthemoongame.com/
12 Stone, Kara. "Time and Reparative Game Design: Queerness, Disability, and Affect." *Game Studies: The International Journal of Computer Game Research,* Vol. 18, No. 3, December 2018.
13 Mallonee, Laura. "Artist Stalks Himself so the FBI Doesn't Have to." *HyperAllergic* 2015, https://hyperallergic.com/225798/artist-stalks-himself-so-the-fbi-doesnt-have-to/.
14 Urist, Jacoba "From Paint to Pixels." *The Atlantic,* May 14, 2015, https://www.theatlantic.com/entertainment/archive/2015/05/the-rise-of-the-data-artist/392399/.
15 Elahi, Hasan. "Tracking Transience." http://trackingtransience.net/.
16 Grother, Ngan, and Hanaoka. "Face Recognition Vendor Test (FRVT) Part 3: Demographic Effects." National Institute of Standards and Technology, U.S. Department of Commerce, 2019.
17 Ulman, Amelia. "Excellences and Perfections." https://webenact.rhizome.org/excellences-and-perfections/.

ANY GIVEN MOMENT
Developing a shared language in multidisciplinary collaborations

▶ John Dieterich and Dr. Carlin Wing

John Dieterich is a guitarist, composer, and producer based in Albuquerque, NM. He plays in the band, Deerhoof, and collaborates on a variety of musical and artistic projects.

Figure 5.5   John Dieterich

Dr. Carlin Wing is an artist, educator, and media scholar. Her work connects everyday gestures to global histories of science, technology, and media. She uis an Assistant Professor of Media Studies at Scripps College.

Figure 5.6   Carlin Wing

Artistic collaborations have been variously understood as mechanisms for experimentation, collectivity, social practice, and radical politics. They can be volatile, generative, short-lived, or enduring. This essay asks what complementary and contradictory understandings of the process of artistic collaboration emerge when we frame it as a practice of interactive storytelling. To this end, we begin by telling the story of our partnership and our exploration of performance, interaction, and improvisation.

We arrived at this collaboration already well into our careers, as an artist and as a musician respectively. We had not met previously, but our paths intersected through a mutual friend who had reached the conclusion that two people unhealthily obsessed with sports and music should know each other. We proceeded to tumble down a compelling rabbit hole of conversations about soccer, music, and art. Supported by our regular, rent-paying gigs – teaching and touring – we were emboldened to pursue hypothetical conversations, to test out stray ideas, to let things happen slowly and indeterminately.

Like many games, our collaboration unfolded carefully and with little indication of the final path that we would discover: to play, of course, is to play with limits, to find rules as they emerge. We started with an open field and with no shared language. We did not have an agreed-upon topic, medium, venue, or audience. Living in different cities required some determination to communicate: initially, we wrote emails, and eventually, we spoke over video chat. For the first two years, we talked once every month, or two, or three, slowly getting to know each other as individuals and as artists: we started building some common language by way of open and often rambling conversations.

This kind of collaboration stages a commitment to discovering through doing. The work emerges out of our back and forth, with each of us trying to pay attention to the things that we both get excited and feel deeply about. but the intention is to say "things we get excited about and feel deeply. Circling (or spiraling) around a wildly broad set of shared interests, we slowly begin to notice things that repeat, and we find things we come back to again and again. So far, this list has included things like bounce, bodies in motion, material histories, sounds, and soccer. We find ourselves asking questions like, "What conscious and unconscious stories do bodies tell? How do they tell them? How do people read gestures? What are the affective possibilities and material politics of physical play, global spectacle, and media broadcasts?"

In the lead up to the 2018 FIFA World Cup, we arrived at a provisional plan: a series of improvisational musical performances using the live television broadcast of FIFA Men's and Women's World Cup games as scores to be read in real-time by musicians. Turning off the broadcast commentary with its pat narratives and instead asking musicians to respond to the live action of the games and the choreographed moves between the cameras would change both the affect and effect of the game. After the live events, we would make video works from the documentation. We decided to call this project *Playing Along*.[1]

[Minutes 28:20–31:02]

"So much is happening at any given moment. 29 minutes into the hour-and-a-half-long video and the music has built into minor chaos. A bleating clarinet announces a free-kick outside of the box as the drums skitter, nervous and frenetic. In the wake of a foul, the French and Croatian players stake out positions at the top of the box – small black and white figures feinting and jostling for space on a grayscale field, with clustered fans in the front rows serving as the backdrop for the camera's view. The French players form a wall, nervously clutching each other as the guitars hover around a minor second ostinato. A head of wild hair passes in front of the gallery camera, briefly blocking the bottom half of the field from view, and the ball flies into play from somewhere offscreen, sending the guitars, trumpet, and clarinet cascading one after the other. A guitar lays out a jagged smattering of notes and another emits an ominous low 4-note pattern. The ball ricochets around the box as a chaotic melee ensues, and then suddenly, somehow, the ball is in the net. The music trills low and high – the clarinet and trumpet taking brief one-note solos to announce the goal. The drums fall silent and the visuals flip into the sudden color of Croatian players in red and white piling on top of each other, the striker pointing the camera to his leg muscle. The guitars form an organ-like cluster as the French players bow their heads. The music drifts into a long collective quiet sustained tone with isolated clarinet and trumpet notes punctuating the increasingly empty soundscape. The cameras cut to the audience in the stadium overlaid with the faces of a few people watching the performance in the gallery. Lisa smiles and scratches the back of her neck. A slow funereal bass drum appears as the trophy animation spins into a slow-motion replay of the goal. Yasi appears mesmerized, circling his head as the ball spins and spins, from one angle and then another, into the net. The guitars join the horns in slow melodic interplay. The music is clearly tonal now, a lament for an oncoming unavoidable train wreck. Just as suddenly, the trophy whirls, and we are out of slow motion and trying to catch up to the game. In between a few quick color close-ups, the ball has been thrown in, whipped back down the field, and just as quickly out of bounds. The instruments are trying to reassemble, take advantage of the pause and stop for a beat. Everyone is mostly waiting, save for a few light plays at lines and some quiet rattling objects. The ball is thrown in, and they are off and running again."

Why the FIFA World Cup? Soccer is *the* global game. You can find soccer fields in almost every corner of the world – in stadiums and parks, prisons and schools, on military bases, attached to factory complexes, medical facilities, corporate campuses, private clubs, and youth detention centers. Founded in 1904 in Paris, FIFA (International Federation of Association Football) held its first men's World Cup competition in Uruguay in 1930. Over the course of the 20th century, it was not uncommon for national football associations to join FIFA before their country joined the United Nations, as if trying on the nation-state form for size in the suspended, half-reality of game space before risking full commitment to political actuality. Today, FIFA has more member states than the UN and recognizes 23 non-sovereign entities – including the United Kingdom's "home nations" (England, Wales, Scotland, and Northern Ireland), Hong Kong, and Palestine. The first unofficial Women's World Cup was held in Mexico in 1971, despite FIFA's efforts to undermine the event. It was another two decades before the first FIFA Women's World Cup competition took place in China in 1991. Today, the FIFA World Cup is one of the great broadcast media spectacles, accounting for six of the top fifteen most-watched television broadcasts of all time (the other nine are the Olympics). The 2015 FIFA Women's World Cup final between the United States and Japan was the most-watched soccer match in US history.

When we watch sports, we learn ways of seeing. Billions of people train their eyes and ears on the broadcast of these games. They listen to the rhythms of the broadcasters' banter, as they follow the cuts between the 33 cameras stationed around the stadium, the strangely swooping cable cam, and the long look of the 360 cam, which shows the shape of the game accompanied by the swelling and subsiding of the crowds' roar. Soccer teaches us its time, and it tells us about ours.

The live broadcast operates as an affective interface, filling our hearts with stories of virtuosity, sacrifice, collapse, and comeback. In the background, the constant beat of tournament sponsorship, broadcast rights, and tele-communication regulations is hypnotic. These games are brutal and beautiful and dumb and crassly corporate; they provide profound examples of what can happen when humans play together. While the broadcast trains our eyes on the field, other stories surround the spectacle: suitcases of cash and rampant cor-ruption, massive pay gaps between men and women, performance enhance-ment programs, hooligan fans taunting opponents with fascist, racist, and homophobic chants, sex trafficking, political protest. Cultural politics and political economy are always present with any global media spectacle. Some people play along in EA's FIFA Ultimate Mode, playing out alternate World Cups in their bedrooms and living rooms. The video game is a mostly silent but constant presence, surfacing in offhand remarks from announcers and podcasters about FIFA rankings and statistics. EA releases their predictions for the tournaments along with their World Cup updates. In EA FIFA, profes-sional players can play as themselves and each other. Sometimes, they complain that their avatars do not do them justice. Of course, the premise of the video game is that everyone gets to play the players.

So, the idea for *Playing Along* is fairly simple. However, once we found it, we faced the work of bringing it into the world in an endless scroll of pragmatics. What kind of space can host a show or a performance? Which broadcasts are we going to project? Is the WiFi fast enough to support three simultaneous livestreams? Will the performance livestreams get shut down by Twitch for copyright infringement? Who should we invite to play? How are we going to pay them, how much, and where does the money come from? What kind of instructions are we going to give the players? Do we need nationally themed pastries? How many breakfast burritos should we make? Some of these questions appear more important than others; some are easier to answer than others.

Our test run took place at a barbeque restaurant in Calgary during the lunch rush as part of the 2018 Sled Island Music Festival. For later iterations, we approached friends and friends of friends who run non-profit art spaces. Our collaboration lives between music and art, so we need spaces that can support both live performance and visual installations. For the first performance, travel and lodging were supported by the music festival. The following performances were supported by Carlin's research funds which we have used to pay the musicians for their performances and for travel, equipment, and materials.

We debated about how to prepare the musicians for the performance. We decided to give them (and the gallery audience) a list of prompts, in the tradition of a performance score. This is a list of things to think about, potential organizing principles and possible ways to approach play:

- Treat the broadcast as a score
- Respond to the expressions on players' faces
- Act as if everything you see is a lie
- See the ball as the center of gravity
- Consider security
- Match the pace and speed of the game
- Celebrate
- Respond to tattoos
- Keep your eye off the ball
- Align yourself with a team
- Consider the referees
- Watch out for style
- Act out the visible advertisements
- Act as if everything that you see is true
- Follow a single player
- Consider the coaches
- See the shapes of the players shift as they orient around the ball
- Play the feel of the game
- Respond to injury
- Follow the lead of the cuts between camera feeds
- Decide whether a fall is a dive
- Be the subconscious of the broadcast
- Respond to fouls
- Take your mind off the game

- Consider the crowds
- Follow the ball
- Be the conscience of the player
- Be the clock
- Respond to hairstyles
- Make music
- Do something else

These are all things that people might already do while watching sports. To our knowledge, none of the musicians have used the prompts during the games, preferring instead to allow themselves to build logic systems on the spot – riffing and interacting with each other. The point of the prompts is not to enforce a set of rules, but to set a tone and to facilitate trust. This trust allows predetermined aesthetics to take a back seat and unexpected resonances to emerge.

Putting these performances together involves imagining other people's imaginations interacting with one another. In the world of musical improvisation, the people playing may not actually have that much in common. They may not even get along, but if they have something to gather around – a shared set of principles or an event like a game – then a shared purpose emerges. The differences then do not so much disappear as become amplified through a shared lens. John describes bringing people together to improvise as a little like trying to create a cult. Both kinds of groups are created quickly and need to resonate deeply on the spot. If you are a cult leader, then you have to invent something to tie meaning to, an illusion of history. If you are bringing people together to improvise, then you are curating the eccentricities of individuals and putting them into relation in order to make something meaningful – something that feels deep and may even be deep.

For each FIFA World Cup performance so far, some of the players had played with each other before, but no one had played with every other person who was there. This meant that there existed some shorthands shared among specific players, but each group has been new as a unit and thus, unique. We decided to give up control at times in order to achieve particular goals and to open up the process to other voices. For example, we asked another collaborator of John's, Rosie Hutchinson, to select and invite the female-identifying ensemble for the Women's World Cup performance in 2019. Once a critical mass of players is reached, a multiplicity of approaches tends to take hold. The hope is for the musicians to trust themselves to be instruments of play and for the audience to encounter and to observe them moving into and out of sustained flow states – all action, interaction, everything all at once, as they float at some remove from their selves.

Watching television is its own kind of virtuosity. And there are so many different ways of watching. At any given moment, one or more of the musicians could be treating the broadcast in a literal way, while someone else might be trying to stitch together a melody from those translations, while someone else is making fun of the referee. The audience can sense the negotiations that are happening in real-time and may start to root for certain musicians' takes on the game as much as they root for any team or player. Everyone in the room – musicians and audience alike – is able to put whatever is happening together in any way that they want. Without the audio broadcast to tailor and direct the focus, everybody becomes unsure of where exactly to look within the frame and what to listen out for. In this liminal space, there is a pervasive feeling of shared purpose which is not about the game at all. Something inexplicable and undetermined is being built, and each person in the room is participating in that generation of meaning.

When it is successful, the project creates a thickly layered experience. It captures the experience of seeing a game but, more than that, it also seemingly captures something closer to what it is like to be alive. The shifts in the improvisations reflect state changes of living, of moving from one feeling to another and feeling all of them piled on top of each other – anxiety, joy, now I want a sandwich, now Ed is playing a really dark line in response to a player writhing on the ground in a way that he and many of us assume is playacting until it turns out to be a real injury and instantly is not at all funny. The video works that we make from the performance documentation fix the improvisations and turn them into 90-minute long songs of sorts. We cut the videos to emphasize the tempo of the broadcast and the gestures of the players (athletes and musicians). This makes the layering tangible, showing the relationship of the song to the broadcast of the game and making easily apparent the musicians' array of responses to what they are watching.

Playing Along is about finding new ways to watch together, to play with and to play against, to reorient to and through play. The performances and video works that we make from them are one way that we have approached shifting the focus to stories that are already there, latent. This collection of gestures helps us learn new ways to solve problems and makes it possible to access the particular, the personal, the intimate, and the political. It guides us to stories that are implicit and emergent in the frame. The closer in that you get, the broader the implications are – the more political and pressing these are – because our bodies are not isolated. They are permeable, and they tell stories.

Our bodies and selves can be choreographed, curated, repurposed, directed, and set loose. Some stories are told on purpose. Players (read: people) do this all the time. We train. We learn the principles of a game. We learn how to see, how to translate, how to improvise, how to pick out a pattern and how to make a new one, how to make sense of the smallest gestures, how to turn on a dime. We try to be ready for any eventuality. But when it comes down to it, we really do not know exactly what will happen – what the substance of any given moment will be. Trained bodies aim to control their stories. Relying on the way gestures and movements are always subject to being misread and mis-recognized; we feint and tell false stories that are meant to deceive. But other stories are always slipping off or getting shaken out of us. We all have tells, whether or not there is anyone around to read them. Movement is telling.

At its core, this project is a commitment to letting things develop at the edges of our respective practices, to being open to opportunity, and to creating openings and opportunities for others. Thanks also to the institutions that have helped support us: Scripps College, Sled Island Music Festival, Potts, Human Resources, and CFA Downtown Studio. Most of all, thanks to all of the people who have participated in our collaboration so far as musicians, curators, pastry bakers, tech wranglers, wordsmiths, and the like: Alicia Beyer, Amanda Broder Hahn, Ariel Muniz, Asha Schecter, Ashley Saywut Moyer, Benjamin Piekut, Cat Hulshoff, Corey Fogel, Cuauhtémoc, Dac Nguyen, Ed Rodriguez, Emily Lacy, George Chen, Greg Saunier, Gregory Uhlmann, Heather Trost, Keiko Beers, Leopoldo Peña, Lisa Haber-Thomson, Liz Mackenzie, Luke Fischbeck, Marisa Demarco, Marya Errin Jones, Maud Salvi, Nick Imparato, Rosie Hutchinson, Rozie Jordan, Sam Lisabeth, Satomi Matsuzaki, Stephanie Richards, Tiffany Defoe, and Yasi Perera.

Note

1 When we named the work, we were describing what the musicians were doing and were not consciously referencing Kiri Miller's excellent book of the same name about the performance of digital games on YouTube. However, our project is aligned with Miller's in its shared interest in its exploration of mediated performance.

ACTIVISM AND INTERACTIVE STORYTELLING

▶ Grayson Earle

Figure 5.9 Grayson Earle

Grayson Earle is a new media artist and educator. He is the creator of Bail Bloc and a member of The Illuminator art collective. He has presented his work and research at The Whitney Museum of Art, MoMA PS1, Radical Networks, the Magnum Foundation, and Open Engagement.

"Alone we go faster, together we go farther." (unattributed proverb)

The word "hacker" today conjures an image of a lonesome and shadowy figure in a basement, maliciously gaining access to personal computers to steal money or information. In reality, the term predates this narrow view, which can more accurately be described as a "security hacker" or "black hat hacker." In truth, "hacking" enjoyed positive connotations for most of its tenure as a word. The creators of what became the first Apple home computer described themselves as hackers, and many of the most renowned computer scientists at MIT and Berkeley continue to do so today. To these people, hacking refers to the creative disregard of the intended use of computers and technology. I too dawn the term with pride, but as an artist and activist, my work further expands upon its definition.

My longstanding love of tinkering with technology combined with my politics has led to my participation in various activist organizations and projects over the past 15 years. I approach activism in the same way that I approach software.

> Activism can be upgraded, shared, open-sourced, blocked by firewalls, zipped, copied, and deleted. It is written in different languages, networked,

> maintained by a rotating cast of characters, and parts of it get infinitely reconfigured and reused in new projects.

I consider my work to be community-engaged new media public art, which is a mouth full of words to describe a practice that encompasses video games, outdoor video projection, political software, and unconventional usage of a range of other emerging technologies to tell stories or communicate ideas. I find it useful to break up the path to creating this kind of work into five steps: engaging a community, identifying problems and solutions, iteration, spreading the word, and maintaining an archive.

An example of creative public storytelling in this vein is the EYEwriter by Graffiti Research Labs. In 2003, a renowned street artist from Los Angeles named Templ1 was diagnosed with ALS – also known as Lou Gehrig's disease – which disables the neurons that enable voluntary control of muscles. The team behind EYEwriter developed software that allowed him to draw onto the architecture of the city without leaving his hospital bed. This entailed developing custom software that tracked his eye movements, as he was unable to move his hands, then used these to move a virtual cursor around a simple drawing application. The drawn graphics were sent over a wireless network to an onsite team with a laptop and projector. The resulting images were drawn live onto buildings around LA, and a video feed looped back to Templ1 in his hospital bed so that he and others could see his creations.

The EYEwriter is a successful project in each of the five steps mentioned above. They engaged a community of street artists of which they were already a part, bringing together artists and software developers. They identified a problem of accessibility (the inability to move one's muscles) and theorized a solution; they iterated the development of software to enact the solution, and finally, they spread the word and created an archive of source code and video documentation to help others who want to use or modify the software.

Accessibility and software go hand in hand; your users (or participants) must be able to access the software in order for it to be useful. Traditionally, we use a mouse and keyboard to interact with a computer, but the goal in this case was to expand this accessibility to people with limited mobility.

In my time as an artist, I have created and participated in dozens of collaborative projects. In my collective, The Illuminator, we use a video projector to project political messages from the roof of a modified cargo van. We have worked with big organizations like Greenpeace, grassroots projects like Black Youth Project, and everything in between. There are ten people currently involved in the project, and everyone fulfills varied vital roles in the collective. Rather than only working on behalf of communities of people, we often create tools that enable people to express themselves. In this way, we amplify the existing concerns of people who are affected by societal problems, thus acting as a support system in a network of grievances.

We take issues of access seriously and work creatively to enable new modes of engagement. During the COVID-19 pandemic, people were encouraged to "shelter-in-place," which made political demonstrations problematic in some instances. Early into the pandemic, our collective was approached by members of the Climate Working Group – a group of scholars and researchers at New York University who had planned a summit to address urgent ecological issues. The summit was moved online amid the pandemic, but the organizers were hoping to host a demonstration online as a way for participants to express their concerns. I worked to create *Protest Generator*, a means of online political demonstration, which I will refer to throughout this chapter.

Communities

Everyone belongs to at least one community. You might think of your immediate geographical location as a community of people. I currently live in Brooklyn, New York, and I see examples of community-engaged work being done all around me. From the small free libraries that people build on the street with a "Give One/Take One" sign, to the In Our Hearts collective that collects free food to redistribute every Friday at the nearby park, there are projects being built and maintained everywhere.

Becoming involved in a community-focused group is a great way to make more connections and share resources. In my work with The Illuminator, for example, we have formed relationships with dozens of activist organizations and have become part of that constellation. This allows us to promote the work that other groups are doing and get the same in return. Because we are now a well-known project, organizations that are familiar with us often connect us to new projects with which we previously had no contact. If you are part of a community garden, then you might ask certain members about creating a small lending library on the sidewalk outside.

Communities are not necessarily tied to physical space. This is probably obvious to anyone reading this, but the internet has enabled new forms and modes of community that allow us to connect with people near and far. As a member of The Illuminator, I created *Protest Generator*, an interactive web application that creates a participatory virtual demonstration. The project website allows participants to draw using the mouse, phone, or keyboard, and submit their design as a "protest sign." The signs are then taken up in real-time via video stream by 3D avatars who create a virtual protest.

Though our group has some popularity, the project would have been mostly ignored if we unceremoniously released it on our website without much of a reason. We saw this as an opportunity to work with an existing event so that it could have the greatest impact. In this case, we collaborated with the Climate Working Group in order to reach a greater audience.

Do your research!

It is easy to come up with a new idea. Far too much credit is given to the "Idea Men," considering that most notable projects involve a team that is often left uncredited for their work. The idea is nothing without a community of people to enact it, and there are likely dozens of organizations just outside your door that could use your support.

Showing up to meetings for local organizations is a great way to make connections and start working quickly. One skill in high demand for community organizations is tech-savvy individuals who can create websites, email lists, social media accounts, and more. I can tell you with absolute confidence that even reaching out to local groups with a cold email and a desire to help out with technical needs will likely result in a very appreciative response, at the very least.

In the case of the *Protest Generator*, we had previously formed a relationship with the Climate Working Group. Trust is a crucial component for projects like this, in which we had a lot of creative control. Your initial collaborations will likely be aimed at facilitating the existing goals of the organization, but if you take the time to grow a relationship, then in the future, you might be able to pitch your own ideas and benefit from the time and energy of the people involved. I was given the freedom to design and code the project, but I counted on the input of the organization to help improve the work. Climate Working Group also promoted the project and gave us an audience, so we both benefited and were able to leverage participation from a wider audience in the end. Making good interactive software also depends on having people test it out, report bugs, and offer ideas to improve the project.

Iterate and playtest

In the development of technology, the term "iterate" is an important one. This just means to create things in increments, experiment, see what works, and repeat. It is okay if something does not work the first time; you should consider any misstep or failure as a learning opportunity. If you are carving stone, then iteration might not be a very appealing idea, but with ideas, software, and pencils, this is rather easy to apply.

Everyone develops a unique creative process, but there are some touchstones that are useful to keep in mind. I tend to sketch out ideas on paper before I begin any digital design. This makes my ideas more communicable to others who are not programmers and can speed things up in the beginning; it is easier to draw a quick sketch of a protester holding a sign than to model it in 3D! Conversely, if you are not a programmer or a digital artist, then paper is a great way to get ideas down, so you can approach people with the necessary skills.

If you are developing something that is intended to be used by others, then you should always ask people to test it out. Do not be offended if their feedback is something like, "This makes no sense to me, how am I supposed to do X?" This is good, useful feedback. As the developer, of course, your creation is going to make sense to you, but it might not make sense to others. This is why video game companies employ game testers – so that they can get feedback from people who did not participate in the development process. By integrating their feedback, they become part of the community of people who are invested in your creation, and you might even recruit some new people to the project.

I cannot possibly list every example of how iterating and playtesting *Protest Generator* helped make the project better, and that speaks to the importance of

Figure 5.7 Image of EYEwriter

this step. It would have been impossible for me to work out these kinks by myself. Other problems included the sign-making interface not working on certain browsers or phones, so having as many people test it as possible was hugely beneficial. Some of these problems you can anticipate, and others you simply cannot. Give yourself time to address these issues, as you do not want to be fixing software problems at the eleventh hour. If you intend for your project to be reused and iterated further after its maiden voyage, consider putting it online as an open-source project for others to help improve and use for their own projects. You can see many of my personal projects and collaborations on my GitHub repository at prismspecs.

Spread the word

"If a tree falls in a forest and no one is around to hear it, then does it make a sound?"

If you have taken the time to craft an idea, develop a project, and solicit the help of friends and strangers, then there is still very important work to be done. I consider this to be the most daunting step because it is outside of my skill set, which is yet another reason to work collectively. I lean on my fellow collective members who are more experienced organizers and social media experts to make sure that our projects reach broad audiences and to contextualize what we are doing.

Leading up to the unveiling of a new project, you will want to develop language around your project so that people know how to engage with it in a meaningful way and to understand what the project is for, to begin with. If your project is taking place in real-time as a public art project, you may also consider how you will communicate with participants as they approach the project.

> Importantly, you should document the project as it happens! Always get permission from people before you photograph them, and consider having someone on the project who is solely concerned with documentation, so that it is not rushed or forgotten. Finally, once you are done, you will want to gather and edit the documentation and write a bit about the project, so people can continue to connect with the work after it has been exhibited.

The importance of documentation cannot be understated. As an artist, you need to be able to show evidence of your creative work. Even if you throw an event for 100 people and only five show up, you can still document the project and submit it as part of your next grant application. Remember, failing is synonymous with learning, if you commit to correcting your mistakes. Even if you do not plan to utilize the project again, documenting your process and results can help others in the future who might benefit from your experience.

With *Protest Generator*, we created video documentation and an open-source repository so that other developers can use its code. I have already included it in a couple of grant proposals so that I can expand and retool it for future opportunities. The more work we put online as a collective, the more people become familiar with what we do, and the amount of resources we are able to leverage increases. The more projects I attempt, even if I fail, the more I grow

Figure 5.8 Image of Protest Generator Split Drawing App and Output

as an artist and programmer. In this way, my creative practice itself is iterative and in dialog with the communities I work within and alongside. As an activist, I do not think of my work as ever arriving but rather, taking what I can from those who came before me, putting this to good use, and offering what I can to those who come after. This is the ethic of the artists, activists, and hackers that I turn to for guidance and inspiration.

COLLECTIVE WISDOM

▶ Katerina Cizek

Figure 5.10 Kat Cizek

Katerina Cizek (she/her/hers) is a two-time Emmy-winning documentarian working across emergent media. She is the Artistic Director and Co-Founder of the Co-Creation Studio at the MIT Open Documentary Lab. At the National Film Board of Canada, she directed the HIGH-RISE and Filmmaker-in-Residence projects. Cizek wrote (with Prof. William Uricchio et al.) Collective Wisdom, a first-of-its-kind field study of the media industry that maps works that live outside the limits of singular authorship.

I was a photojournalist at a student newspaper at McGill University 30 years ago, and I ended up behind the barricades at what is now known as the Oka Crisis or the Kanehsatake uprising. Kanehsatake, a Mohawk community north of Montréal, refused a neighboring white town from building a ninth hole of their golf course on an ancient burial ground. They put up a barricade on a gravel road. The Quebec police came in. It was a summer day, and a lot of dust rose from the skirmish. It was very dusty, very cloudy. Shots rang out. Nobody could see anything, but when the dust settled, there was one police officer dead on the ground (years later, it was confirmed that it was a police bullet that killed the officer). The army was called in. That began a 76-day standoff between the Mohawk warriors and the Canadian Army. It was very much like the Standing Rock struggle over the pipelines. Behind the barricades, as a student journalist, what I saw on mainstream television compared to what I witnessed with my own eyes were two different realities. I committed to the notion of community media – the notion of people being able to tell their own stories in their own ways. That was an eye-opener for me.

I have always been platform and media agnostic, as I have never really cared about what kind of tools to use. When the internet arose, I had already been exposed to it quite a bit because my father is a quantum physicist, and he brought a modem and terminal home to access the mainframe at the university to conduct his computations. He used high-level computing that was available at the university for his own work in quantum physics. Accordingly, once the digital revolution came, I was not surprised.

I became attracted to documentaries and journalism. I worked in newsrooms. I appreciate long-form journalism. I appreciate the news and the ability to report accurately and quickly on time. However, documentaries really appealed to me. I noted that John Grierson defined documentary as "the creative treatment of actuality." There is absolutely no platform that is attached to that definition. Documentaries were always my passion for community-based ethics through whatever platform or medium is necessary at the time.

As filmmakers creating linear work, we are thinking: what does the audience need to know and when? How does it make sense emotionally, factually, and intellectually? What are the building blocks, and how do we put them together? We are still creating something, and we are still making choices about how that happens. The same happens in digital work and interactive work; it is just a different playing board. It is still about the ability to think about what your user is experiencing and when. Great filmmakers show their films often to people and watch their reactions carefully. Good editors do that too. Interactive storytelling is just on a different scale, and there are a lot more unknowns in the sense that you have a lot more building blocks.

A lot of my early works were across many platforms – one involved seven projects based on my work at a hospital in downtown Toronto, called the Filmmaker-in-Residence program at the National Film Board of Canada. The hospital was committed to healthcare outside of the walls of the hospital – both the community in Toronto and global health. For instance, we worked with a group called "Young Parents With No Fixed Address." Hospitals, shelters, and the child welfare system are all involved in patchwork and oppressive ways. They are all systems that do not account for user experience. I was really impressed to encounter the innovative nurses working together to meet young parents and give healthcare where they are in the streets of Toronto. As opposed to expecting people to go into hospitals. Accordingly, these nurses got together with people involved in both prenatal and postnatal care for women in the margins or at risk of not having homes. They think, "What can we do to make this a better experience, with better health outcomes for both the mother and children? Both parents and children?" When I came along, they were so excited because they felt that the media was a wonderful way to potentially involve young parents in the process and to teach the systems about the user experience. The project started off as a five-week participatory project where the young women created photo blogging and stories. It turned into a five-year process where they became advisors to the hospital, the mayor of Toronto, and the provincial government of Ontario.

It was an incredible opportunity to think about media as a tool of creative expression and also a social and political tool within this specific healthcare problem and how we can work together differently to come up with better solutions. I felt like I have met so many people along the way that we are working in these co-created methods that put people formally known as subjects – people formally known as audiences – and acknowledging their role in the creative process and having agency in their own lives. I am not saying that there is no author. Point of view is important especially for historically marginalized communities. I also think that, in a time of fake news and epistemological crisis, it is very important to be able to trace how we know what we know. Authorship is a big part of that. I am not trying to erase authorship, but there are other forms of collective creation that have been deprioritized yet are also important to fund, recognize, credit, and understand.

I was invited, along with Producer Gerry Flahive, to continue to explore these methodologies, these kinds of tools, interactive digital formats, and also the processes of collective creation at a higher level at the National Film Board of Canada. That is how *Highrise* started. *Highrise* was a seven-year project. We widely explored the density of our cities and how we are citizens of the web. How are we citizens of the city and the internet? How do those two things intersect in high-rise communities around the world? During *Highrise*, I was a visiting artist at the MIT Open Documentary Lab. My colleagues, Dr. William Uricchio and Sarah Wolozin asked, "What are you thinking of doing next?" I replied that I was interested in a co-creation studio because I noticed that there are many of us in the world employing co-creative practices, yet all of us are always reinventing the wheel, because the work is so underrecognized. They said, "Come, bring it to us. This could work really well in our lab." That was five years ago. Together with the principal investigator, William Uricchio and Sarah Wolozin, the founding director of the documentary lab, I founded the Co-Creation Studio at MIT.

With the help of MacArthur and Ford Funding, we researched and wrote a two-year field study called *Collective Wisdom*, co-creating media within communities across disciplines and without the ribbons. It is a treaty, one of the first-of-its-kind field studies that documents precisely what we are talking about. These methodologies are already in place, and so many parts of our field put the user at the center of the practice and working within communities. These are works not made "about" people or "about" a subject, but rather "with." That is one way that George Stoney, legendary filmmaker and founder of the Challenge for Change program at the National Film Board, talked a lot about his work and influenced a lot of what we did. Another way to think about it is any kind of work that is the ideation of it. The actual concept comes from a relationship. It is not one person, one discipline, or one organization rounding up people saying, "I have got an idea. How can you fit into my idea?" It is more about people coming together and coming up with the idea collectively.

The same can be said about technology, technological systems, or algorithms. For example, we spoke with 30 artists working with biological environments, planetary-scale systems, or technological systems such as artificial intelligence. We asked them, "Are you co-creating with these systems?" Some of them said, "No, these systems are tools for us – the same way a paintbrush is for an artist." However, most of them said that it is co-creative, because the process becomes a feedback loop. Those are two key ways of thinking about co-creation. We also identified six important risks involved in co-creation. The first one is about the threat to editorial integrity and artistic freedom in terms of "too many cooks in the kitchen" or a committee decision. Those things can weaken or kill projects. Another is calling things "co-creative" at a time when people have been denied access to funding, people from the historically marginalized communities. Now, suddenly, everything is co-creative.

There are plenty of reasons why we need to think about co-creation in the context of an emergent, local conversation about access to these funds. You have also seen big companies using "co-creation" as a word, an excuse, or as a so-called "community consultation," when in fact, it really is not. It is about stealing and exploiting labor and ideas for more profit for Google, Facebook, or whatever. We need to be clear about those risks. For our study, we interviewed 166 people to identify those risks and their strategies to mitigate them. What are the tools and processes that people use to make sure that their co-creation is ethical, just, equitable, and fair? Maybe not all of the processes are "co-creation." Some of it is, and, in reality, some of it is not.

We need to be transparent and upfront about our intentions and our governance. All of those are those issues come into play. I will give you an example of some of them. The first one is deep listening and dialog. Rather than going into, "I am going to make a 43-minute film about this subject, and I am going to find the people that fit my film," the starting point for co-creative processes tends to be more about deep listening. Therefore, rather than going out looking for access to a story, a co-creator might identify what their skills are and what their expertise is, but then seek out to understand what is going on and build a project together. Often, when I am beginning co-creative processes, I am in dialog and in deep listening mode with many folks.

In *Highrise*, for example, the first year consisted of deep listening with architects, residents, urban planners, policymakers, and residents in high-rise buildings. I went in, and I said, "I do not know what your life is like, so please share, and we will figure it out together." On the technology side, I am deep listening with the people cutting into these technologies. I am not saying, "I want to make this, this, and this." How would I know? They know what the technology is. Then eventually, in specific projects, these two streams of conversations start coming together.

The moment when we say, "Yes, let us work together." is fascinating because we have great expertise at the table. It is about spending time developing a statement of mission and a statement of principles. I will give you an example with a film called *The Edge of the Knife* from the Haida Gwaii – an Indigenous nation on the west coast of Canada. It was a co-creation between an Inuit film company, a university, and the Haida Gwaii government. These are three organizations that do not work in the same fields. They are from completely different sectors. Each of them brought something different to the table. The Inuit film company wanted to make sure that they made a festival-ready film. The university was a community planning group that had been working with Haida Gwaii for many years and was interested in using film as a tool for community development. How do they bubble up stories that matter? How do they give training to people? Then, the Haida Gwaii government was specifically interested in language revitalization and economic development. There are only 26 people left speaking the Haida Gwaii dialect, so they wanted to use the film for economic development. They saw the film as a potentially interesting way of bringing jobs to the community. They had extraordinary locations; they are up the coast from Hollywood and in the same time zone. They were interested in training community members in filmmaking and also in revitalizing the language. The film was shot entirely in the two dialects of Haida. The story of the film was done through community storytelling workshops. They found the scriptwriters in the community and built up the story.

> Before they got to all that, the three organizations sat down and wrote a list of ten principles and what collectively mattered to them the most. Was making a film more important than revitalizing the language, or was it more important than hiring inside the community? They all agreed that hiring from within the community was more important to put first when issues arose. That is one example, and I have certainly done that kind of thing, especially when co-creators come from different worlds.

Once you are past the missions and principles, a lot of people will begin to develop contracts. For example, when we worked with the Detroit Narrative Agency on this project for collective wisdom, we built a portion of the research within Detroit. They asked us to sign a Community Benefit Agreement, which was all about the terms of engagement between MIT – one of the most powerful and complicated universities in the world – and a small community group. Who paid? How? When? How are decisions made? Who has control? All of these kinds of things were spelled out, and we signed to it. This action says that these are the things that matter to us.

Training and including community engagement in learning the tools is central to much of the co-creative practice.

A lot of the work is connected to design, but it is also a critique of design thinking. In fact, one of my colleagues at MIT, Sasha Costanza-Chock, has just published a book called *Design Justice*. It is about rethinking and critiquing this so-called co-design world, which you can easily argue is co-operative and does not really put justice and equity at the center of the work. When you say "user-centered," who are you considering as the user? Design justice encourages, or demands, this notion that you need to design for the most vulnerable and for the most marginalized people in our society. That is when you are really doing design justice. Otherwise, you are just perpetuating marketing or "tech-solutionism." It is so prevalent. It has been driven by engineers. We have placed engineers at the top of a hierarchy.

Our lab is situated in the humanities and social sciences section of MIT. We argue that humanities and social sciences need to be a part of these approaches. It is about the product, but it is also about the process. Absolutely, there are outcomes – often, multiple iterations of different things – that fit into different audiences or communities differently. In fact, in *Highrise,* we made a lot of media content that you would have never seen online. We published a newsletter with the community. We would spend a lot of time in our workshops publishing a newsletter. We considered that an important part of our work, but it was not central to international audiences. On the flip side, the web documentaries that garnered international attention were of less interest to the residents living in the buildings. They cared about the project because of what it can contribute and build up in the community.

Sometimes, people think that co-creative practices are associated with the digital revolution, the speed of technology, and the way that technology has been built up until recently. In fact, we argue that co-creation is ancient. In the theater for example, for thousands of years, the troupe or the ensemble – everybody did everything in theater. At a certain point in time, you see that the producer is born. You see the progression of theater as it specializes in the Industrial Revolution.

Definitely, this moment that we are in – technology's affordances give rise for co-creative practice to reemerge, largely through the internet. Therefore, it is both those things. It is something that we have done for a long time. It has also been accelerated by this technology. Technology is largely human-made and hand-made. When we think of the internet, we think of robots, servers, and nonhuman entities but, in fact, there are so many people doing stuff all of the time. Whether it is this illusion of AI, the reality is that many companies use humans. Some rely on wherever labor is cheap to read your email, because it is easier, faster, and cheaper than developing the algorithm that they claim they have made. In fact, even our technology is remarkably human. It is touched by humans all the time. It is something that we are doing. When we talk about community and being transparent about our structure and who does what, all of those things equally applies to technology. If that helps situate technology in a community-based practice.

We tend to fall back on binaries and polarities, but the analog-digital binary is highly limited. We are missing the nuance and the complexity of the way that we exist in the world and the layers of systems that structure our lives. Whether or not I am plugged into my computer, there are parts of my life that are digital. They continue going on without me interacting with them. I would argue the same about our creative process. One of the things that I am seeing over and over again in some of the high-level conversations that I am having with policymakers or people trying to understand the digital arts and the digital world approach is that everything is digital.

> The more that we remove our technologies from actual devices, we cannot think of technology as devices. They are systems.

Just because you are alone in your room writing a novel does not mean that you are not a part of society that shapes that novel you write. It is simple to understand.

CONCLUSION PERFORM

Interactive storytelling for the screen

Sylke Rene Meyer and Gustavo Aldana

Interactive storytelling has the potential to empower an individual identity for an intrademographic community by inhabiting a shared story world. User-oriented, interactive storytelling not only challenges our tradition of following narrative timelines, but also our tradition of using written language to compose stories. In the past, the terms "storyteller" and "writer" were often used synonymously. Interactive stories of the 21st century may not be written but instead, evolve through the users' decisions and movements in the narrative space. Furthermore, the languages of interactive storytelling are more tied to oral composition when created in an analog space like improvisational and immersive theater or in the binary system of computer codes that design digital games.

Interactive storytelling empowers the user as a self-authorized protagonist of a simulated reality where everybody can be what they want – and in which winning and growing are not the maxim of actions. Out of new narrative-ludic hybrids, two different forms and aesthetics of participations evolved or renewed prominence. On one hand, we have forms of immersive theater, LARPs, theme parks, artivism, etc., where the players participate in and through their human bodies. On the other hand, in the digital realm, participation requires a digital apparatus and includes digital virtual worlds, digital games, social media, and any participation where the players participate in and through their digital avatar.

Although this book presents a wide range of examples, the full scope of interactive storytelling includes many more aspects of communication: human communication, intelligent machine communication, and intraspecies communication. Interactive storytelling is defined not by a field of narrative or playful entertainment, but by the process of participation. In other words, while linear, traditional storytelling addresses a group and provides a collective experience, the interactive narrative is determined by the role of the individual and how the individual experience intersects with the community. The importance of the human author in creating interactive narratives is at the center of attention of the developers and researchers of interactive narrative systems; presenting information is not limited to form but is an aspect of art that is necessary to create an interactive experience.

The core quality of interactivity lies not so much in the lack of narrative predetermination but in the relationship between authorship and recipients. In this sense, an interactive narrative can be seen not as a form of representation of story but as either a simulation or imitation of roles and space within a network of recipients. Play and playfulness occupy a key role in our understanding of interactive storytelling. Interactive storytelling is primarily understood as a narrative form that (1) privileges space and user-participation over linearity and authorship and (2) exists in a formative dialog with digital games yet thrives as a narrative tool in the non-digital sphere. An interactive narrative can be defined as the random process of unintentional storytelling in space where at least two users have come to play a key role as the producers of a narrative trajectory.

The frontiers of interactive storytelling continue to expand, and those new frontiers offer many opportunities for creativity. Interactive storytelling is inherently a collaborative process between the creator and the audience, and because of the ever-evolving nature of the modes of interactive storytelling, creators are afforded the freedom to continuously surprise audiences with innovative techniques and approaches. In commercial applications, creators in interactive storytelling have the ability to present novel forms of storytelling in unique ways – the rules of interactive storytelling are constantly being updated and rewritten. This spirit of freedom and innovation in interactive storytelling can also be utilized to tackle the important burgeoning social issues and get audiences to participate in and engage with those issues. As an interactive storyteller, you are positioned to be at the vanguard of artistic and narrative innovation.

ABOUT THE EDITORS

Sylke Rene Meyer

Sylke Rene Meyer is a writer, director, media artist, performer, educator, and co-founder of the performance group Studio206 in Berlin (2007), extended in LA (2019). In 2018, she also co-founded the performance group "Family Room Collective" in Los Angeles. Her practice is informed by and engages with film, media history, theory, and criticism, encompasses feature and documentary filmmaking, as well as writing and collaborative experimentation across theater, new media, and digital platforms. Her work has garnered numerous awards such as an Emmy Award and Best Film Awards at major festivals such as Seattle, Chicago, and Montréal. She is a Professor of Creative Writing and Director of the Institute for Interactive Arts, Research, and Technology at California State University in Los Angeles.

Gustavo Aldana

Gustavo Aldana is a musician, media artist, and educator. Their projects have involved the combination of electronic music, interactive visuals, and the creative use and manipulation of myriad forms of digital media as forms of resistance. They are interested in the utilization of emergent media and education as praxis. Their focus is on the intersection of media studies and political activism. They are a graduate student in Television, Film, and Media Studies at California State University, Los Angeles.

Anna Weinstein is a screenwriter based in Atlanta, Georgia where she works as a writer-for-hire to develop features and television series. Ten of her feature-length screenplays have won awards and placed in dozens of international film festivals and screenwriting competitions – such as Script Pipeline, Page International, the Austin Film Festival, American Zoetrope, and in the top 5% of the Academy Nicholl Fellowship. She is on the screenwriting faculty in the Department of English at Kennesaw State University where she works with undergraduate and graduate creative writing students. Anna is the Founding Editor of the *PERFORM: Succeeding as a Creative Professional* book series.

INDEX

NOTE: *f* indicates a figure; *n* indicates a note